CRIMINAL
LAW
AND
THE
CANADIAN
CRIMINAL
CODE

CRIMINAL LAW
AND
THE
CANADIAN
CRIMINAL CODE

Kenneth L. Clarke, LL.B.
Richard Barnhorst, LL.B.
Sherrie Barnhorst, LL.B.

McGraw-Hill Ryerson Limited

Toronto Montreal New York St. Louis San Francisco
Auckland Bogotá Düsseldorf Johannesburg London
Madrid Mexico New Delhi Panama Paris
São Paulo Singapore Sydney Tokyo

Criminal Law and the Canadian Criminal Code

ISBN 0-07-082553-X

2 3 4 5 6 7 8 9 0   AP   6 5 4 3 2 1 0 9

Printed and bound in Canada

Care has been taken to trace ownership of copyright material contained in this text. The publishers will gladly take any information that will enable them to rectify any reference or credit in subsequent editions.

TABLE OF CONTENTS

PREFACE

This book was written for persons who are not lawyers but who need a basic knowledge of the fundamental principles of criminal law and the offences in the Canadian Criminal Code. Such persons include police officers, security personnel, probation officers, parole officers, criminologists, law clerks, and others who are involved with the criminal justice system.

The book is intended primarily as a community college textbook but it would also be appropriate for use in police college courses, some university programs, and in-service training classes.

The subject matter is divided into two main parts:

Part A, which is approximately one-third of the book, is concerned with an introduction to criminal law. It includes a brief discussion of general principles of criminal law and various defences available to an accused person. Part A ends with a description of criminal procedure, with the emphasis on the powers of arrest and search.

Part B is devoted in its entirety to a discussion and analysis of the actual offences contained in the Canadian Criminal Code. Each chapter contains a reproduction of relevant Code sections and where necessary, each offense is explained first in general terms. Then, the constituent elements of the offence are identified and key words and phrases are defined. The discussion of each offence includes summaries of actual cases which deal with the particular Code section in question.

A brief appendix dealing with drug offences contained in federal statutes such as the *Narcotic Control Act* and the *Food and Drug Act* completes the book.

Space did not permit a consideration of every Criminal Code offence. Therefore, we have attempted to select only the more significant offences.

Finally, it should be noted that because we have limited our discussion of offences to those in the Criminal Code and other federal statutes, we have necessarily excluded violations of provincial statutes (e.g., provincial highway traffic laws and liquor laws).

GLOSSARY

Abbreviations for Case Reports
(Unless indicated all reports are Canadian)

All.E.R.	All England Reports (English)
C.C.C.	Canadian Criminal Cases
Cr. App.R.	Criminal Appeal Reports (English)
C.R.	Criminal Reports
C.R.N.S.	Criminal Reports New Series
Cox's C.C.	Cox's Criminal Cases
D.L.R.	Dominion Law Reports
E.R.	England Reports
K.B.	King's Bench (English)
M.P.R.	Maritime Provincial Reports
O.W.N.	Ontario Weekly Notes
Q.B.	Queen's Bench (English)
R.L.	La Revue Légale (Quebec)
S.C.R.	Supreme Court Reports
Upper Can. Q.B.	Upper Canada Queen's Bench

PART A

THE
CRIMINAL
LAW

Chapter One

An Introduction To Law

A. THE NATURE OF LAW

Before beginning the subject of this book, the criminal law, it will be helpful to briefly consider the nature of the law in more general terms. Let us first start with a definition. Law can be defined as that body of rules which regulates the conduct of members of society and is recognized and enforced by the government. There are, of course, many rules which regulate our conduct which are not, by this definition, part of the law. For example, the rules of a private club regarding the duties of club members are not part of the law. Likewise, the moral values which govern a person's conduct are not part of the law; although moral convictions and legal rules often, but not always, overlap. These types of rules are not rules of law for at least two reasons. First, they are not officially recognized by the government as laws applying to all members of society. Second, their violation does not involve a penalty or other legal consequence imposed by the government.

1. Functions of the Law

The definition given above, although suitable for our purposes, does not indicate the wide range of functions served by the law. The law not only tells us what our rights, privileges and obligations are, but also determines the structure of our government and assigns duties and powers to its various branches. The law even tells us how and by whom laws are to be made. An example of a law-making law is the British North America Act. This statute, which is Canada's primary constitutional document, creates our federal system of government. The B.N.A. Act divides the authority to make law on various subjects between the Federal Parliament and provincial legislatures. For example, certain areas such as property and civil rights are given exclusively to the provinces. This means a federal law on the topic of provincial civil rights would be *ultra vires,* or beyond the scope of the federal government's authority. If a statute is *ultra vires,* it will not be enforceable. Similarly, if a province enacts a law which touches an area given to the federal government by the B.N.A. Act, that law is also *ultra vires* and unenforceable.

2. Classes of Law

The two main classes of law are: (1) *public law* and, (2) *private law.* Public law consists of the rules which govern the relations between various branches of the government, and between the government and private citizens. The main types of law within the class of public law are constitutional law, criminal law and administrative law. Private, or civil law, as it is also known, consists of the rules governing the relations between private persons or groups. Types of private law include contract law, property law, and tort law.

3. Substantive and Procedural Law

Each class or type of law consists of *substantive rules* and *procedural rules.* Substantive rules of law are the laws with which most people are probably more familiar. This is the law which describes our rights and duties. For example, the substantive part of the criminal law defines certain prohibited forms of conduct from which society has a right to be protected. Procedural law is the law which tells us how the substantive law can be enforced, that is, how our rights can be protected and our wrongs redressed. Thus, the rules which must be followed when an arrest is made are part of the law of criminal procedure. Whether an accused has a jury trial or not is a matter of procedure. Most of the material in the following chapters is concerned with substantive law. For example, specific criminal offences will be defined and discussed. However, some areas of criminal procedure will also be covered. In the next chapter, such procedural matters as the classification of offences and methods of trial will be examined. Chapter Five discusses other topics of procedure such as the powers of arrest and search.

4. Sources of Canadian Law

A. COMMON LAW AND CIVIL LAW There are two major systems of law in the western world today. Most English-speaking countries have what is called a *common law system.* The second type is called the *civil law system.* It should be noticed that the term "civil law" has two meanings. It may refer to civil or private law, which was discussed above, or it may refer to the system of law which is used by many continental European countries. Except for Quebec provincial law, which has adopted the civil law system, Canadian law is part of the common law tradition.

The civil law system is the older of the two. Its beginnings can be traced to the law of the Romans. Justinian, a Roman emperor in the 6th century A.D., compiled a code or book of law which contained all of the great Roman laws. This code was then used as the law in the areas of Europe under Roman control. After the fall of the Roman Empire, many of the people of Europe continued to use *Justinian's Code* or laws derived from it. In the early 19th century, Napoleon had written a similar code which was then adopted by many European countries. The *Napoleonic Code* also influenced greatly the writers of the *Quebec Civil Code*.

From about 55 B.C. to 412 A.D., England was occupied by the Roman army and naturally Roman law was used. However, in the fifth century A.D., various Anglo-Saxon tribes invaded the country, forcing the Romans to withdraw their troops. These invasions largely erased the influence of Roman law in England. For many centuries after the departure of the Romans, England was occupied by diverse tribes and groups who had little contact with each other. Each community had its own law based on its traditions and customs. Thus there was no body of law that could be called English law.

It was not until William, the Duke of Normandy, conquered England in 1066 that a unified England started to come into existence. One of William's first tasks was to set up a centralized government for the purpose of effectively controlling his new land. Part of the strong central government developed by William and his successors consisted of a royal court system. Under this system, the king's judges would travel through the country holding court in large villages and trading centres. Each judge's route was called a *circuit* and court sittings were known as *assizes*. It is interesting that today high court judges in Canada still travel to county or district seat towns and hold assizes.

These early judges were in the difficult position of not having a set of rules or a code of law to guide them when making decisions. Sometimes Norman Law and at other times local law could be used. Often, though, neither was appropriate and the judges had to rely on their common sense and base decisions on what seemed to them principles of justice and fairness. Eventually, the judges began discussing among themselves the cases they had heard and the decisions they had made. Gradually, it became a practice of the judges to follow the decision made in an earlier case if the case being heard and the earlier case had the same or similar facts involved. In other words, rather than rely only on his own judgement, a judge would think back to previously decided cases. If he found one that matched, or was very similar to, the case presently before him, he would make the same decision as that made in the first case. Of course, the facts in one case were frequently not the same or even very similar to the facts in other cases, so the judges could not always find a case to follow. But each time a decision was made in a particular situation, it created a *precedent,* or example, to be followed in future cases. The principle that was emerging was that like cases should be treated alike. Even today, we accept this principle as a basic rule of justice.

Once accurate written reports of cases became available to judges in about the 16th and 17th centuries, it became much easier for judges to follow precedent. By the 19th century, this practice became a strict and binding rule called *stare decisis* which means literally "to stand by." Today, judges in Canada still follow precedent. What this means, generally speaking, is that lower courts must follow the decisions of higher courts and courts of equal rank should try to follow each other's decisions if at all possible. Thus, by the process of making decisions in case after case, guided by the rule of precedent, these early English judges created a body of law that applied to all the people in England. This law was then common to all, or the *common law*. Since the common law consists of the decisions of judges in particular cases it is also sometimes called *case law*.

B. STATUTE LAW Another way to make law is to pass a statute or an Act that contains all the rules on a particular subject. As mentioned previously, the B.N.A. Act divides the authority to make statute law, which is also called legislative law, between the Federal Parliament and the provincial legislatures. Municipalities also make a type of legislative law. Municipal laws are called by-laws.

In Canada, statute law always has priority over case law. In other words, if there is a conflict between a court decision and a statute, the statute will overrule the court decision. In fact, it is the obligation of judges to apply statute law, where it exists, regardless of what the case law has been on the same topic.

Statutes do not always conflict with case law. Sometimes statutes only *codify* the case law. That is, all the principles of law that are contained in a number of cases are put into one statute. Statutes may also clarify an area that has been left unclear by case law. There are also statutes which are concerned with modern topics that have never been dealt with by case law. However, we still have large areas of law in the form of case law which have never been the subject of a statute and are still being developed by the courts. For example, much of the law of evidence which consists of the rules for presenting evidence in court is still in case law form.

An important point to be mentioned is that the judges' law-making function does not end once an area has been put into statute law. Statutes quite frequently need interpreting and this becomes the responsibility of the courts. The interpretations given to statutes, in turn, become part of the law. Why do statutes need interpreting? First, because statutes usually contain only general rules and it may be questionable how the general rule applies to specific situations. Second, because legislators, like all other people, do not always communicate clearly. Even if a statute seems quite straightforward, it still may be possible to read in more than one meaning. In either situation, the judge becomes the final interpreter who must decide the intent of the legislators when enacting the statute.

An interesting example of a court's interpretation of a statute is given by an Ontario County Court decision[1] regarding the offence of soliciting for the purpose of prostitution. Section 195.1 of the Code defines the offence as follows:

195.1 Every person who solicits any person in a public place for the purpose of prostitution is guilty of an offence punishable on summary conviction.

The question to be answered was whether a man who impersonated a female and solicited men for sexual purposes could be convicted of the offence described in s.195.1. The answer depended on the court's interpretation of the term "prostitution." The court decided that since traditionally only women were considered prostitutes, this offence could not be committed by a man. Since the court which heard the case was not a high level court, its decision does not carry much weight as a precedent. In fact, one year after the Ontario decision, the British Columbia Supreme Court reached the opposite conclusion.[2] It is, however, an interesting illustration of the court interpreting an apparently clear section in an unexpected way.

C. ADMINISTRATIVE LAW Administrative law is a growing source of law created by the executive branch of government. It consists largely of the decisions and regulations made by administrative boards and tribunals. For example, the decisions of the Workmen's Compensation Board in determining the eligibility of an injured workman for compensation form part of administrative law. Administrative law is not generally concerned with criminal law and will not be dealt with in this book.

B. FINDING THE LAW

1. Statute Law

After a statute is passed by either Parliament or a provincial legislature, it is published by the official government press. Usually all the statutes (or Acts) passed in one legislative session are contained in one volume. About every ten years, all the statutes are revised and consolidated into one set of volumes. Parliament then repeals the former statutes and enacts as law the newly revised ones. Revisions are necessary mainly to correct any errors in the original statutes and to incorporate into each any subsequent amendments. The last revision of the federal statutes occurred in 1970. So, a law first passed in 1965 can be found in the 1970 revised statutes. Here, each Act is given a separate chapter number and is listed alphabetically. A statute passed in 1976 will be found in the sessional volume for that year. These are usually listed in order of enactment. At the back of each sessional volume is a Table of Public Statutes which lists the acts by title or subject matter. These tables are very useful for locating statutes and checking for amendments.

The titles of the volumes are often referred to in abbreviated form. Revised statutes are abbreviated R.S. followed by the initial of the province or a "C" for Canada. If a sessional volume is referred to, the R. is dropped. Next the year of enactment is given. Thus, R.S.C. 1970 stands for Revised Statutes of Canada enacted in 1970. If a particular statute is mentioned, its chapter number is given after the year. Statutes are divided into sections. If a section is referred to, a small "s" followed by the section number is written after the chapter number.

Example: Narcotic Control Act R.S.C. 1970, c.N-1 s.24.

2. Case Law

There are many different series of case reports including national, regional, and provincial series. Some of these are official publications, while others are printed by private publishing companies. Only the more important cases are contained in these reports. The cases which would typically be reported would be the decisions in cases that have been appealed, cases which set precedents, and cases involving unclear areas of law. Not everything that has occurred in a case is reported. Usually, only the judge's written decision, which may often include a recital of the facts and the reasons for his decision, is reported. If more than one judge has heard the case (an appeal court frequently has more than one judge sitting) and there is a *dissenting opinion,* this will often be included in the report. A dissenting opinion results when the judges who have heard the case fail to reach a unanimous decision. In this situation the decision agreed to by a majority of the judges becomes the official decision of the court. The decision of the minority becomes the dissenting opinion. The court's decision is often referred to as the "holding" in the case. Similarly, a reference may be made to what the judge (or court) "held" in a case.

The most frequently referred to case series in the following pages will be Canadian Criminal Cases, abbreviated C.C.C. and Criminal Reports, abbreviated C.R. A glossary located in the beginning of the book gives a complete list of the names and the accepted abbreviations of other mentioned series.

To locate a case it is important to understand the case citation. The following chart indicates the form used for citing cases and the meaning of each element of the citation.

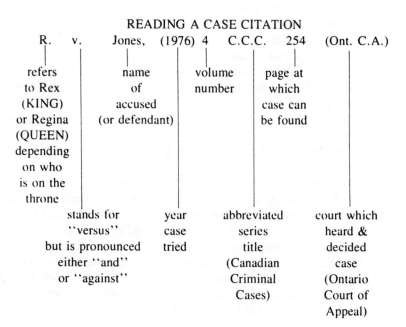

READING A CASE CITATION

R.   v.   Jones,   (1976) 4   C.C.C.   254   (Ont. C.A.)

| refers to Rex (KING) or Regina (QUEEN) depending on who is on the throne | name of accused (or defendant) | volume number | page at which case can be found |

| | stands for "versus" but is pronounced either "and" or "against" | year case tried | abbreviated series title (Canadian Criminal Cases) | court which heard & decided case (Ontario Court of Appeal) |

Notice that the first name given in the case is Rex or Regina, which indicates that the state or the Crown is proceeding against (i.e. prosecuting) the accused. If the court's decision is appealed to a higher court, the name of the *appellant* (the party appealing) is given first, followed by the name of the *respondent* (the party responding to the appeal).

QUESTIONS FOR REVIEW AND DISCUSSION

1. Define the term "law".
2. a. Why are the rules of a private club not considered law?
   b. Can you think of other types of rules which govern our conduct but are not considered law?
3. What are some functions served by the law? (try to think of specific functions not mentioned in the chapter).
4. a. What are the two main classes of law?
   b. Define each class.
5. a. What is the difference between substantive law and procedural law?
   b. Indicate whether the following are types of procedural or substantive law:
      (i)   the legal definition of murder
      (ii)   the law which states how a search warrant can be obtained
      (iii) the law which requires the appeal of a court decision to be made within a certain time limit
      (iv)   the law which requires parents to support their children.
6. a. Explain the origin of the common law system.
   b. Why is this system called the common law system?
7. a. Explain the operation of the rule of *stare decisis*.
   b. What is a precedent?
8. How does a judge make a law?
9. How should the following statutes be abbreviated:
   a. Juvenile Delinquents Act, Chapter J–3, 1970, Revised Statutes of Canada.
   b. Criminal Law Amendment Act, 1972, Chapter 13, 1972, Statutes of Canada.
   c. Ontario Highway Traffic Act, 1970, Chapter 202, Revised Statutes, section 172.
10. What should be the citations for the following cases?
    a. John Smith was prosecuted by the Crown Attorney on behalf of the State. The decision of the court was reported in Canadian Criminal Cases, the fifth volume at page 27. The trial was held in 1974 in the province of New Brunswick in Magistrates Court.
    b. After being found guilty Smith appealed the decision of the court to the County Court for the County of Addington. The decision of the appeal court was reported in volume twelve at page 305 of Canadian Criminal Cases. The appeal was heard in 1975.

c. In 1972 Sharon Brown was prosecuted by the Crown Attorney, on behalf of the State, in Ontario Provincial Court (Criminal Division). The decision of the court finding her guilty was reported in volume 7 of Criminal Reports at page 46.

[1] *R. v. Patterson* (1972), 9 C.C.C. (2d) 364, 19 C.R.N.S. 289 (Ont.Co.Ct.)
[2] *R. v. Obey* (1973), 11 C.C.C. (2d) 28, 21 C.R.N.S. 121 (B.C.S.C.)

Chapter Two

An Introduction to Criminal Law

A. THE NATURE OF THE CRIMINAL LAW

1. A Definition

Crimes are unlawful acts, or failures to act, which are wrongs committed against society. In other words, when a person commits a criminal act, not only the victim but also the community suffers. Why do we say that the community is harmed by criminal acts? Consider the situation of a rash of muggings in a local park. Unless the offender is found and punished, people will be afraid to walk through the park, will look suspiciously at others, and a general feeling of uneasiness will prevail. Consider also the concern of the public when it is announced that the crime rate is rising. Clearly, crime and its control are community concerns. Therefore, the primary aims of the criminal law are protecting the public and preserving the peace. In fact, as we will see later, some criminal offences have no particular victim except the community.

2. The Distinction Between Criminal and Civil Proceedings

Where there is an individual victim of a crime, the victim may seek a remedy in private law through what is called a civil proceeding.

In the early days of the English law, there was little distinction drawn between a civil wrong and a criminal wrong. If a person or his property were injured, either that person or his family would seek revenge. Consequently, blood feuds between families were not infrequent events, although the community migh. encourage the victim to accept compensation in the form of money.

At the same time, the idea of the king's peace was becoming establish. king could put certain people or property under his protection. If anyone injui persons or property being protected by the king, he would have to pay the ki. money fine. Some offences were so serious that a fine would be inadequate. In ti. case, the offender's "life and limbs" would be at the king's mercy. Gradually, the king extended the area of his peace so that it finally encompassed all the territory and persons under his rule. Since the wrong was an offence against the king, breaches of the peace came to be prosecuted by the king's agents in the name of the king.

Today, most prosecutions are undertaken by Crown Attorneys (i.e. prosecutors) who are the agents of the Attorney General. The Attorney General's (or Solicitor General's) office is occupied by a person appointed by the executive branch of the government. His role is to act as the government's legal advisor and counsel. There are a limited number of situations in which a criminal offence can be prosecuted by a private individual (i.e. private prosecutions). These situations will be mentioned during the discussion of the classification of offences.

While the criminal law was taking shape, the civil law was also developing. As mentioned previously, the civil law governs the interactions of private persons. For example, the law of contract consists largely of the rules which must be followed before an agreement between private parties will be enforced by the courts.

A breach of a civil rule of law is considered a civil wrong. Many civil wrongs are also criminal wrongs. For example, if A is accused of taking B's car without B's permission, A may have committed both the criminal offence of theft and the civil offence of trespass to goods. This civil wrong is a type of offence called a tort. Very briefly, torts are acts (or omissions) which all people have a duty to refrain from committing against other people. The usual remedy a victim of a tort may seek through a civil proceeding is compensation (e.g. money) for the loss he has suffered. So, in the above example, A may be *prosecuted* (proceeded against) in a criminal court and if *convicted* (found guilty), *sentenced* to a suitable punishment. If A is found not guilty he will be *acquitted* and the criminal charge *dismissed*. If B wishes to seek his civil remedy he must *sue* (or proceed against) A in a civil court. If B is successful and wins his case, *judgment* (the court's decision) will be given in his favour, or against A, and he will be *awarded* suitable compensation. If B is not successful, judgment will be given in favour of A.

There are many differences between criminal and civil proceedings other than terminology. It is not necessary to discuss these differences extensively, but a brief mention of two important differences should be made. First, where a possibility of a civil action exists, the community has no interest in whether the victim decides to go to court. However, where a crime has occurred, except where private prosecutions are possible, it is the Crown Attorney's decision whether or not to prosecute, even if the victim would rather not take any steps against the offender. Second, an important aim of the criminal law is to punish convicted offenders (e.g. by fine or imprisonment). However, the civil law generally only permits a victim to be compensated, or repaid, for his actual loss from the wrongdoer.

B. CRIMINAL LAW IN CANADA

1. Jurisdiction

The authority to enact legislation in the area of criminal law has been assigned to the federal government by the B.N.A. Act, although the provinces are authorized by the Act to organize the courts of criminal jurisdiction. The provinces have, however, been given the power to impose punishment by fine, penalty or imprisonment for the purposes of enforcing provincial laws. Strictly speaking then, all criminal law is federal. However, it is common for people to think of provincial offences as criminal, particularly because of the types of punishment possible. In Ontario for instance, a person may be imprisoned for "two years less a day" for violating a provincial law. Since the topic of this book is the criminal law, provincial offences will not be dealt with in any depth.

2. Sources of Canadian Criminal Law

The main source of both substantive and procedural criminal law in Canada is the Criminal Code. This is a federal statute which was first enacted in 1869. At that time, it attempted to consolidate the English common law crimes applicable to Canada and the Colonial laws. A significant addition was made in 1953 by s.8, which states in part:

> **8. Notwithstanding anything in this Act or any other Act, no person shall be convicted**
> **(a) of an offence at common law ...**

This section was necessary to clarify the question of whether a person could be convicted of a common law offence that was not in the Code. It should be mentioned however, that s.7(3) of the Code preserves all common law defences. Thus, for example, the law regarding the use of intoxication as a defence is in case law form.

Although the main focus of this book will be on the Criminal Code, there are many other federal statutes which create criminal law. Some of these will be discussed in the Appendix.

C. THE CRIMINAL CODE

1. Structure

The Criminal Code contains twenty-five parts. The sections within each part are related to each other by subject matter. For example, Part VII consists of offences against the rights of property.

The official Criminal Code can be found in the 1970 Revised Statutes of Canada. Later sessional volumes must be checked for amendments. Private companies also publish up-to-date editions of the Code each year. One very helpful study aid is an *annotated code*. Codes which are annotated list after each section a brief description of important cases which interpret and apply the section. Annotated codes are useful since the Code, like other statutes, is constantly being interpreted and applied by the courts, and reference to these court decisions is necessary to fully understand the meaning of the Code.

2. Classification of Offences

The Code divides offences into two categories: (1) indictable offences and (2) offences punishable upon summary conviction. Generally speaking, the difference between the two is that indictable offences are considered more serious crimes, and so, for example, a more involved and formal trial procedure is used. Conversely, summary offences are tried in a "summary" fashion, that is, quickly and informally. Examples of indictable offences are murder, kidnapping, and robbery. Causing a disturbance in or near a public place and common assault are types of summary offences. There is one other group of offences which may be either indictable or summary. These are sometimes called *hybrid* offences. The decision as to whether a hybrid offence is treated as an indictable offence or as a summary offence is made by the prosecutor. The prosecutor may base his decision on facts such as whether the offence is a first-time occurrence to be treated less seriously, or a second offence to be treated more seriously. The existence of mitigating or, on the other hand, aggravating circumstances will also influence the prosecutor's decision.

3. Differences Between Indictable and Summary Offences

The specific differences between indictable offences and summary offences are mainly related to matters of procedure and to the types of penalties possible. The following discussion will only touch upon some of the more important differences between, and main characteristics of, indictable and summary offences. Further comparison will be made in Chapter Five, where powers of arrest and search are discussed.

A. SUMMARY OFFENCES Part XXIV of the Code describes the procedure to be used for the trial of offences punishable upon summary conviction. Section 723 provides that to begin a court proceeding (i.e. the trial), an *information* must be laid before a justice of the peace. This means that the *informant* swears, under oath, in an affidavit either that he has personal knowledge, or that he has reasonable and probable grounds for believing that an offence has been committed by a certain person. The information is then signed by the informant and the justice of the peace. If the accused is present, either personally or represented by counsel or agent, the trial can proceed immediately. If the accused is not personally present and not represented by counsel or agent, the justice of the peace can issue a warrant for the arrest of the accused, or a summons which orders the accused to appear in court on a certain date.

Although informations are usually laid by police officers, any person may lay an information. Since s.720 includes the informant in its definition of "prosecutor", private prosecutions are possible for summary offences. However, most offences are prosecuted by the Crown Attorney, the agent of the Attorney General.

Unlike most indictable offences, summary offences must be prosecuted within a certain time. Section 721 (2) states that proceedings can not be started more than six months after the time when the "subject-matter" of the proceedings arose. In other words, the information must be laid within six months of the happening of the complained-of act.

Trials of summary offences are held before "summary conviction courts" as defined in s.720. Usually the trials are held before a justice of the peace or magistrate. In some provinces magistrates are called provincial court judges. Jury trials are never permitted in summary proceedings. Similarly preliminary hearings are never held. A preliminary hearing is an inquiry which takes place before the trial to determine if there is enough evidence to commit the accused to trial. This hearing is only used in connection with indictable offences.

After the information has been laid, and with both the accused (or his agent or counsel) and the prosecutor present, the accused is *arraigned*. The procedure used for arraignment is set out in s.736. It provides that the substance of the information must be stated to the accused. He is then asked whether he pleads guilty or not guilty. If he pleads guilty, the court will convict him. If he pleads not guilty, the court will proceed with the trial. This means that the prosecutor will present his evidence, through the testimony of witnesses, and the accused may present evidence in his defence. Both parties also have an opportunity to cross-examine each other's witnesses.

Once the court has heard the prosecutor, the accused and the witnesses, it will decide whether to convict the accused or dismiss the information.

Where the accused is convicted, the penalties which may be imposed are limited by s.722. This section allows punishment by fine of up to $500.00 and/or imprisonment for not more than six months.

B. INDICTABLE OFFENCES Brief reference to the origins of the procedure used for indictable offences should be made at this point.

Starting in the 12th century, the English method for bringing suspected criminals to justice was by the *presenting of an indictment* by a grand jury. The jury consisted of members of the local community whose duty it was to report all suspected crimes committed by their neighbors to the king or his agent. This report, which would accuse certain persons of specific crimes, was called an indictment. At first the jurors based their report on their own personal knowledge. Gradually, as the jury system evolved, the grand jurors became persons without direct knowledge of the crime, who based their report upon the testimony of witnesses to the offence.

The modern practice, which is set out in sections 503 – 506 of the Code, is for the Attorney General, or some one authorized by him or the court, to *prefer,* (i.e. present) a bill of indictment before a grand jury. The jury will then hear the testimony of witnesses called by the prosecutor. The accused and his counsel are not present during the hearing. In fact, the proceedings are conducted in complete secrecy. One reason for the secrecy is to protect the reputations of innocent persons falsely accused of crimes.

After hearing the evidence presented by the prosecutor, the jurors must decide whether there is enough evidence to send the accused to trial before a judge and *petit jury.* If a majority of the jurors decide that there is enough evidence for a trial, the foreman of the jury will endorse the indictment with the words "true bill." If a majority of the jurors decide that there is insufficient evidence for a trial, the indictment is endorsed "no bill."

The grand jury system was originally adopted in Canada by all the provinces except Saskatchewan and Alberta. Also, the territories have never had grand juries. Today, however, the only province which still requires indictments to be presented by grand juries is Nova Scotia. In all other provinces, to commence the trial of an indictable offence, the Attorney General, his agent, or someone with his consent or the consent of the court (e.g. a private person) prefers the written indictment before the court. This means, in effect, that the Attorney General or his agents are performing the functions that had been performed by the grand jury.

There are three methods of trial for indictable offences:
1. by magistrate (or provincial court judge)
2. by a judge without a jury
3. by a judge and jury.

Some offences in the Code must be tried by a magistrate. Other offences must be tried by a judge and jury. For the majority of offences, however, the accused can elect his method of trial, i.e. whether before a magistrate, judge alone, or judge and jury. The one situation where the accused may lose his right of election is where the offence is punishable by more than five years imprisonment. In this situation s.498 allows the Attorney General to require the accused to be tried by judge and jury.

Section 483 lists the indictable offences which must be tried before a magistrate. These are the less serious indictable offences such as theft where the value of the goods does not exceed $200.00, keeping a gaming house, bookmaking and betting. These offences are tried like summary offences in that formal indictment is not necessary and preliminary hearings are not held.

Since preliminary hearings are generally required for those indictable offences not tried by a magistrate, a brief discussion of the purpose of the hearing at this point would be helpful.

A preliminary hearing is usually held before a magistrate or justice of the peace after the accused has been charged with an offence. The main purpose of the hearing is to determine if there is enough evidence to commit the accused to trial. During the hearing the prosecutor presents evidence through the testimony of witnesses. The accused has a right to present evidence and to make a statement on his own behalf. Each party can also cross-examine each other's witnesses. After considering the evidence, the justice or magistrate will decide whether or not there is enough evidence to commit the accused to trial. Where an accused has been committed to trial, it is important to point out that this does not mean that the justice or magistrate has found him guilty. Being committed to trial after a preliminary hearing just means that there is "sufficient evidence" for a trial to be held. This procedure serves a somewhat similar purpose as that served by the grand jury in that weak cases can be disposed of without the time and expense of a full trial. For the accused, the preliminary hearing has the added advantage of allowing him to determine the nature and strength of the case against him.

Preliminary hearings are held before the indictment is preferred. The relevant Code sections on preliminary hearings are sections 463 – 481 and sections 485 (1) and 485 (3) (a).

Section 427 lists the offences which must be tried in a *superior court of criminal jurisdiction*. This court is the province's highest ranking trial court with criminal jurisdiction. Section 2 gives the name of the superior criminal court for each province. Usually it is called the Supreme or Superior Court of the province (e.g. Supreme Court of Ontario). Generally, all trials before superior criminal courts are by judge and jury. The one exception is that in Alberta the accused may consent to being tried by a superior criminal court without a jury. This exception is set out in s.430.

The offences contained in s.427 are considered the most serious offences. They include: treason, sedition, piracy, and murder.

All other offences in the Code are electable except where, as mentioned above, the Attorney General can require a trial before judge and jury. If the accused elects to be tried by judge without a jury, he will be tried by a judge as defined for each province in s.482. Generally, the judges listed in this section are county or district court judges. Part XVI of the Code, which starts with s.482, describes the procedure to be used where the trial is without a jury and before either a judge or magistrate.

Where the accused elects to be tried by judge and jury he may be tried by a superior court of criminal jurisdiction or a court of criminal jurisdiction. Courts of criminal jurisdiction are defined in s.2. Generally, they are courts of general or quarter sessions of the peace presided over by a county or district court judge.

Unlike summary offence proceedings, the accused must be personally present (unless the court orders otherwise) for the trial of an indictable offence. Generally speaking, during the trial each party calls its own witnesses who give evidence under oath. Each party also has a right to cross-examine the other party's witnesses. After both the accused and the prosecutor have finished presenting evidence, each one has the right to sum up the evidence and make closing arguments to the jury, if there is one, or to the judge.

If the trial is before a jury, the judge will then sum up the case for the jury. He will instruct them on questions of law and may express his opinion regarding credibility of witnesses or the importance of the evidence.

If there is a jury, it will return a verdict of guilty or not guilty. If the trial is before a judge only, he will make the finding of guilty or not guilty. Depending on the verdict, the accused will either be convicted or acquitted by the court. If the accused is convicted, the judge will then sentence the accused to a punishment.

The possible penalties for indictable offences are much harsher than those allowed for summary offences. The Code sets out maximum terms of imprisonment for each offence, such as life, 14 years, or 10 years. Section 646 allows the court to impose fines in addition to, or instead of, imprisonment.

4. Appeals

Whether the decision of a court can be appealed, and if so, what procedure is used, depends upon a number of factors. The most important factor is the class of the offence, i.e. whether it is indictable or summary. The following discussion will, however, only give a very general overview of the grounds and procedure for appealing both classes of offences. A detailed examination of this subject is beyond the scope of this book.

In every trial there are two main issues which must be determined: the *facts* of the case, and the *law* which applies to those facts. The grounds for most appeals are usually based on *questions of fact, questions of law,* or *questions of mixed fact and law*. For example, A is charged with murdering B by shooting him. Whether A was the person who aimed and fired the gun at B is a question of fact. Given the facts of the case, whether the offence of murder has been committed is a question of law. That is, assuming that A intentionally shot B, does this conduct constitute the offence of murder as defined by the Code? When an accused is tried by judge and jury, it is the jury's function to determine the facts of the case while the judge's function is to determine what law applies to the facts. If the trial is before a judge alone he performs both of these functions.

Generally, both parties to a proceeding (i.e. the accused and the prosecutor) have a right to appeal in certain situations. The accused may be able to appeal from his conviction or against his sentence. In other words, he can appeal the decision of the court finding him guilty or only the punishment imposed by the court. So for example, A is convicted of common assault and sentenced to six years imprisonment. A can appeal his sentence on a question of law because s.245(1) of the Code provides that the maximum term of imprisonment for common assault is five years.

The prosecutor can appeal a dismissal of the information, the acquittal of the accused, or the sentence ordered by the court.

If the appeal court agrees that the trial court decision was wrong, it may *allow* the appeal. If the appeal court finds that the trial court decision was proper, it will *dismiss* the appeal. Where the appeal is allowed, the appeal court can do such things as: order a new trial, direct an acquittal, enter a verdict of guilty (except where there has been a jury trial), or vary the sentence.

An appeal court decision can sometimes be appealed to a higher court. The final and highest court of appeal in Canada is the Supreme Court of Canada.

5. Hierarchy of Persons and Courts with Jurisdiction Over Criminal Matters

One way of picturing the criminal justice system is to imagine a pyramid. At the top of the pyramid is the Supreme Court of Canada. At the base of the pyramid are the justices of the peace. Lower levels of the pyramid are occupied by trial courts. Upper levels are occupied by appeal courts which only review cases appealed from trial courts. At the middle of the pyramid are those courts in which both trials are held and appeals heard. Generally speaking, as the offence becomes more serious or as an offence is appealed it moves up the pyramid.

The following is a brief description of some of the main functions of the several levels of judicial authority in criminal matters, starting with the lowest level. This is only a general description since each province is responsible for the administration of criminal law in the province and provincial variations are common.

Title	Duties
Justice of the Peace	— receives informations. — issues summonses and warrants for arrest. — holds hearings in bail, and preliminary hearings. — tries summary offences.
Magistrate (or Provincial Court Judge)	— exercises all the duties of a justice of the peace. — tries less serious indictable offences.
County or District Court	— trials of certain indictable offences, either with or without jury are held here. — hears appeals of summary offences.
Supreme or Superior Court	— the province's highest level trial court. — trials of the most serious indictable offences are held here always before judge and jury, except in Alberta where the accused can elect trial by a superior court judge without jury.

	— hears some appeals involving summary offences.
Court of Appeal	— the province's highest appeal court, hears appeals from the trial courts and lower level appeal courts.
Supreme Court of Canada	— hears appeals from provincial Courts of Appeal.

QUESTIONS FOR REVIEW AND DISCUSSION

1. What is a crime?
2. Discuss the differences between civil wrongs and criminal wrongs.
3. What is the main source of criminal law in Canada?
4. a. Discuss the main differences between indictable offences and summary offences.
   b. What is a hybrid offence?
5. What is the purpose of a preliminary hearing?
6. What are the three methods of trial for indictable offences?
7. What is the difference between a question of fact and a question of law?
8. What is the highest court of appeal in Canada?

Chapter Three

Some General Principles

A. THE ELEMENTS OF A CRIME

In general, every crime has a physical element and a mental element. If either element is missing, then no crime is committed. In the first part of this chapter we will discuss the physical element and in the next part we will discuss the mental element.

1. The Physical Element of a Crime: *Actus Reus*

The physical element of a crime is usually referred to as the *actus reus*. *Actus reus* is a Latin term which is loosely translated as "guilty act" or "wrongful act". Although the term frequently refers to prohibited acts, it is more accurate to say that it refers to all the parts of the crime other than the *mens rea* or the state of mind of the accused.

In order to determine what is the *actus reus* of a particular offence, it is necessary to look at the definition of the offence. For example, consider s.244:

> **244. A person commits an assault when**
> **(a) without the consent of another person .... he applies force intentionally to the person of the other, directly or indirectly, ...**

In this offence of assault, the *actus reus* or physical element consists of (1) applying force to another person (2) without the other person's consent. These are the parts of the crime which do not pertain to what was going on in the mind of the accused. Rather, they pertain to a physical occurrence (applying force) and a circumstance (without consent). The mental element or *mens rea* of the offence largely consists of the intention to apply force. This is indicated by the word "intentionally." This intention is clearly something which relates to what was going on in the mind of the accused and therefore, is not part of the *actus reus*.

In general, the *actus reus* of a crime consists of a certain type of *conduct*, a *consequence* of that conduct, and *circumstances* surrounding the conduct. Each of these terms will be discussed separately.

A. CONDUCT The conduct involved in a crime may be an act, an omission, or a "state of being," depending on the particular crime.

Most crimes require that some *act* be committed. In criminal law, an act is a voluntary movement. For example, when A throws a punch at B, A is voluntarily moving his arm. Or, when C shoots a gun, he is committing an act if he voluntarily pulls the trigger.

An *omission* is the failure to act when there is, under the criminal law, a duty to act. For example, s.197(1)(a) refers to such a duty:

> **197.(1) Every one is under a legal duty**
> **(a) as a parent, foster parent, guardian or head of a family, to provide necessaries of life for a child under the age of sixteen years.**

In brief, a parent has a legal duty to provide food and shelter for his children. If a parent omits or fails to perform this duty, then he may be in violation of the criminal law.

Another example of a duty is the duty to assist a police officer when requested to do so:

> **118. Every one who ...**
> **(b) omits, without reasonable excuse, to assist a public officer or peace officer in the execution of his duty in arresting a person or in preserving the peace, after having reasonable notice that he is required to do so ....**
> **is guilty of an indictable offence and is liable to imprisonment for two years.**

It is clear that s.118 is not prohibiting an act. Rather, it creates a duty and makes it an offence for a person to omit or fail to perform this duty, unless there is a reasonable excuse.

Some offences require neither an act nor an omission. Rather, they simply require a state of being. For example, s.312 prohibits a person from "having in his possession" anything which was obtained by crime:

312.(1) Every one commits an offence who has [anything] in his possession . . .knowing that [it] was obtained . . .
  (a) [by] the commission in Canada of an offence punishable by indictment, or
  (b) [by] an act or omission anywhere that, if it had occurred in Canada, would have constituted an offence punishable by indictment.

For example, if a person is wearing a stolen watch, then he has it in his possession. Simply having it is enough. It is not necessary that there be some act or omission for this offence to occur.

Another example of a state of being is found in s.185(2)(a):

185.(2) Every one who
  (a) is found, without lawful excuse, in a common gaming house or common betting house, . . .
is guilty of an offence punishable on summary conviction.

Again, no act or omission is necessary. Simply being "found in" a common gaming house or common betting house is sufficient.

A state of being is not really conduct. But, it has been mentioned here to indicate that it forms part of the *actus reus* of crimes which do not require some act or omission.

(i) voluntariness

It is a general principle of criminal law that a person's act or omission must be voluntary if he is to be held responsible for it. An act was defined above as a voluntary movement. If a movement is involuntary, then under the criminal law, there is no act and, therefore, no criminal responsibility.

An example of an involuntary (or automatic) movement is the beating of a heart. Other examples are the bodily movements of a person undergoing an epileptic fit, or the actions committed while sleep-walking. The general point is that if a person has no control over his conduct, then he will not be held criminally responsible for it.

If the conduct which forms part of the *actus reus* of a crime is not voluntary, then the accused can use the defence of automatism. Automatism, along with other defences, is discussed in Chapter Four.

(ii) innocent agent

A person will not escape criminal responsibility by using the innocent actions of someone else to achieve unlawful purposes. For example, A might try to sell drugs to B by using his 12-year-old son to deliver a package containing the drugs and collect the payment. The son may have no idea that he is delivering drugs and thus would be innocent of any wrongdoing. However, A could be found guilty of trafficking even though he was not involved in the actual sale. Under the criminal law, the acts of A's son are considered to be the acts of A and thus A is held responsible for the *actus reus* of the crime.

B. CONSEQUENCES Another part of the *actus reus* or physical element of a crime is a consequence. The consequence involved in a crime is the result of an act or an omission. For example, the consequence or result in homicide is the death of a human being:

> **205.(1) A person commits homicide when, directly or indirectly, by any means, he causes the death of a human being.**

Another example is mischief in which the "consequence" part of the offence is damage to property:

> **387.(1) Every one commits mischief who wilfully**
> **(a) destroys or damages property.**

In both these examples, the Code section does not mention any particular conduct which must cause the consequence to occur. In other words, a person may cause the death of a human being by shooting him, by stabbing him, by throwing a bomb in his car or by some other act. Regardless of which act is done, the person will have committed homicide if his act caused another person to die. Similarly, a person commits mischief if he causes damage to property such as a house by throwing rocks through the windows, by breaking down the front door, or by some other destructive act.

The point here is that the definitions of most crimes mention a consequence, but they do not mention any particular act or omission. In most situations, this distinction between conduct and consequence is not necessary. For example, it is usually precise enough to say simply that A killed B or that A damaged B's property. However, the distinction can be very helpful when trying to understand the concepts of causation, intention, and recklessness, which are discussed below.

C. CIRCUMSTANCES Conduct (an act or omission) is usually not criminal unless it is committed under certain circumstances which form part of the *actus reus* of a crime. For example, s.249(1) includes many circumstances:

> **249.(1) Every one who, without lawful authority, takes . . .an**
> **unmarried female person under the age of sixteen years out of**
> **the possession of and against the will of her parent or guardian**
> **is guilty of an indictable offence.**

The relevant circumstances which must be present for this particular offence to be committed are: (1) the taker must not have lawful authority (an example of a taker with lawful authority might be a social worker acting under a court order); (2) the taken person must be female; (3) she must be unmarried; (4) she must be under the age of sixteen; (5) at the time of the taking, she must have been in the possession of her parent or guardian; and (6) the taking must have been against the will of her parent or guardian. If any one of these circumstances is not present, then the *actus reus* is not complete and, thus, the offence is not comitted.

Another example of relevant circumstances in a crime can be found in s.173, trespassing at night:

> **173. Every one who ...loiters or prowls at night upon the property of another person near a dwelling-house situated on that property is guilty of an offence....**

Here, the circumstances which form part of the *actus reus* are (1) the loitering or prowling must occur at night, (2) it must occur on another person's property, (3) it must occur near a dwelling-house and (4) the house must be situated on that property. All these circumstances must be present for the offence to be committed. For example, if the loitering or prowling occurs during the day or if there is no dwelling-house on the property, then there is no *actus reus* and thus, no offence under s.173.

D. CAUSATION When the *actus reus* of a crime includes certain consequences, the crime is committed only if the conduct of the accused caused the consequences to occur. So, if A is charged with murdering B, then it must be shown that A's conduct caused the death of B. In most criminal cases, there is no problem in establishing a causal link between the conduct of the accused and the consequence. For example, A punches B, breaking his nose. It is clear that there is a direct cause and effect relationship between A's act and B's broken nose.

In some cases, the question of causation is not so clear. In *R. v. Wilmot,*[1] the accused was charged with "causing the death of a human being by means of an unlawful act" (manslaughter). The accused was driving his car on a highway when he collided with a person on a bicycle who was riding in the opposite direction. The collision killed the bicycle-rider. The accused was intoxicated at the time of the accident. Just before the collision, the accused was driving at a moderate, not excessive, rate of speed. At the moment of impact the car was standing still or practically so and it was slightly across the centre line on the wrong side of the road. Also, the bicycle-rider, who had a carton of empty beer bottles on the handle bars, swerved or wavered into the left-hand front corner of the car. The court found the accused not guilty because it was not proven that there was a causal relation between the unlawful act of driving a car while intoxicated and the killing of the bicycle-rider. The court said that it is not enough to show that while a person was doing an unlawful act another person was killed. It must be proven that the act (driving while intoxicated) was a direct cause or at least a contributing cause of the death. Neither the fact that the accused was intoxicated nor the other facts in the case proved that his driving caused or brought about the death of the bicycle-rider.

In *R. v. Dubois*[2] the problem was whether the accused had indirectly caused the death of a person. The accused, Dubois, started a fight with Miron in a tavern. After the fight was over, Dubois left the tavern to get into his car. A few minutes later, Miron ran out and fired a shot at Dubois. The shot missed Dubois but killed Petit, an innocent passer-by. Miron was convicted of manslaughter. Dubois was then charged with murder. The prosecution argued that Dubois had indirectly caused the death of Petit by assaulting Miron. The court found the accused not guilty because, in law, there was no causal relation between the assault of Dubois on Miron and the death of Petit. The connection between the conduct and the consequence was too remote.

Other causation issues are covered in special Code provisions regarding the causing of death, discussed in Chapter Nine.

2. The Mental Element of a Crime: *Mens Rea*

As mentioned above, there is a general rule that a crime consists of both an *actus reus* or physical element and a *mens rea* or mental element. If either one of these elements is missing, then no crime is committed. In general, the *actus reus* of a crime refers to certain conduct of a person, the consequences of that conduct, and surrounding circumstances. In this part of the chapter, another general rule will be discussed: the person's conduct must be committed with a certain state of mind (i.e. *mens rea)*. In his mind, the person must *foresee* the consequences of his conduct and be *aware* of the circumstances mentioned in the definition of the crime.

There are three types of *mens rea*[3]: (1) intention, (2) knowledge, and (3) reck-lessness. Each of these will be discussed separately.

A. INTENTION In most crimes, it is necessary that the accused person intended to cause a certain wrongful consequence. This means that he "meant to" cause the consequence. For example, if A hits B without B's consent, then he will be guilty of assault, but only if he intended or meant to hit B. If A accidentally hit B, then he would not have intention and thus no assault would be committed.

Many Code sections clearly require intention by using such words as "intentionally", "wilfully" or "means to". For example, one type of assault is defined in s.244(a) as:

> **244. A person commits an assault when, without the consent of another person or with consent, where it is obtained by fraud,**
> **(a) he applies force *intentionally* to the person of the other, directly or indirectly . . . .**

Another example is the offence of obstructing a peace officer in the execution of his duty:

> **118. Every one who**
> **(a) resists or *wilfully* obstructs a public officer or peace officer in the execution of his duty or any person lawfully acting in aid of such an officer . . . .**
> **is guilty of an indictable offence.**

In the offence of obstructing a peace officer, a person is guilty only if he intends or means to wrongfully obstruct or interfere with the officer.

Even if the Code section does not use a word such as "wilfully", intention usually will still be required. For example, in s.118 above, a person may be charged with resisting a peace officer rather than wilfully obstructing the officer. The section does not indicate that the person must "wilfully" or "intentionally" resist. However, despite the absence of these words, the person will be guilty of the offence only if he intended or meant to resist the peace officer.

(i) specific intent

Some offences require a special or specific kind of intent. These are called specific intent offences. In general, specific intent offences are indicated by the words "with intent" or similar words such as "for the purpose of."[4] For example, consider s.306(1)(a):

> **306.(1) Every one who**
> **(a) breaks and enters a place** *with intent to commit an indictable*
> *offence* **therein...**
> **is guilty of an indictable offence....**

In this offence, it must be shown not only that the accused intended to break and enter but also that he did it with the specific intent to commit an indictable offence such as theft. If it could be shown that he broke into a place in order to obtain shelter from a storm, then he would not have violated s.306(1)(a). On the other hand, it is not necessary to show that he actually committed an indictable offence. It is enough to show that he broke and entered with the intent to commit an indictable offence.

Another example of a specific intent offence is robbery. One form of robbery is found in s.302(c):

> **302. Every one commits robbery who**
> **(c) assaults any person** *with intent to steal* **from him.**

To violate this provision, a person must not only assault someone but he also must do the assaulting with the intent to steal from his victim. If it could be shown that A assaulted B, but it could not be shown that he had the specific intent to steal, then A would be guilty of assault, but not robbery.

Offences, such as assault, which do not require a specific intent are called *general intent* offences. The distinction between a general intent offence and a specific intent offence has been explained in the following way:

> *In considering the question of* mens rea, *a distinction is to be drawn between "intention" as applied to acts done to achieve an immediate end on the one hand and acts done with the specific and ulterior motive and intention of furthering or achieving an illegal object on the other hand. Illegal acts of the former kind are done intentionally in the sense that they are not done by accident or through honest mistakes, but acts of the latter kind are the product of*

> *preconception and are deliberate steps taken toward an illegal goal.*
> *The former acts may be purely physical products of momentary pas-*
> *sion, whereas the latter involve the mental process of formulating a*
> *specific intent.* [5]

Briefly, in a general intent offence the acts are done to achieve an immediate consequence or result. For example, assault is committed when A throws a punch at B in order to hit him and he does hit him without B's consent. In a specific intent offence, the acts are done with some additional or further intention in mind. For example, A's further intention in hitting B might be to steal B's money.

The distinction between general intent and specific intent is important for at least two reasons:

(1) A greater burden of proof is placed on the prosecution in a specific intent offence. That is, the prosecution must prove not only that the accused intentionally committed the prohibited act, but also that he committed the act with a specific intent.

(2) The defence of intoxication (by alcohol or drugs) can be successfully used with a specific intent offence. It is not a defence to a charge of committing a general intent offence.

(ii) intention and motive

Intention is different from motive. Motive refers to some purpose for committing the crime. It is not part of the *mens rea* of a crime. A person may commit a crime for a good motive and still be found guilty. For example, a man may want to free his father from the pain of cancer. So he gives his father a poisonous drug which results in the death of his father. Here the *actus reus* (killing the father) and the *mens rea* (intending to kill his father) of murder were both present and thus the crime was committed. The motive, to put his father out of his misery, was irrelevant to the issue of criminal responsibility and the son would be guilty of murder.

The important point to remember is that the motive is not part of the actual crime. Therefore, if the *actus reus* and the *mens rea* of a crime were present, then it makes no difference to criminal responsibility whether the accused acted with a good or bad motive.

However, motive can be relevant in at least two general ways. First, it can be used as evidence to help prove the intention of the accused. For example, if the prosecution can show that A would inherit $100,000 when B died, then it can be seen that A would have a motive or purpose for killing B. This evidence of motive could be important in establishing whether A intended to kill B.

A second way in which motive is relevant concerns sentencing. An accused who has been found guilty of a crime may receive a lighter sentence from the judge if he acted with a good motive rather than a bad one. For example, A might receive a lighter sentence for murdering B if he did it as an act of mercy (e.g. "mercy killing") rather than as an act of greed (e.g. to inherit money).

(iii) intention and voluntariness

Intention is part of the *mens rea* of a crime and it should be distinguished from the voluntariness of a person's conduct which is part of the *actus reus* of a crime. In general, voluntariness refers to control over bodily movements. Intention refers to the state of mind regarding the consequences or results of those bodily movements. For example, a person may voluntarily shoot a gun but he may not be intending to kill someone. His act of shooting is under his control and, therefore, is voluntary. But, if he did not intend human death or serious bodily harm as a consequence of his act, then he did not have the *mens rea* or criminal intent of murder.

B. KNOWLEDGE In many crimes it is necessary that the accused have knowledge or awareness of certain circumstances. This is sometimes indicated by the word "knowing" or "knowingly" in the definition of the crime. For example, s.120 states:

> **120. Every one commits perjury who, being a witness in a judicial proceeding, with intent to mislead gives false evidence,** *knowing that the evidence is false.*

If a person gives false evidence at a trial but he does not realize that the evidence is false, then he has not committed perjury. Without knowledge of this circumstance, there is not *mens rea* and thus no offence is committed.

The general rule is that the word "knowingly" in the definition of an offence applies to all the elements of the *actus reus*. In *R. v. Rees,*[6] the accused was charged with contributing to juvenile delinquency, contrary to s.33(1) of the Juvenile Delinquents Act:

> **33.(1) Any person ...who,** *knowingly* **or wilfully, ...does any act producing, promoting, or contributing to a child's being or becoming a juvenile delinquent, ...is liable on summary conviction ....to a fine ....or to imprisonment.**

The accused had sexual intercourse with a female who was 16 1/2 years old. Prior to the intercourse, she told the accused that she was 18 years old and he thought that she looked at least that old. In British Columbia, a person under the age of 18 years is a "child" within the meaning of the Juvenile Delinquents Act. The court held that, because of the word "knowingly," the accused could not be found guilty. Since he made an honest mistake about the female's age, he did not have the knowledge required to commit the offence.

Even if "knowing" or "knowingly" is absent from the definition of the offence, knowledge of relevant circumstances will usually be required. For example, in *R. v. McLeod,*[7] the accused was charged with assaulting a police officer, contrary to what is now s.246(2)(a):

246.(2) Every one who
(a) assaults a public officer or peace officer engaged in the
execution of his duty, or a person acting in aid of such an
officer ...
is guilty of an indictable offence.

The police officer, dressed in plain clothes, tried to stop a fight between two youths. The accused was one of the many bystanders watching the fight. When the officer tried to stop the fight, the accused, not knowing that he was a police officer, pushed the officer and told him to mind his own business. The court held that the accused was not guilty because he lacked the necessary knowledge to commit the offence. Without the knowledge that the person interfering was a police officer, the accused had no *mens rea*.

In the definitions of some offences, knowledge of a circumstance may be clearly excluded. For example, s.146(1) states:

146.(1) Every male person who has sexual intercourse with a
female person who
(a) is not his wife, and
(b) is under the age of fourteen years, *whether or not he be-*
lieves that she is fourteen years of age or more, **is guilty of an**
indictable offence ...

In this offence, lack of knowledge of the female's age will not be a defence to the charge.

C. RECKLESSNESS Recklessness is a third type of *mens rea* or mental element of a crime. In some offences it is not necessary that the accused actually intended to commit the offence. Instead, it may be enough for criminal responsibility that he was reckless about committing the offence.

In general, a person is reckless when he is extremely or grossly careless. The Supreme Court of Canada has been more specific. It has ruled that a person is reckless when he foresees the possibility of a harmful consequence and then takes the risk that the harm will not result.[8] In other words, the person must be aware of the danger involved. If he does not have this awareness or foresight, then he is not reckless. For example, A wants to practice his target shooting. So, he attaches a target to a tree in a public park. He sees that the tree is in front of a children's play area and that the area is being used by a few children. A's first shot misses the target and wounds one of the children. A was clearly reckless because he foresaw the possibility of injury even though he had no intention to cause injury. He did not intend the harmful consequence but he foresaw the possibility of it and took the risk.

It also seems that to be reckless, the risk which is taken must be an unjustifiable one. Some risks are justifiable. For example, when a person drives a car he foresees that he might cause injury to a pedestrian or another driver, but it is not reckless for him to take the risk. Or, the doctor who performs heart surgery foresees the possibility of causing the death of his patient, but he is not being reckless by operating. In both cases, the risks are reasonable or justifiable. On the other hand, in the target shooting example above, it was not reasonable or justifiable for A to take the risk.

Some courts have said that a person may be reckless even though he does not foresee the possibility of a harmful consequence. These courts have stated that the question is not whether the accused actually foresaw the consequence. Rather, the question is whether a reasonable person, in the position of the accused, would have foreseen the consequences. This view is discussed in depth in regard to criminal negligence in Chapter Ten. The problem of foresight of consequences also comes up in regard to driving offences in Chapter Eleven.

Some Code sections clearly require recklessness by using the word "reckless." An example is s.202 which defines criminal negligence:

> **202.(1) Every one is criminally negligent who**
> **(a) in doing anything, or**
> **(b) in omitting to do anything that it is his duty to do,**
> **shows wanton or *reckless* disregard for the lives or safety of other**
> **persons.**

When knowledge of circumstances is part of the *mens rea* of a crime, a reckless state of mind may be sufficient, despite the absence of the word "reckless." For example, in *R. v. Blondin,*[9] the accused was charged with importing narcotics, contrary to s.5 of the Narcotic Control Act which states:

> **5.(1) .... no person shall import into Canada or export from**
> **Canada any narcotic.**

Twenty-three pounds of hashish were found inside a scuba-diving tank which the accused was trying to bring into Canada. The accused admitted that he knew that there was something illegal in the tank but stated he did not know that it was a narcotic. Knowledge that the substance being imported is a narcotic is an essential ingredient of the offence of importing narcotics. The court held that this requirement was satisfied if it was proven that the accused had been reckless about what the substance was or had wilfully shut his eyes as to what it was.

D. CONCURRENCE OF *MENS REA* AND *ACTUS REUS* It is a general principle of criminal law that for an offence to occur, both the *mens rea* and the *actus reus* must be present at the same time. In most cases, there are no problems with this principle. For example, in the case of theft, the act of stealing and the intent to steal usually occur at the same time. However, in some cases, it is not so clear. For example. A picks up a coat in a restaurant thinking that it belongs to him. When he gets home, he realizes that the coat does not belong to him. He also realizes that the coat is a much better and more expensive coat than his own. So, he decides to keep it. Here the *actus reus,* the taking of the coat, occurred at the restaurant, but the *mens rea,* the intention of depriving the owner, did not occur until later. The question is whether A should be found not guilty because the *actus reus* and *mens rea* did not occur at the same time. In answering this question, the criminal law relies on the fiction that the act of taking the coat continued until the point at which A formed the *mens rea* to commit the crime. Thus, A would be guilty of theft.

In an English case,[10] the accused accidentally drove his car on to a police officer's foot. When he learned of the officer's predicament, he refused to move the car. The accused was convicted of assault based on the fiction that the act continued until the intention to assault occurred.

E. STRICT LIABILITY Despite the general rule that *mens rea* is an essential element of an offence, some offences do not require *mens rea*. These are called strict liability offences. In other words, only the *actus reus* or physical element is necessary for a conviction for a strict liability offence. This means that in regard to these offences a person may be convicted of the offence merely because of his conduct, and it is not necessary to consider whether he was reckless or had an intention to commit the offence. Strict liability offences are often created by statutes dealing with health, safety, and the general welfare of the public (e.g. the Food and Drugs Act).

It is a general rule that the language of a criminal law statute must be very clear in excluding *mens rea* as a requirement of the offence. If the statute is silent in regard to *mens rea,* then it will usually be interpreted as requiring *mens rea*. For example, the offence of driving while disqualified has been interpreted as requiring *mens rea:*

> **238.(3) Every one who drives a motor vehicle in Canada while he is disqualified or prohibited from driving a motor vehicle by reason of the legal suspension or cancellation, in any province, of his permit or licence ...is guilty of an indictable offence ....**

In *R. v. Jollimore,*[11] the accused was charged under s.238(3). His defence was that he had not received notice of the cancellation and therefore, did not have *mens rea*. The court dismissed the charge because of the general rule that *mens rea* is required unless there is clear language which excludes it.

B. PARTIES TO A CRIME

In general, parties to offences are certain persons who are involved in a crime either before or during the commission of the offence. All persons who are classified as parties are subject to the same penalty. In determining who is a party, it is necessary to look at Code sections 21 and 22.

1. Aiding and Abetting

> **21.(1) Every one is a party to an offence who:**
> **(a) actually** *commits* **it,**
> **(b) does or omits to do anything for the purpose of** *aiding* **any person to commit it, or**
> **(c)** *abets* **any person in committing it.**

The person who actually commits an offence is a party to the offence. He will be referred to as the principal offender or simply the principal. A person who acts through an innocent agent is considered to actually commit the offence himself and, thus, is a principal.

Parts (b) and (c) of s.21 mean, in general, that anyone who helps or encourages another person to commit an offence is a party and is thus responsible for its commission. More specifically, "aid" means to help or give assistance and "abet" means to encourage another to commit a crime.

In order to find a person guilty of aiding or abetting, "it is only necessary to show that he understood what was taking place and by some act on his part encouraged or assisted in the attainment thereof."[12] The encouragement or the assistance given by the person must be intentional. If the conduct of a person has the effect of helping the principal to commit a crime, but he did not intend to help the principal, then he would not be aiding or abetting.

For example, A lends his tools to B because he thinks B needs them for house repairs and B uses them to break into a shop. A would not be guilty of aiding or abetting the commission of the offence. Or, A, a bank security officer, forgets to lock the door to the bank. This omission helps B to steal money. A would not be guilty of aiding or abetting because he did not intend to help in the commission of the crime.

In general, a person who is merely present at the commission of an offence will not be guilty of aiding and abetting. There must be some active assistance or encouragement. Simply being present and not objecting to the offence is not aiding and abetting. In *R. v. Salajko,*[13] the accused was charged with aiding and abetting on the ground that he was present when fifteen men raped a girl. The victim admitted that the accused did not have intercourse with her. But there was evidence that he was near her with his pants down while others raped her. He was found not guilty of aiding and abetting because there was no evidence that he had actively assisted or encouraged the rapists. On the other hand, the accused in *R. v. Harder,*[14] was convicted of rape because he helped subdue the girl while others had forcible intercourse with her. Here, unlike *Salajko,* the accused was actively assisting in the commission of the offence.

A "look-out man" is an aider and abettor. In *R. v. Cunninghan,*[15] the accused was stationed at the entrance of a common betting house for the purpose of signalling to the keepers of the house if the police approached. The court held that the accused was assisting in the continued operation of the house by preventing the police from obtaining evidence.

In some cases, the issue of whether there is active assistance or encouragement is more difficult. For example, in *R. v. Kulbacki,*[16] the accused, a 20-year-old man, allowed a 16-year-old girl to drive his car. While he was sitting beside her, she drove the car over 90 m.p.h. and the accused did not do or say anything to stop her. He was charged with aiding and abetting the commission of the offence of dangerous driving. His defence was that he did nothing to encourage the commission of the offence, but was merely a passive observer, and, therefore, should not be liable for aiding and abetting. The court held that the failure of the accused to try to stop or prevent the girl from committing the offence, when he was in a position to do so and when he had the authority to do so, amounted to encouragement and, thus, he was aiding and abetting. The court also pointed out that every passenger in an unlawfully driven car is not necessarily an aider and abettor because he might not have any authority over the car or any right to control the driver.

An aider and abettor may be charged with aiding and abetting in the commission of a particular offence or he may simply be charged with the particular offence. In *R. v. Harder,* the accused was charged with rape but his only involvement was assisting another person to commit rape. The Supreme Court of Canada held that the accused was properly convicted of rape and that it was not necessary to spell out in the charge that the accused only assisted and did not actually rape the victim.

2. Common Intention

A person is also a party if his conduct falls within s.21(2):

> **21.(2) Where two or more persons form an intention in common to carry out an unlawful purpose and to assist each other therein and any one of them, in carrying out the common purpose, commits an offence, each of them who knew or ought to have known that the commission of the offence would be a probable consequence of carrying out the common purpose is a party to that offence.**

To convict someone under this section, certain requirements must be met: (1) there must be a common intention formed by the accused and at least one other person; (2) the intention must be to carry out an unlawful purpose and to help each other in doing so; (3) one of them in carrying out the purpose must commit an offence; (4) the offence must be one which they knew or should have known would probably result from carrying out their common purpose. If all of these requirements are met, then all persons involved are equally responsible for the offence committed.

In *R. v. Trinnear,* [17] A and B planned to rob C. B knew that A had a hunting knife with him when they took C to a secluded spot to commit the robbery. While B remained in the car, A took C some distance from the car where he stabbed her to death and robbed her. Under s.213 a person commits murder if while committing robbery he causes bodily harm for the purpose of facilitating the robbery and death results from the bodily harm. Both A and B were convicted of murder. The Supreme Court of Canada held that B was properly convicted if it was shown that B knew or ought to have known that it was probable that bodily harm would be inflicted on C as a consequence of carrying out the robbery.

It is possible to avoid criminal responsibility under s.21(2) by withdrawing from the plan to carry out the unlawful purpose. The party who is withdrawing must do more than merely change his mind or leave the scene of the crime before the crime is committed. Where practicable and reasonable, he must communicate, by words or otherwise, his intention to withdraw to the others involved in the plan. [18]

3. Counselling and Procuring

> **22.(1)** Where a person counsels or procures another person to be a party to an offence and that other person is afterwards a party to that offence, the person who counselled or procured is a party to that offence, notwithstanding that the offence was committed in a way different from that which was counselled or procured.
>
> **(2)** Every one who counsels or procures another person to be a party to an offence is a party to every offence that the other commits in consequence of the counselling or procuring that the person who counselled or procured knew or ought to have known was likely to be committed in consequence of the counselling or procuring.

To "counsel" means to advise or recommend. To "procure" means to get or obtain.

The general idea in s.22 is that a person is a party to an offence if he advised or got another person to commit a crime, even if the crime was committed in a way different from what he suggested. He will also be a party to any other offence committed if he knew or should have known that it was likely to be committed as a result of his counselling or procuring.

Counselling or procuring may be an offence in itself. In *Brousseau v. R.*,[19] a municipal councillor tried to get a contractor to offer him a bribe so that he would use his influence to get contracts with the city for the contractor. The contractor did not try to bribe the councillor. However, the Supreme Court of Canada held that the councillor had committed the offence of counselling the commission of an offence.

In *R. v. Gordon and Gordon*,[20] A and B counselled C to burn the stores of two of their business competitors. C did not burn the stores. The two accused were convicted of counselling.

If the offence counselled or procured is *not* committed, the accused is subject to being punished under s.422. The punishment for counselling an indictable offence is the same as for attempting to commit the offence, or being an accessory after the fact (see below). The person who counsels another to commit a summary conviction offence is guilty of an offence punishable on summary conviction.

If the offence counselled or procured *is* committed, the accused is punishable as a party and, thus, may be punished as severely as if he had actually committed the offence himself.

4. Accessory After the Fact

Section 23 creates a separate offence of helping someone who has committed an offence. The person who provides such assistance is not a party to the offence but may be convicted of being an accessory after the fact (i.e. a helper after the offence has been committed) if his actions fall within s.23.

23.(1) An accessory after the fact to an offence is one who, knowing that a person has been a party to the offence, receives, comforts or assists him for the purpose of enabling him to escape.

There are three main requirements of this section. First, there must be *knowledge* that the other person has been a party to an offence. In *R. v. Vinette*,[21] the accused did not deny having assisted another person in disposing of a corpse by throwing it to the bottom of a flooded quarry in a weighted trunk. The court decided that this was enough in itself to indicate that the accused had knowledge that the other person had been a party to the crime of homicide.

Second, the accused must *assist* the party to an offence. In general, assistance is anything which goes beyond a mere omission to aid in the capture of the criminal. In *Young v. R.*,[22] the accused told two murderers that their names were known to the police and that the police had the licence number of the murderers' car. This information would help them to avoid apprehension by the police. The court held that this was assistance because it went beyond a mere omission to aid in their capture.

Third, the assistance must be given with the *intention* of helping the criminal to escape. Normally, this requirement is easily satisfied if the other two requirements have been met. However, it is possible that A may know that B stole some goods and A may agree to sell them for him. But, his intention in selling the goods may be not to help B escape but rather to make a profit for himself. An English judge has held that in such a case, A would not be guilty as an accessory after the fact.[23]

The penalty for being an accessory after the fact varies depending on the seriousness of the offence involved. An accessory after the fact to an offence punishable by life imprisonment is liable to imprisonment for 14 years. If the offence involved is punishable by imprisonment for 14 years or less, the accessory is liable to imprisonment for a term that is one half of the longest term to which a person who is guilty of that offence is liable. If the offence involved is a summary conviction offence, the accessory is punishable on summary conviction also.

C. CONSPIRACY

In general, a conspiracy is an agreement (or "common design") by two or more persons to do an unlawful act or to do a lawful act by unlawful means. It is immaterial whether the unlawful act is committed or not. Even though the conspirators may change their mind, or may not get the opportunity to perform the unlawful act, they commit the offence of conspiracy when their agreement is reached. Thus, if A and B agree to kidnap C and they are arrested before they can carry out the kidnapping, both of them would be guilty of conspiracy.

Assume A and B made the same agreement as above but B only pretended to agree. That is, he agreed but had no intention of carrying out the agreement. In such a situation there would not be a conspiracy. Neither B *nor* A could be found guilty of conspiracy. This is because the essence of the crime of conspiracy is an agreement and it is impossible to have an agreement without at least two participants. If B was only pretending, then he was not really a participant and thus no agreement was reached.

A husband and wife cannot be found guilty of conspiring with each other. However, if a third person is involved, then all three can be convicted of conspiracy.

The main section dealing with conspiracy is s.423:

423.(1) Except where otherwise expressly provided by law, the following provisions apply in respect of conspiracy, namely,

(a) every one who conspires with any one to commit murder or to cause another person to be murdered, whether in Canada or not, is guilty of an indictable offence and is liable to imprisonment for fourteen years;

(b) every one who conspires with any one to prosecute a person for an alleged offence, knowing that he did not commit that offence, is guilty of an indictable offence and is liable

(i) to imprisonment for ten years, if the alleged offence is one for which, upon conviction, that person would be liable to be sentenced to death or to imprisonment for life or for fourteen years, or

(ii) to imprisonment for five years, if the alleged offence is one for which, upon conviction, that person would be liable to imprisonment for less than fourteen years;

(c) every one who conspires with any one to induce, by false pretences, false representations or other fraudulent means, a woman to commit adultery or fornication, is guilty of an indictable offence and is liable to imprisonment for two years; and

(d) every one who conspires with any one to commit an indictable offence not provided for in paragraph (a), (b), or (c) is guilty of an indictable offence and is liable to the same punishment as that to which an accused who is guilty of that offence would, upon conviction, be liable.

(2) Every one who conspires with any one

(a) to effect an unlawful purpose, or

(b) to effect a lawful purpose by unlawful means,

is guilty of an indictable offence and is liable to imprisonment for two years.

Section 423 (1)(a), (b), and (c) provide for specific conspiracy offences, that is, conspiracy to commit a murder or to unlawfully prosecute another person, or to conspire to induce a woman to commit adultery or fornication.

Section 423 (1)(d) makes it an offence to conspire to do any indictable offence.

Section 423 (2) has wider application. This subsection makes it an offence to conspire to effect any unlawful purpose, or to effect a lawful purpose by unlawful means. An "unlawful purpose" is not restricted to summary conviction offences in the Criminal Code. Offences created by other federal statutes and by provincial laws are included in the definition of "unlawful purposes".

Section 423(3) and (4) further provides:

> **423.(3) Every one who, while in Canada, conspires with any one to do anything referred to in subsection (1) or (2) in a place outside Canada that is an offence under the laws of that place shall be deemed to have conspired to do in Canada that thing.**
> **(4) Every one who, while in a place outside Canada, conspires with any one to do anything referred to in subsection (1) or (2) in Canada shall be deemed to have conspired in Canada to do that thing.**

In other words, if the conspiracy itself occurred in Canada, even though the object of the conspiracy was to commit an offence in the United States, the conspirators would be guilty of conspiracy in Canada. If the conspirators were in the United States and conspired to commit an offence in Canada, they would be considered to have committed the conspiracy in Canada for the purpose of s.423.

An example of a conspiracy case is *R. v. Chapman and Grange*.[24] The accused, G, was the president of a company which was in the business of supplying trucks and drivers for other companies whose drivers were on strike. In 1971, the International Chemical Workers Union went on strike against the Redpath Sugar Company. Redpath Sugar engaged G's company to assist in transporting its products. A few weeks later, a Union member (International Chemical Workers) on duty at Union headquarters had a telephone conversation and suspected that the phone was tapped. He checked the telephone line and located a wire attached to the Bell telephone junction box on the outside of the building. This wire led to a tape recorder hidden under a crate on the ground adjacent to the building. The Union decided to "stake out" the tape recorder. That same night, the accused C was caught collecting the tape on the tape recorder.

It turned out that C, who was an off-duty policeman, was a good friend of the accused G. The evidence indicated that G wanted to know what the Union was planning. Therefore, he and C reached an agreement whereby C would tap the Union phones and provide the tapes to G. In such circumstances, G and C were charged with a conspiracy to obtain and use information passing over a telephone line not intended for them, contrary to s.423(2)(a). The court concluded that the circumstances in the case led to the inescapable conclusion that C and G were fellow conspirators and both were convicted as charged.

D. ATTEMPTS

A person can commit an offence by merely trying to commit an offence. The offence of attempting a crime is defined in s.24.

> **24.(1) Every one who, having an intent to commit an offence, does or omits to do anything for the purpose of carrying out his intention is guilty of an attempt to commit the offence whether or not it was possible under the circumstances to commit the offence.**
>
> **(2) The question whether an act or omission by a person who has an intent to commit an offence is or is not mere preparation to commit the offence and too remote to constitute an attempt to commit the offence, is a question of law.**

There are three essential elements to an attempt: (1) the intent to commit an offence; (2) some act or omission toward committing the offence, and (3) non-completion of the offence attempted.

The *intent* required in an attempt is the same as the intent required in the completed offence. For example, in an attempted theft there must be the intent to steal; in an attempted murder there must be the intent to kill or cause serious bodily harm. Thus, if A shoots at B, intending to kill him but he misses, then he can be convicted of an attempt to murder.

In addition to the criminal intent, there must also be some *act or omission* done for the purpose of carrying out the intent. The general rule is that the act or omission must amount to more than mere preparation to commit the crime. It must be immediately, not remotely, connected with the commission of the crime. In other words, if a person is only preparing to commit a crime, then no offence is committed. But, if he commits some act or omission which amounts to more than mere preparation, then he may be guilty of an attempt.

There is no rule of law for determining in all cases when the conduct of a person goes beyond mere preparation and becomes an attempt. The decision depends upon the circumstances of each case.[25] However, the act must go so far toward committing the offence that if there had not been some intervention or interruption the offence would have been committed.[26] Consider the following examples:

In *Henderson v. R.*,[27] the accused and two others planned to rob a bank. They obtained the equipment they felt was necessary, including guns and ammunition. On their way to commit the robbery, they saw a police car parked in front of the bank. They drove away in another direction and were later apprehended by police. The Supreme Court of Canada ruled that the actions of the accused amounted to an attempt to commit robbery.

In *R. v. Cline*,[28] the accused disguised himself in large, dark sunglasses and approached a 12-year-old boy in a dark area of a street and asked him if he would carry his suitcases. The accused had no suitcases with him. The boy refused and ran away. The accused chased the boy, caught up with him, and then let him go after telling the boy not to tell anybody of the incident. Evidence at the trial showed that the accused had previously tried to lure boys into dark alleys by asking them to carry his suitcases. On some of these previous occasions, the accused succeeded and committed indecent assaults. The appeal court held that no indecent assault was committed but the accused was guilty of attempting an indecent assault. The court distinguished the acts of preparation from the actual attempt in the following way: the accused chose a time and place where he might obtain a victim; he went to that place at the chosen time; he disguised himself and then waited for an opportunity. These were all acts of preparation and he was then ready to embark on the course of committing the crime. When he approached the boy and tried to lure him away, the accused was going beyond mere preparation and, thus, these actions amounted to an attempt to commit the crime of indecent assault.

Section 24(1) makes it clear that it is no defence to an attempt charge that it was impossible under the circumstances to commit the offence. In *R. v. Smith*, [29] the accused was charged with attempting to use a substance called slippery elm to bring about an illegal abortion. The court held that in order to convict the accused of the attempt, it was not necessary to show that it was possible to bring about the abortion by using slippery elm.

The penalty for attempts is contained in s.421 and is determined in the same manner as the penalty for accessories after the fact is determined. That is, the penalty depends on the seriousness of the offence attempted.

Section 24(2) states that the issue of whether the act of the accused is an attempt or mere preparation is a question of law. This means that it is the judge's function to decide whether the actions of the accused, as found by the jury, amount to an attempt.

E. PROOF OF A CRIME

In the course of a trial, there are certain general principles involved in establishing the guilt or innocence of the accused. Some of these principles will be discussed in this section.

1. Proof of Intention

Unless a person confesses, it is practically impossible to know for certain what was in his mind at the time he committed an act. So, it is necessary to look at his conduct in order to get some idea of his state of mind.

In criminal law, there is the general rule that a jury may infer that a person intends the natural consequences of his acts. This rule is based on a common sense notion: since a person is usually able to foresee the natural consequences of his acts, it is usually reasonable to infer that he did foresee them and intend them. So, for example, if A points a gun at B's head and fires it, it is reasonable to infer that A intended to kill B or at least to cause him serious bodily harm. However, the jury is not required to make this inference. There may be other facts in the case which might lead to a different conclusion. For example, it may be established as a fact that A did not know that the gun was loaded and thus did not have the intention to kill B.

2. Presumption of Innocence

Another general principle is that the accused is presumed innocent until proven guilty. This presumption of innocence is contained in s.5 of the Code:

5.(1) Where an enactment creates an offence and authorizes a punishment to be imposed in respect thereof,
(a) a person shall be deemed not to be guilty of that offence until he is convicted thereof ....

It is also contained in s.2(f) of the Canadian Bill of Rights which states that, unless Parliament expressly provides otherwise, no law shall be interpreted to

deprive a person charged with a criminal offence of the right to be presumed innocent until proved guilty according to law in a fair and public hearing by an independent and impartial tribunal ....

The general meaning of the presumption is that an accused person will be considered not guilty until enough evidence is produced which proves that he is guilty.

3. Burden of Proof

The effect of the presumption of innocence is that, in general, the *burden of proof* at a criminal trial is on the prosecution. This means that it is the responsibility of the prosecution to prove that the accused is guilty. The accused does not have the responsibility of proving that he is innocent.

The prosecution has the burden of proving the guilt of the accused *beyond a reasonable doubt*. If, at the end of a case, the jury has a reasonable doubt as to whether the accused committed the offence, then the prosecution has failed to prove its case and the accused is entitled to be found not guilty. Reasonable doubt is very difficult to define but it has been explained in the following way: "By reasonable doubt as to a person's guilt is meant that real doubt ...which an honest juror has after considering all the circumstances of the case and as a result of which he is unable to say: 'I am morally certain of his guilt'. Moral certainty does not mean absolute certainty."[30]

The doubt must be based on the evidence given at the trial. Also, it is not necessary that the prosecution disprove every possible defence which the accused could raise. But, if the accused does raise a defence which is supported by some evidence, then the Crown must disprove the defence beyond a reasonable doubt.

The burden of proof in a criminal case is much higher than the burden of proof in a civil action. In a civil action, the plaintiff must prove his case only by a balance of probabilities. This means that he must show that it more likely than not that his claim is true. For example, A claims that B negligently drove his car and caused damage to A's car. So, A sues B in order to be repaid for the costs of repairing his car. A must prove that it was more likely than not that B drove his car in a negligent manner and caused damage to A's car. It is not necessary that A prove B's negligence beyond a reasonable doubt. However, if B were charged with murdering A, then the prosecution would have to prove B's guilt beyond a reasonable doubt. If it could only be shown that B probably killed A or that it was more likely than not that B killed A, then B would be entitled to be found not guilty of murder.

Sometimes, the burden of proof is shifted to the accused by a *reverse onus clause*. Section 309(1) contains such a clause:

> **309.(1) Every one who, without lawful excuse,** *the proof of which lies upon him,* **has in his possession any instrument suitable for house-breaking ...., under circumstances that give rise to a reasonable inference that the instrument has been used ....for house-breaking ... is guilty of an indictable offence ....**

The phrase, "proof of which lies upon him," is a reverse onus clause. The prosecution must prove that the accused had an instrument which could be used to break into a house and that he had it under suspicious circumstances. The accused, on the other hand, must prove that he had some lawful excuse for having the instrument (e.g. the instrument may be a tool used in his work as a carpenter). If he can prove a lawful excuse, then he should be found not guilty.

There is an important difference between the burden of proof on the prosecution and the burden of proof which is placed on the accused by a reverse onus clause. As discussed above, the burden on the prosecution is proof beyond a reasonable doubt. When the burden is on the accused, it is a burden of proof by a balance of probabilities. In other words, where a reverse onus clause is involved, the standard used in civil actions applies. That is, in the example above, the accused must show only that it is more likely than not that he did have a lawful excuse for possessing the house-breaking instruments. He is not required to prove beyond a reasonable doubt that he had a lawful excuse. There are numerous other examples of reverse onus clauses in the Code, but these will be discussed throughout the book when the particular sections which contain such clauses are considered.

QUESTIONS FOR REVIEW AND DISCUSSION

1. Define *actus reus* and *mens rea*.
2. What can constitute the *actus reus* of a crime?
3. What are the types of *mens rea?*
4. What words are often used in the Code to indicate that *mens rea* is required? If these words are not used, is *mens rea* required?
5. What is an "act" in criminal law? Give an example.
6. Why were the accused found not guilty in *R. v. Wilmot* and *R. v. Dubois?*
7. What is the difference between a general intent offence and a specific intent offence? Give an example of each.

8. At a trial, what is the general rule for determining whether an accused had the intention to commit a crime?

9. Explain the difference between the intention to commit an offence and the motive for commiting an offence.

10. Explain the difference between an intentional act and a voluntary act.

11. How is recklessness different from intention?

12. What is a strict liability offence?

13. What are the essential elements of aiding and abetting? Give an example.

14. What are the essential elements of being an accessory after the fact? Give an example.

15. What is counselling?

16. What are the essential elements of an attempt?

17. Explain the meaning of: (1) presumption of innocence, (2) burden of proof, (3) beyond a reasonable doubt, and (4) reverse onus clause.

18. What is the difference between a charge of conspiracy and a charge of aiding and abetting?

19. Mrs. M. asked Sarah to take care of her infant boy for a few days. Mrs. M. also asked Sarah to give the infant a teaspoonful of "medicine" every night. In fact, the medicine was poison. Sarah did not think that the infant needed medicine so she did not give it to him. She put the "medicine" on the mantlepiece in her room. Later, Sarah's five-year-old son gave the infant a large dose of the "medicine" and the infant died. Mrs. M. was charged with murder. Should she be convicted? What else, if anything, do you need to know?

20. A and B are walking through the park with eight of their friends when they see their enemy C. They decide to "have some fun" with C. So, B holds C while A punches and kicks him. The friends stand around watching, laughing and yelling their support to A and B. Meanwhile D, who is walking his dog, stops momentarily to see what is going on and decides not to get involved. A is convicted of assault causing bodily harm. Should B be convicted of aiding or abetting A? What about the friends? What about D?

21. A, B (A's wife), and C agree to steal some money from X's clothing store. They also agree that X will not be harmed and that no weapons will be used. A enters the store and gets X's attention by asking him questions about an article of clothing. Then B enters the store and walks toward the cash register while C acts as a look-out near the store entrance. X notices B reaching into the drawer of the cash register and he yells loudly. C panics, pulls out a gun and shoots X, wounding him in the arm. A, B and C run from the store (without the money) and go to D's apartment around the corner. D agrees to let them use his car and A, B and C drive to a hiding place. Should A, B and C be convicted of conspiracy? Is B guilty of an attempted theft? If so, are A and C guilty of aiding and abetting B in his attempt? Who is legally responsible for the wounding of X? Is D an accessory after the fact? Explain your answers to these questions.

[1] (1940), 74 C.C.C. 1 (Alta.C.A.).

[2] (1959), 32 C.R. 187 (Que).

[3] Intention and knowledge are often referred to as one type of *mens rea:* intention. However, for the purpose of this chapter, they will be discussed separately.

[4] However, this is not always the case. A notable exception is murder (s.212).

[5] *R. v. George* (1960), 128 C.C.C. 289, 34 C.R.I. (S.C.C.).

[6] (1956), 115 C.C.C. 1, 24 C.R. 1 (S.C.C.).

[7] (1954), 111 C.C.C. 106, 20 C.R. 281 (B.C.C.A.)

[8] *O'Grady v. Sparling* (1960), 128 C.C.C. 1, 33 C.R. 293 (S.C.C.)

[9] (1970), 2 C.C.C. (2d) 118 (B.C.C.A.)

[10] *Fagan v. Metropolitan Police Commissioner* (1969) 1 Q.B. 439 (Queen's Bench).

[11] (1962), 32 C.R. 300 (N.S.S.C.).

[12] *Preston v. R.* (1949), 93 C.C.C. 83 (S.C.C.).

[13] (1970) 1 C.C.C. 352 9 C.R.N.S. 145 (Ont. C.A.).

[14] (1956), 114 C.C.C. 129 (S.C.C.).

[15] (1937), 68 C.C.C. 176 (Ont. C.A.).

[16] (1966) 1 C.C.C. 167 (Man. C.A.).

[17] (1970) 3 C.C.C. 289 (S.C.C.).

[18] *R. v. Whitehouse* (1941), 75 C.C.C. 65 (B.C.C.A.).

[19] (1917), 29 C.C.C. 207 (S.C.C.).

[20] (1937), 79 C.C.C. 315 (Sask. C.A.)

[21] (1974), 19 C.C.C. (2d) 1 (S.C.C.).

[22] (1950), 98 C.C.C. 195 (Que. C.A.).

[23] *R. v. Rose* (1962), 46 Cr.App.R. 103 (Eng.).

[24] (1973), 11 C.C.C. (2d) 84, 20 C.R.N.S. 141 (Ont.C.A.).

[25] *R. v. Brown* (1947), 88 C.C.C. 242 (Ont.C.A.).

[26] *R. v. Quinton* (1947), 88 C.C.C. 231 (S.C.C.).

[27] (1948), 5 C.R. 112 (S.C.C.).

[28] (1956), 115 C.C.C. 18 (Ont. C.A.).

[29] (1961), 34 CR 207 (B.C.C.A.).

[30] *R. v. Sears* (1947), 90 C.C.C. 159 at 163 (Ont.C.A.).

Chapter Four

Defences

A defence is a justification or excuse for conduct which would otherwise be criminal. In this chapter, several of the defences available to accused persons will be discussed.

The possible defences to criminal charges are contained in the Criminal Code and the common law. According to s.7(3) of the Code, all common law defences apply to criminal charges, except in so far as they are changed by Parliament:

> **7.(3) Every rule and principle of the common law that renders any circumstance a justification or excuse for an act or a defence to a charge continues in force and applies in respect of proceedings for an offence under this Act or any other Act of the Parliament of Canada, except in so far as they are altered by or are inconsistent with this Act or any other Act of the Parliament of Canada.**

Examples of defences which are contained in the Code are insanity (s.216), self-defence (ss.34–37) and provocation (s.215). Examples of common law defences (i.e. defences which are not contained in the Code) are intoxication, automatism and mistake of fact.

The general rule is that an accused does not have to prove his defence. It is sufficient if merely some evidence is produced which could raise a reasonable doubt in the mind of the jury. For example, A is charged with murder and his defence is that he was too drunk to form the specific intent to kill his victim. It is not necessary that A prove his intoxication beyond a reasonable doubt or even on a balance of probabilities. It is enough if A shows some evidence of his intoxication which could lead a jury to have a reasonable doubt as to whether or not he had the specific intent to kill his victim. If the jury does have a reasonable doubt, then the prosecution has failed to prove its case and A should be acquitted.

One major exception to the general rule mentioned above concerns the defence of insanity. If an accused is relying on the defence of insanity, he must prove on a balance of probabilities that he was insane at the time of the alleged offence.

Another exception is the "reverse onus clause" which was discussed in Chapter Three.

A. INCAPACITY OF CHILDREN

Sections 12 and 13 of the Criminal Code state:

> **12. No person shall be convicted of an offence in respect of an act or omission on his part while he was under the age of seven years.**
> **13. No person shall be convicted of an offence in respect of an act or omission on his part while he was seven years of age or more, but under the age of fourteen years, unless he was competent to know the nature and consequences of his conduct and to appreciate that it was wrong.**

The law presumes that children under the age of seven do not have the mental capacity to understand the nature and consequences of their acts and to distinguish between right and wrong. Without this mental capacity there can be no *mens rea* or "guilty mind" and thus, no offence.

A child between the ages of seven and fourteen is also presumed not to have the mental capacity to be considered guilty of a crime. However, with children of this age group, the prosecution is given the opportunity to prove that the child does have the necessary mental capacity. The child can be convicted of an offence only if this capacity is proven.

Any person over fourteen years of age is presumed to have the mental capacity to understand the nature and consequences of his acts and to distinguish between right and wrong.

Section 147 states that a male person under the age of fourteen years cannot be convicted of the following sexual offences: rape, attempted rape, sexual intercourse with a female under fourteen or between fourteen and sixteen, and incest. The presumption in this section is that a boy under fourteen does not have the *physical* capacity to commit these crimes. In other words, even if it is clear that a 13-year-old boy had forcible intercourse with a female, he could not be convicted of one of these offences.

B. INSANITY

1. The Test of Insanity

The main provisions dealing with the defence of insanity are contained in s. 16:

> **16.(1) No person shall be convicted of an offence in respect of an act or omission on his part while he was insane.**

> **(2) For the purposes of this section a person is insane when he is in a state of natural imbecility or has disease of the mind to an extent that renders him incapable of appreciating the nature and quality of an act or omission or of knowing that an act or omission is wrong.**

Subsection (1) establishes that insanity is a valid defence and subsection (2) lays down the test of insanity. According to this test, a person is insane if
(1) he is in a state of natural *imbecility* or has a *disease of the mind* which makes him
(2) incapable of *appreciating the nature and quality of his act* or
(3) incapable of *knowing that his act is wrong*.
In brief, there must be one of the mental incapacities mentioned in (2) and (3). And the mental incapacity must be caused by either imbecility or a disease of the mind. If the disease or the imbecility caused the accused *either* to be incapable of appreciating the nature and quality of his act *or* to be incapable of knowing that his act was wrong, he is considered to have been legally insane at the time of the alleged offence. The important terms and phrases included in the test of insanity will be discussed separately.

A. NATURAL IMBECILITY Natural imbecility refers to a state of incomplete mental development. A severely retarded person may be described as being in a state of natural imbecility.

B. DISEASE OF THE MIND Diseases of the mind include a number of mental disorders. Schizophrenia, senile dementia, paranoia, melancholia, and certain types of epilepsy are examples of diseases of the mind which have been the subject of insanity pleas in Canadian criminal courts. As a general rule, personality disorders that are not caused by diseases of the mind *cannot* be used as grounds for insanity.

A psychopathic condition has been considered to be a disease of the mind.[1] In *R. v. Leech*[2] the following description of the psychopath was given:

> *The psychopath is asocial. His conduct often brings him into conflict with society. The psychopath is driven by primitive desires and exaggerated craving for excitement. In his self-centred search for pleasure he ignores the restrictions of his culture. The psychopath is highly impulsive. He is a man for whom the moment is a segment of time detached from all others. His actions are unplanned and guided by whims. The psychopath is aggressive. He has learned few socialized ways of coping with frustration. The psychopath feels little, if any, guilt. He can commit the most appalling acts, yet do them without remorse. He has a warped capacity for love. His emotional relations when they exist are meagre, fleeting, and designed to satisfy his own desires. The last two traits, guiltlessness and lovelessness, conspicuously mark the psychopath as different from other men.*

C. APPRECIATING THE NATURE AND QUALITY OF AN ACT The following passage, taken from a Royal Commission Report on the law of insanity in Canadian criminal law, explains the meaning of "appreciating the nature and quality of an act":

> ....*was the accused person at the very time of the offence — not before or after, but at the moment of the offence — by reason of disease of the mind, unable fully to appreciate not only the nature of the act but the natural consequences that would flow from it? In other words, was the accused person, by reason of disease of the mind, deprived of the mental capacity to foresee and measure the consequences of the act?*[3]

For example, if a man stabs someone with a knife and he is unaware that such an act could injure his victim, he does not appreciate the nature and quality of his act. Or, if a mother kills her baby by putting him in an oven, thinking that the baby is a roast, she does not appreciate the nature and quality of her act. In each of these examples, the person did not have the necessary appreciation because of a mental incapacity to foresee the consequences of an act.

In *R. v. Craig*[4] the accused was charged with rape and he raised the defence of insanity. It was established by medical evidence that he was a psychopath. However, simply having a disease of the mind was not enough. The important question in the case was whether the accused appreciated the nature and quality of his act. The court held that he did appreciate or realize that he was raping his victim. Therefore, the defence of insanity failed and he was found guilty.

D. KNOWING THAT AN ACT IS WRONG A person may appreciate the nature and quality of his act, but if he is not capable of knowing that the act is wrong, he still may be found insane.

There is disagreement in the cases as to the meaning of "wrong." In *R. v. Cardinal*,[5] the Alberta Court of Appeal held that "wrong" meant contrary to law (i.e. "legally wrong"). In *R. v. Laycock*,[6] the Ontario Court of Appeal held that the word should be given the wider meaning of "morally wrong." The Supreme Court of Canada has not yet decided the issue and until it does, this area of law will probably remain unsettled.[7]

The facts in *Laycock* demonstrate the difference between the two interpretations. The accused was charged with murdering his neighbour K, and the accused raised the defence of insanity. There had been many disputes between the accused and K. These disputes mainly involved charges by the accused that K trespassed on his property. On one occasion, the accused shot and killed K. The accused was 66 years old, and had been a soldier in World War I and had tried to serve in World War II but was not accepted. He regarded K as an enemy of democracy and justice and as a Hitler or Mussolini. He believed that when he shot K he was fighting for justice, liberty, and freedom and that he was protecting democracy from a dictator. A psychiatrist testified that the accused was suffering from a disease of the mind. He went on to state that *although the accused knew the act was against the law, he believed it was the right thing to do.* The accused felt that he was morally obligated to undertake the mission of stopping the dictator and that the killing was absolutely justified. The court concluded that this was evidence which could indicate that the accused was incapable of knowing that his act was wrong.

2. Delusions

Section 16(3) states:

> **16.(3) A person who has specific delusions, but is in other respects sane, shall not be acquitted on the ground of insanity unless the delusions caused him to believe in the existence of a state of things that, if it existed, would have justified or excused his act or omission.**

If an accused suffers from a specific delusion he may plead not guilty by reason of insanity. A delusion is a belief that is not in touch with reality. The delusion must cause the accused to believe in a situation which, if it were real, would make his act legal.

Suppose, for example, that an accused suffered from the specific delusion that he had a million dollars in his bank account. In actual fact, he had less than a hundred dollars deposited. If the accused wrote "bad" cheques as a result of his delusions, he could plead insanity pursuant to s.16(3). This is because if he actually had a million dollars in his account, his cheques would not have been "bad."

In one of the few reported cases involving a specific delusion,[8] the accused was under the delusion that he was suffering from a fatal and incurable disease. He and his wife made a suicide pact and each took poison with the intention of committing suicide. The wife died but the accused recovered from the effects of the poison. He was charged with counselling his wife to commit suicide. His defence was that, although he was sane in other respects, he was insane at the time of the offence because of his specific delusion that he was suffering from an incurable disease. The court held that despite the delusion the accused did not meet the legal test of insanity. He could not be acquitted unless the delusion caused him to believe in a state of things which, if it existed, would have justified or excused his act. Even if it had been true that the accused was hopelessly ill, this would not have justified his counselling his wife to kill herself. The court went on to find that the accused was capable of appreciating the nature and quality of his act and that he knew his act was wrong. Therefore, he was convicted.

3. Presumption of Sanity

Section 16(4) states:

> **16.(4) Every one shall, until the contrary is proved, be presumed to be and to have been sane.**

The effect of this presumption is that, in general, the burden of proving insanity is on the accused. The accused's lawyer does not have to establish the insanity of the accused beyond a reasonable doubt. It is sufficient to prove that it is probable that he was insane at the time the offence was committed.

If an accused is found not guilty by reason of insanity, he is not released. He is held in custody until it can be demonstrated that he has regained his sanity. It is possible that he will be in an institution for the rest of his life. Therefore, the defence of insanity is rarely used in cases other than murder.

C. AUTOMATISM

When *actus reus* was discussed in Chapter Three, it was mentioned that there is a general rule that for a person to be guilty of a crime, his conduct must be voluntary. In other words, the person must have conscious control over his bodily movements.

If a person's conduct is involuntary, he may be able to rely on the defence of automatism. Automatism refers to a state in which a person has no conscious control over his bodily movements. In other words, his behaviour is "automatic." Examples of involuntary, unconscious behaviour are acts done while sleepwalking and acts done while suffering from an epileptic seizure.

In general, for automatism to be a defence, the cause of the automatism must be something other than a disease of the mind or intoxication (by alcohol or drugs). If an involuntary, unconscious act is caused by a disease of the mind, the defence is insanity, not automatism. Similarly, if the involuntary, unconscious act is caused by intoxication, the defence is, in most cases, intoxication, not automatism.

Automatism caused by a physical injury was a successful defence in *Bleta v. R.*[9] In that case, the accused was charged with murder. Several witnesses testified that they watched a fight between G and the accused which culminated in the accused stabbing G fatally in the neck. Although the stories of the eyewitnesses differed as to the details of the fight, it is clear that blows were exchanged between the two men. The accused was knocked down or fell down striking his head forcibly on the pavement. G started to walk away when the accused, having regained his feet, followed him and pulled out a knife with which he delivered the fatal blow. Two of the onlookers observed that when the accused got up, he staggered and appeared to be dazed, and one police officer also commented on his apparently dazed condition.

The accused contended that the blow to his head when it struck the sidewalk, deprived him of all voluntary control over his actions. In other words, the accused was saying he was in a state of automatism when he stabbed G.

A psychologist gave evidence which supported the accused's defence. The trial judge summarized the psychologist's evidence as follows:

> *The doctor says that the actions of the accused when he stabbed the deceased were purely automatic and without any volition on the part of the accused. He was, in fact, in the condition of a sleepwalker or an epileptic and since he had been in a fight, he automatically continued it.*

Dr. S. considered all of the circumstances and the actions of the accused both before and after his arrest, and gives as his opinion, and without doubt on his part, that this is a true case of automatism.

The jury believed that the accused was in a state of automatism when he stabbed G and he was acquitted on the charge of murder.

Automatism may also be used as a defence if an involuntary, unconscious act results from taking a drug without knowing its effect. For example, in *R. v. King*[10] the accused was charged with impaired driving. He had been given an injection of a drug from his dentist. He did not know the drug's effects nor was he made aware of the effects. Shortly after driving away from the dentist's office the drug caused the accused to become unconscious and he ran into a parked car. His act of driving while impaired was considered to be an involuntary act and he was found not guilty. The result would have been different if the accused had known that the drug would produce unconsciousness.[11]

If an accused was aware that he was subject to states of unconsciousness, automatism will not be a successful defence. For example, in *R. v. Shaw,*[12] the accused was suffering from a physical disability which, the court concluded, was probably epilepsy. Although the accused knew that he was subject to attacks which caused unconsciousness, he continued to drive his car. On one occasion, he suffered an attack while driving. He slumped or fell and caused the car to accelerate. The car went off the highway and collided with a tree. Two passengers were killed and three others were injured. Unlike the *King* case, the accused in this case was aware that he could become unconscious while driving and the court held that he could be found criminally responsible for his conduct.

A person who is sleepwalking is considered to be in a state of automatism. For example, in *R. v. Cogdon*[13] the accused dreamed in her sleep that the Korean War was taking place around her house. She dreamed that soldiers were in her daughter's bedroom and that one was on the bed attacking her. In a sleepwalking state, the accused mother got out of bed, picked up an axe, entered her daughter's room and hit her daughter on the head two times with the blade of the axe, thus killing her. At her trial, the defence of insanity was not raised, but she was found not guilty because her acts while sleepwalking were not considered voluntary, conscious acts. Because she did not have conscious control over her bodily movements, she could not be held criminally responsible for them.

The possibility of automatism being caused by a severe psychological blow was recognized by the court in *R. v. K.*[14] The accused killed his wife and was charged with manslaughter. The trial judge summarized the testimony of the accused as follows:

He gave evidence concerning his depression in the months before this tragedy and following the sale of his farm. He described the affection he had for his wife . . . . He described his worry over his own depression and the problem that he was facing, whether he was going to lèave with his family to go to Vancouver or not. He also described his actions on the day of the tragedy: the telephone call from Mrs. S. saying repeatedly, 'your wife is leaving, your wife is leaving', how he went outside looking for the girls (his daughters), met his wife on the street, returning home, going upstairs and then coming down again, and then seeing his wife and putting his arms around his wife, saying to her, 'please don't leave'. To the accused, in his evidence, the rest is like a dream. He remembers falling and getting up, his wife being on the floor calling for help.

People who saw the accused after the incident agreed that he appeared to be in shock. His eyes were glazed and he repeatedly answered questions by saying that he did not know what had happened.

A psychiatrist supported the accused's evidence by stating that, in the days before the incident, the accused had become extremely depressed about the problems of having sold his farm and the possibility of his wife leaving him. The psychiatrist felt that a state of automatism was caused by the severe psychological blow of learning that his wife was leaving him. This psychological blow produced a state in which "the mind registered little, and from then on the accused did not know what was happening, his mind no longer being in control of his actions."

The judge instructed the jury that if they accepted the above evidence, they should find the accused not guilty. However, if they believed that the state of automatism was caused by a disease of the mind, they should find the accused not guilty by reason of insanity. The jury returned a verdict of not guilty.

There are some important legal differences between the defences of automatism and insanity. First, if an accused is found not guilty because he was in a state of automatism at the time he committed the offence, he is immediately released from custody. If he is found not guilty by reason of insanity, he remains in custody, possibly for the rest of his life.

Second, the burden of proof on the defence of insanity is usually on the accused. In other words, it is usually up to the accused to prove that it was more likely than not that he was insane at the time he committed the offence. With automatism, the accused must only show enough evidence to raise a reasonable doubt about the voluntariness of his act. The prosecution then has the burden of proving beyond a reasonable doubt that the act of the accused was voluntary.

Third, automatism is a defence to a charge of committing a strict liability offence. As mentioned in Chapter Three, a strict liability offence involves an *actus reus* (physical element) but no *mens rea* (mental element). The *actus reus* of an offence only occurs if the act is voluntary. The acts of a person in a state of automatism are not voluntary and therefore no *actus reus* occurs. On the other hand, the defence of insanity is useful only in regard to offences which require *mens rea*. Thus, it is not a defence to a charge of committing a strict liability offence.

D. INTOXICATION

In general, intoxication by alcohol or drugs is not a defence to a criminal charge.

However, it may be a defence to a charge of commiting a specific intent offence. That is, if it can be shown that the accused was too intoxicated to form the specific intent required, then he will not be guilty of the offence.

As discussed in Chapter Three, specific intent offences in the Code are often indicated by the words "with intent." Examples of specific intent offences are theft, robbery, murder, and assault with the intent to commit an indictable offence. With these and other specific intent offences, the accused may raise the defence of intoxication. If the offence is a general intent offence, such as common assault or manslaughter, intoxication will not be a defence.

In *R. v. George*[15] the accused was charged with robbery and the included offence of common assault. The accused had violently manhandled an 84-year-old man. The man was badly injured, dumped into a bathtub and then pulled out when he agreed to give the accused his money. The accused raised the defence of intoxication by alcohol. He was found not guilty of robbery because robbery requires the specific intent to steal and the accused was too drunk to form this specific intent. However, the accused was guilty of common assault because assault requires only the general intent to apply force to another person. As discussed below, it is possible that a person could be too drunk to know that he is applying force to someone else, but in such a case, his defence would be insanity, not intoxication. In this case, insanity was not suggested and the accused clearly admitted that he knew that he was applying force to his victim.

It should also be noted that if a person drinks in order to give himself the courage to commit an offence, he can not rely on intoxication as a defence. In such a situation the relevant intent would be the intent the accused possessed *before* he became drunk.

1. Degree of Intoxication Required

The Supreme Court of Canada, in *Perrault v. R.,*[16] considered to what extent an accused must be intoxicated before he can successfully use drunkenness as a defence. The court quoted with approval a statement made by a British judge, Lord Denning:

> *... If a man is charged with an offence in which a specific intention is essential (as in murder, though not in manslaughter), then evidence of drunkenness, which renders him incapable of forming the intention, is an answer. This degree of drunkenness is reached when the man is rendered so stupid by drink that he does not know what he is doing, ... as where a drunken man thought his friend (lying in his bed) was a theatrical dummy placed there and stabbed him to death. In this case it would not be murder but it would be manslaughter.*

In another case, *R. v. Reece,*[17] the trial judge explained the relationship between drunkenness and criminal responsibility in the following terms:

A man may drink, he may drink to excess, he may become quarrel-some, vicious, nasty, belligerent — none of that makes any differ-ence. He is still criminally responsible if he knows what he is doing, if he knows what he is doing even through an alcoholic haze. It is a matter of mind. It may be that he gives way to temptation more readily after drinking and after drinking to excess. That makes no difference to his criminal responsibility, if he knows what he is doing.

In *R. v. Bucci*[18] the accused was charged with theft of a motor vehicle. His defence was intoxication caused by drugs. The accused had been standing in a small crowd of people beside a car which had been driven into a ditch. The operator of a tow truck asked the accused to put the car in neutral; the accused did so and the tow truck pulled the car out of the ditch. When the car was released from the tow truck the accused promptly drove it into the ditch again. When it was again pulled out of the ditch, the accused drove the car into the back of the tow truck. The accused then made a maneouver with the car which the tow-truck driver assumed was to be an attempt at parking it nearby. Instead, the accused drove off. The tow-truck operator gave chase and caught up with the accused about a block and a half away when the accused again drove the car into the ditch. The accused ran away but was ap-prehended by the truck driver.

The accused testified that on the day of his arrest he had taken some valium pills in order to get a "high." Within a two hour period he swallowed at least 16 valium pills (10 mg. each or 160 mg. in total) and drank some whiskey. He said he recalled nothing of the events of the next four days except driving a car around a curve, his body going limp, the car going into the ditch, his putting the key in the ignition and getting into the police car.

Several witnesses testified about his condition. The truck driver said the accused was "tripping all over the place, like tripping over his own two feet." Both police officers who testified said the accused seemed to be under the influence of some-thing — his speech was incoherent, slow and slurred, his walk was a little unsteady. There was no odour of alcohol. He seemed to understand a direction from one of the officers to get into the police car.

Another witness said the accused was "stoned" during the afternoon of the day on which these events occurred. She said he walked "funny," his eyes were red, and he was not "himself." When they parted a friend took or led him up the steps of the bus he was taking and more or less put him on a seat in the bus.

A professor of pharmacology testified that valium was a minor tranquilizer used in the treatment of anxieties. He said the normal daily dosage prescribed was 10 to 30 mg. In his opinion an ingestion of 100 mg. would be very high. He stated that he would expect profound effects in a person who had consumed 150 mg. of valium over an eight-hour period, including euphoria, depression, a desire for sleep, loss of memory, depression of the normal activity of the central nervous system with resulting loss of inhibitions. He likened its effects to those of alcohol. He said a person might do things while under the influence of valium which he might not otherwise do.

In his reasons for judgement the judge pointed out that a charge of theft (s. 283) requires proof of a specific intent — the accused must have the specific intent of depriving the owner of his property, either permanently or temporarily. The judge found that the accused was unable to form this intent because of the drugs he had consumed. He stated:

> *Normally, the prosecutor would have the benefit of the presumption that a man intends the natural and probable consequences of his acts, with the result that when the accused was, for instance, driving the motor vehicle away from the place where it had been driven into the ditch, he was then intending to deprive the owner of the use of his motor vehicle. But such presumptions are easily displaced. The evidence here points very strongly to the fact that the accused's mental processes were deeply affected by the drug he had taken and I have no hesitation in reaching the conclusion that the presumption has been displaced in this case . . .there being no positive proof of the specific intent on the part of the accused to deprive the owner of his motor vehicle, I hold that the prosecution has failed to prove this ingredient of the first charge and I acquit the accused on the charge of theft.*

2. Delirium Tremens

It is possible for an accused to argue that he had drunk so much alcohol, or consumed such a quantity of drugs, that he brought on a distinct *disease of the mind*. That is, because of his intoxication he was temporarily insane and was therefore incapable of appreciating the nature and quality of his act, or of knowing that it was wrong. Disease of the mind caused by intoxication is frequently called "delirium tremens." If an accused is relying on "delirium tremens" he must plead insanity and use s. 16 of the Code. This defence can be used in regard to charges of specific intent offences and also general intent offences.

3. Summary

Briefly, the limitations of the defence of intoxication are as follows:
(a) In general, the offence must be a specific intent crime.
(b) The degree of intoxication must be such that the accused was unable to form a specific intent, or that it caused him to become temporarily insane (delirium tremens).
(c) Evidence of intoxication which merely shows that the accused more readily gave way to some temptation is no defence.

E. DURESS OR COMPULSION

Section 17 of the Criminal Code provides that in certain circumstances a person who has been *forced* to commit an offence may be excused for committing that offence.

Section 17 reads:

> **17. A person who commits an offence under compulsion by threats of immediate death or grievous bodily harm from a person who is present when the offence is committed is excused for committing the offence if he believes that the threats will be carried out and if he is not a party to a conspiracy or association whereby he is subject to compulsion, but this section does not apply where the offence that is committed is treason, murder, piracy, attempted murder, assisting in rape, forcible abduction, robbery, causing bodily harm or arson.**

It is clear that before an accused can rely on the defence of compulsion or duress as outlined in section 17 it must first be established that:

(1) he committed an offence *other* than those specifically listed in section 17;

(2) he committed the offence because of threats of *immediate death* or *immediate grievous bodily harm;*

(3) threats were delivered by a person who was present at the time the accused committed the offence; and

(4) he was not a member of a group planning to commit the offence.

In *R. v. Carker,*[19] the accused was charged with having unlawfully and wilfully damaged public property. The damaged property consisted of plumbing fixtures in the accused's prison cell. The accused testified that he committed the offence during a disturbance in the course of which a substantial body of prisoners, shouting in unison from their separate cells, threatened the accused, who was not joining in the disturbance, that if he did not break the plumbing fixture in his cell he would be kicked in the head, his arms would be broken and he would get a knife in the back at the first opportunity.

The court decided that although there was little doubt that the accused committed the offence under the compulsion of threats of death and grievous bodily harm, they were not threats of *"immediate* death" or *"immediate* grievous bodily harm." The court arrived at this decision because it was virtually impossible that immediate death or grievous bodily harm could come to the accused as the persons who were uttering the threats were locked up in separate cells.

F. CONSENT

In limited circumstances an accused may use as a defence the fact that the victim consented to the accused's act. For example, if the accused engaged in a fight with another individual, and as a result of the fight was charged with assault (s.244), he might be able to argue that the other person consented to the fight. If it can be established that both parties consented to the fight, the accused may be entitled to an acquittal.[20] Consent in such circumstances does not include the consent to use excessive force. In other words an accused cannot violently "beat-up" someone and use the consent of the victim as his defence.

1. Specific Offences for which Consent Is *Not* a Defence

The victim's consent to be killed is no defence to a murder charge because s.14 states:

> **No person is entitled to consent to have death inflicted upon him, and such consent does not affect the criminal responsibility of any person by whom death may be inflicted upon the person by whom consent is given.**

Section 140 provides that an accused charged with having sexual intercourse with a girl under the age of 14 (contrary to s.146) cannot use the girl's consent to the act as a defence.

Section 140 also states that if an accused is charged with the offence of indecently assaulting a female under age 14 (contrary to s.149) or indecently assaulting a male under age 14 (contrary to s.156), the consent of the child is not a defence.

Section 249 of the Code (abduction of female under 16) states that the fact the girl being taken is consenting cannot be used as a defence to a charge under s.249.

2. Specific Offences for which Consent Is a Defence

In general, consent will be a defence to a charge of taking or damaging another person's property. For example, A takes B's car and is charged with theft. If A had B's consent to take the car, then he would be not guilty. Similarly, if A has B's consent to cut down B's tree for firewood, then A would not be guilty of the offence of wilfully damaging B's property.

Consent also will be a defence to some offences involving contact with the body of another person. In addition to certain non-sexual assaults, there are several sex offences which require the lack of consent by the victim. For example, s143(a) states:

> **143. A male person commits rape when he has sexual intercourse with a female person who is not his wife,**
> **(a) without her consent ....**

It is clear that an essential element of rape under s.143(a) is that the female victim did not consent to the intercourse. If she did consent, no offence is committed.

Other sex offences in which consent is a defence include homosexual acts between two adults in private, indecent assault and attempted rape.

3. Consent by Fraud or Threats of Bodily Harm

When consent is available as a defence, the consent of the victim must be a real or valid consent. If the consent is obtained by fraud, it will not be considered real and therefore it will not constitute a defence. For example, a doctor tells a woman patient that in order to cure her ailment, it is necessary that he have sexual intercourse with her. So, she consents to the intercourse. In fact, the "treatment" was simply for the doctor's pleasure. He could be convicted of rape because, although the woman consented, the consent was obtained by fraud.

A similar result occurs if the consent is obtained by threats of bodily harm. For example, a man with a gun threatens to kill a woman if she will not consent to sexual intercourse. Her consent would not be a real or valid consent and therefore the offence of rape would be committed.

For a discussion of cases involving consent as a defence to charges of rape and indecent assault, see Chapter Seven: Sexual Offences, Obscenity and Disorderly Conduct.

G. PROVOCATION

The defence of provocation only arises in a case of murder. If provocation is proved the accused will be found guilty of the reduced charge of manslaughter.

Section 215 of the Criminal Code provides:

> **215.(1) Culpable homicide that otherwise would be murder may be reduced to manslaughter if the person who committed it did so in the heat of passion caused by sudden provocation.**
>
> **(2) A wrongful act or insult that is of such a nature as to be sufficient to deprive an ordinary person of the power of self-control is provocation for the purposes of this section if the accused acted upon it on the sudden and before there was time for his passion to cool.**
>
> **(3) For the purposes of this section the questions**
> **(a) whether a particular wrongful act or insult amounted to provocation, and**
> **(b) whether the accused was deprived of the power of self-control by the provocation that he alleges he received,**
> **are questions of fact, but no one shall be deemed to have given provocation to another by doing anything that he had a legal right to do, or by doing anything that the accused incited him to do in order to provide the accused with an excuse for causing death or bodily harm to any human being.**

In general, culpable homicide refers to causing the death of another person by an unlawful act or criminal negligence. The three types of culpable homicide are murder, manslaughter, and infanticide.

Provocation as defined in s.215 consists of the following elements:
(1) a wrongful act or insult;
(2) sufficient to deprive an ordinary person of the power of self-control;
(3) the offender acts upon it on the sudden; and
(4) before there has been time for his passion to cool.
These four elements form the two tests that are to be used in determining whether or not provocation existed. The accused must satisfy *both* tests before a defence of provocation will be successful.

1. "Wrongful Act or Insult"

The first test is whether the wrongful act or insult was of a nature sufficient to deprive *an ordinary person* of his self-control. The test is not whether the wrongful act or insult deprived the accused of his self-control but whether it is sufficient to deprive any ordinary person of the power of self-control. A common or casual verbal insult, or act, will not be considered provocation. Even a confession of adultery will usually be considered insufficient to amount to an insult that would deprive an ordinary person of self-control for the purposes of provocation. However, if a spouse is caught by the other spouse in the act of committing adultery, the adultery would probably be considered a wrongful act or insult sufficient to deprive an ordinary person of self-control.

The first test was considered in *R. v. Clark.* [21] The accused killed his girlfriend and was charged with murder. The accused testified that his girlfriend had provoked him into shooting her. He described what happened in these words:

> *Well I've been going with this woman about eight years and I don't think any man took the guff I did from her. This is running around with other guys, you know. I really loved her. Everytime my back was turned she was running around with other guys going to the beer parlour. Myself, I had no interest in any other woman. Friends of mine told me to get away from her — she was just ruining my life. When I first met her I even bought a house, got hold of every cent I could get to put into this house and I lived with her. And many times I'd come home from work and she would be gone and wouldn't come back all night. I had to quit two jobs because of lack of sleep — enough to drive you hairy. This has been going on for eight years. I lived with her for about five years. Because of this she moved out of my house and I rented it out, but I continued to go with her. I could not even get interested in another woman. That's about it until last night. I took her, her small daughter and her grand-daughter to a drive-in and before we left her apartment a man phoned her and she told him she couldn't come out because she didn't have a babysitter — she lied to everybody. When we got home and into bed, we got into an argument about her cheating.* She told me what she did was her own business. Said she didn't give a damn what I thought about it. *I just flipped my lid I guess and it all piled up so damn much I shot*

> *her. As far as I can see she ruined my life — even my friends told me that.*

The accused contended that the emphasized words amounted to an insult of such proportion that he lost control of himself and shot the woman.

The judge stated, "in my opinion such words are not capable of being construed as an insult by *an ordinary person.*" The judge then continued: "However assuming that I am wrong, and such words can be construed as an insult, then they are not of such a nature as to be sufficient to deprive an *ordinary* person of the power of self-control."

The accused's defence of provocation therefore failed.

2. "Upon the Sudden"

If the accused can meet the first test for provocation it is still necessary that he satisfy the second.

The second test is that the accused must act upon *the sudden* and *before his passion has time to cool.* In other words the accused must react almost instantaneously after the insult. If he sees his wife in bed with another man; runs down to the basement to get his rifle; loads it; and returns to the bedroom and shoots his wife, it is likely that a court would say in such circumstances that his "passion had time to cool." This is because of the time interval between the "seeing" and the "shooting".

The meaning of "sudden" was considered in *R. v. Tripodi.*[22] The accused was married in Italy. In 1952 he came to Canada, leaving his wife and two infant children in Italy. In letters from friends and relatives in Italy he was told that his wife had been unfaithful to him and had obtained an abortion. In spite of this information, he arranged for his wife and children to come to Canada. Upon their arrival, the accused took them to the home of his brother with whom he had been living. After lunch he and his wife went upstairs. He admitted that he asked her to go for the purpose of sexual intercourse. While she did not refuse, her attitude was rather cold toward him and she said, "I cannot have any more children." In reply to his question asking the reason, she explained that "she was in hospital and had an abortion." Because of this admission on the part of his wife the accused said he lost his self-control and he seized her by the neck and strangled her to death.

The court stated: "There can be no doubt, upon the evidence, but that the accused had committed culpable homicide and the real issue turned upon whether he had suffered such provocation as would reduce his offence from murder to manslaughter."

The court rejected the accused's defence of provocation because they decided he had not acted "on the sudden." The court concluded that in order for provocation to be sudden, the wrongful act or insult must strike upon a mind unprepared for it and make an unexpected impact which takes the accused by surprise. In this case the words of the wife did not furnish the defence of provocation to the accused because he was already aware of her adultery and he killed her as a result of a "pent-up" determination to do so.

H. SELF-DEFENCE

1. Against an Unprovoked Assault

Section 34 provides that a person may use force in order to protect himself against an *unprovoked* assault:

> **34.(1) Every one who is unlawfully assaulted without having provoked the assault is justified in repelling force by force if the force he uses is not intended to cause death or grievous bodily harm and is no more than is necessary to enable him to defend himself.**
>
> **(2) Every one who is unlawfully assaulted and who causes death or grievous bodily harm in repelling the assault is justified if**
>
> > **(a) he causes it under reasonable apprehension of death or grievous bodily harm from the violence with which the assault was originally made or with which the assailant pursues his purposes, and**
> >
> > **(b) he believes, on reasonable and probable grounds, that he cannot otherwise preserve himself from death or grievous bodily harm.**

An accused can rely on s.34 as a defence only if he did not provoke the other person to assault him. If he did provoke the other person to assault him, then he may be able to rely on s.35, discussed below. For the purposes of s.34 and s.35, provocation includes provocation by blows, words or gestures (s.36).

The general principle regarding self-defence is that the force used must be no more than is necessary under the circumstances. Under s.34(2) a person who kills another in self-defence is justified if:

(1) he was under a reasonable fear of death or serious bodily harm, and

(2) he believed that there was no other way to save himself.

The first test, the reasonable fear of death, is an objective test. That is, this test will only be satisfied if an ordinary reasonable person in the position of the accused would have been in fear of death or serious bodily harm.

The second test, the accused's belief that he cannot otherwise save himself, is a subjective test. That is, this test is satisfied by looking at the accused's state of mind at the time he killed his assailant. The question to be asked is: did the accused believe, on reasonable and probable grounds, that he could not otherwise save himself from death or serious bodily harm? If he did have such a belief, he would be not guilty of culpable homicide. If he did not have such a belief, he must have used excessive force and, thus, would probably be guilty of culpable homicide. With this test, the belief must be based on reasonable and probable grounds, but it is not necessary to consider whether or not an ordinary reasonable man would have held the same belief. Rather, the important question is whether or not the accused himself actually believed that there was no other way to save himself.

In *R. v. Cadwallader*,[23] a 14-year-old boy was charged with the manslaughter of his father. His defence was self-defence. The boy lived alone with his father. Although their relationship seemed normal and healthy to outsiders, the boy had been living in fear of his father for several months. The boy testified that there had been over twenty incidents in which the father seemed to want to do away with him or to kill him. The report of the facts continues as follows:

> *About 1:30 p.m. father and son had a light dinner together, after which the father went outside to repair the fence. The boy went upstairs to lay down on his bed again as he was not feeling well. About 3:30 p.m. the boy heard his father make a lot of noise on the doorstep, he mumbled as he entered the house, slammed the door, and he was heard to say: I'm going to kill that God Damned little bastard. The father walked noisily to his room (situated roughly beneath the boy's room), started loading a 30-30, pumped a shell into the barrel, and walked noisily again across the kitchen towards the stairway. The boy arose from his bed and peeked over the edge of the stairway; he saw his angry and determined father start up the stairs with the 30-30 rifle in his hand. The boy figured this was it — that his father was coming up to get him. The boy returned to his bed, quickly grabbed the magazine on the nail keg as well as his semi-automatic Cooey rifle leaning against the east wall, and slipped the magazine into the gun. The boy swung around and saw his father up the steps aiming at him with his 30-30 rifle. The boy took a quick shot without aiming; there followed four other shots . . . .*
> *[T]wo shots followed quickly after the first one before or as the father and his gun started to fall back down the stairs. The fourth shot was fired with the boy standing near the top or about three quarters of the way up the stairs, the father was still partly on the stairs and the bullet struck him in the back. The father was still moving around and the boy says he was still scared of his ability to shoot. The accused followed down the stairs and fired the fifth and last shot in the neck of the deceased from a distance of about three inches. Either the fourth or fifth shot could have been fatal whereas the first three shots were not.*

The prosecutor agreed that the accused boy had acted in self-defence, but he argued that the force used by the accused was excessive (i.e. more than necessary) and that there should be a conviction for manslaughter.

It was clear that the first test of self-defence was satisfied because the boy was under reasonable apprehension of death or serious bodily harm. The important issue in the case was whether or not the second test was satisfied. On this point, the court said:

> *. . .[I]f one believes he is in danger of life or limb he is entitled to use such force as would effectually put his assailant out of action. Where the means of defence used is not disproportionate to the severity of the assault, the plea [of self-defence] is valid although the defender*

fails to measure with nicety the degree of force necessary to ward off the attack and inflicts serious injury. The test as to the extent of justification is whether the accused used more force than he on reasonable grounds believed necessary. It is not an objective test; the determination must be made according to the accused's state of mind *at the time. The question is: Did he use more force than he on reasonable grounds believed to be necessary? . . . The boy was trapped and he reacted in the only way it seems to me that an ordinary person would under the circumstances . . . .It is clear that he acted in self-defence . . . .he used only sufficient force as he reasonably thought necessary under the circumstances to put his assailant out of action.*

2. Against a Provoked Assault

Section 35 deals with situations in which a person provokes an assault on himself by another person (e.g. by insulting the other person or by assaulting him):

> **35. Every one who has without justification assaulted another but did not commence the assault with intent to cause death or grievous bodily harm, or has without justification provoked an assault upon himself by another, may justify the use of force subsequent to the assault if**
> **(a) he uses the force**
> > **(i) under reasonable apprehension of death or grievous bodily harm from the violence of the person whom he has assaulted or provoked, and**
> > **(ii) in the belief, on reasonable and probable grounds, that it is necessary in order to preserve himself from death or grievous bodily harm;**
> **(b) he did not, at any time before the necessity of preserving himself from death or grievous bodily harm arose, endeavour to cause death or grievous bodily harm; and**
> **(c) he declined further conflict and quitted or retreated from it as far as it was feasible to do so before the necessity of preserving himself from death or grievous bodily harm arose.**

In other words, to justify the use of force under s.35 the accused must satisfy the following criteria:
(1) he must have assaulted another or in some other way provoked an assault on himself;
(2) he must at no time have intended to cause death or grievous bodily harm;
(3) after being assaulted he must have been in reasonable danger of death or bodily harm;
(4) he must have believed on reasonable and probable grounds that the force used was necessary to prevent his death or grievous bodily harm occurring to himself; and

(5) before he used force he must have exhausted all other ways, such as retreat, of avoiding the use of force.

R. v. Doiron[24] is a case in which the accused, without excuse, assaulted another person (the victim). The victim then broke a beer bottle and attacked the accused. The accused shot the victim with a pistol, and wounded him slightly. The accused argued that he fired his pistol in self-defence using s.35 as his justification. The court held that the accused had reasonable grounds to fear at least that the victim would cause him grievous bodily harm *and* that firing the pistol was necessary, on reasonable and probable grounds, to stop the accused from injuring him. The court concluded, therefore, that the accused's actions were justified by s.35 and he was acquitted of the charge of discharging a firearm with intent to wound.

3. Defence of Others

Although it is not specifically mentioned in s.34 and s.35, apparently the right of self-defence extends to the defence of others under a person's protection. In *R. v. Wiggs*[25] the accused was charged with assaulting a boy who, with several other boys, attacked the accused's son. They threw him to the ground, sat on him, and punched and kicked him. The accused father rushed to the defence of his son and in stopping the attack struck one of the boys, causing injury to his face. The court found the father not guilty because in defending his son he had used no more force than was necessary in the circumstances.

4. Preventing an Assault

Sections 34 and 35 deal with situations in which an assault actually occurred. Section 37 is concerned with situations in which force is used to *prevent* an assault from occurring. It authorizes a person to use force in order to prevent himself or any one under his protection from being assaulted:

> **37.(1) Every one is justified in using force to defend himself or any one under his protection from assault, if he uses no more force than is necessary to prevent the assault or the repetition of it.**
>
> **(2) Nothing in this section shall be deemed to justify the wilful infliction of any hurt or mischief that is excessive, having regard to the nature of the assault that the force used was intended to prevent.**

In one of the few reported cases concerning this section, the court held that it was possible that s.37 could apply to a situation in which the accused had been earlier attacked and threatened with physical harm and death by another person.[26] The court went on to say that it was for the jury to decide whether the use of force by the accused was necessary to protect himself from assault. If the jury decided that the force was necessary, then they would have to consider whether the amount of force used was more than necessary (i.e. excessive).

I. DEFENCE OF PROPERTY

The defence of property applies to two types of property: real property and movable property. Real property refers to land and structures attached to the land. Movable property refers to things which can be moved such as a car, a television set, a chair, etc.

1. Movable Property

Sections 38 and 39 pertain to a person's right to defend movable property which is in his possession:

> **38.(1) Every one who is in peaceable possession of movable property, and every one lawfully assisting him, is justified**
> **(a) in preventing a trespasser from taking it, or**
> **(b) in taking it from a trespasser who has taken it,**
> **if he does not strike or cause bodily harm to the trespasser.**
> **(2) Where a person who is in peaceable possession of movable property lays hands upon it, a trespasser who persists in attempting to keep it or take it from him or from any one lawfully assisting him shall be deemed to commit an assault without justification or provocation.**
> **39.(1) Every one who is in peaceable possession of movable property under a claim of right, and every one acting under his authority is protected from criminal responsibility for defending that possession, even against a person entitled by law to possession of it, if he uses no more force than is necessary.**

Both these sections apply to persons in possession of movable property. This does not necessarily mean that they own the property. For example, A may be renting furniture from B. Even though A does not own the furniture, if he is in peaceable possession of it, he has a right to defend it.

Under s.38(1) force may not be used to prevent a trespasser from taking the movable property. Under s.39(1) force may be used, even against the lawful owner, but only if the person in peaceable possession has possession under a claim of right. In other words, he must honestly believe, on reasonable grounds, that he has a right to possess the property. Thus, a possessor under a claim of right is in a much stronger position than a possessor who does not have some basis for claiming that he has a lawful right of possession.

Under s.38(2) a trespasser commits an assault if he tries to take movable property from a person in peaceable possession if the possessor puts his hands on the property. In *R. v. Doucette,* [27] C had failed to make his payments on a television set which he was purchasing under a conditional sales agreement. Three bailiffs, acting for the seller of the television, entered C's house to repossess the set. They were not acting under the authority of a court order and C told them to leave. While C was leaning on the television set, the bailiffs grabbed it and began carrying it away. C followed "in a threatening manner" and the bailiff Doucette, believing that C was about to strike him, hit C in the mouth knocking him to the floor. Doucette was charged with assault. In its decision the court found the accused guilty and made the following points:

(1) It was illegal for the bailiffs to repossess the television set by the use of force.

(2) C was a peaceable possessor of movable property under a claim of right and was protected from criminal responsibility for resisting the taking of the property.

(3) The bailiffs were trespassers at least from the point at which C protested against their being in his house.

(4) Apart from the actual force applied to C, they could be held for having committed an assault under s.38(2) because they persisted in taking the property after C had leaned on it.

2. Real Property

Sections 40 and 41 pertain to a person's right to defend real property (including his dwelling-house) which is in his possession:

40. Every one who is in peaceable possession of a dwelling-house, and every one lawfully assisting him or acting under his authority, is justified in using as much force as is necessary to prevent any person from forcibly breaking into or forcibly entering the dwelling-house without lawful authority.

41.(1) Every one who is in peaceable possession of a dwelling-house or real property and every one lawfully assisting him or acting under his authority is justified in using force to prevent any person from trespassing on the dwelling-house or real property, or to remove a trespasser therefrom, if he uses no more force than is necessary.

(2) A trespasser who resists an attempt by a person who is in peaceable possession of a dwelling-house or real property or a person lawfully assisting him or acting under his authority to prevent his entry or to remove him, shall be deemed to commit an assault without justification or provocation.

Section 40 allows a person to use as much force as is necessary to prevent a person from forcibly entering his home without lawful authority.

Section 41(1) is broader in that it allows a person to use force to remove trespassers not only from his home but from any part of his real property. For example, a person could forcibly remove a trespasser from his front lawn. However, the force used must be no more than is necessary.

In *R. v. Ryan*[28] the accused was charged with unlawfully assaulting a police officer. His defence was that the police officer was a trespasser and that he was using reasonable force in the defence of his property against the trespasser. The facts were summarized by the court as follows:

> *A report was received at the police station . . . that a store selling*
> *electrical appliances . . . was keeping open to an hour later than that*
> *permitted by the city by-law. Accordingly, two women, who were*
> *police officers, one in uniform, were sent to investigate. These offic-*
> *ers arrived at the store at approximately 6:55 p.m., entered and*
> *found there the accused, who was the general manager and in*
> *charge of the store, two other employees, and a man, woman and*
> *two children. The accused asked the officers to leave . . .(one officer)*
> *refused and insisted she was going to another part of the store to*
> *interview the man and the woman. The accused, having asked her to*
> *leave then stood in the aisle to prevent her going to interview these*
> *people. She endeavoured to force her way past the accused and he*
> *put his hands on her arms to stop her.*

The court found the accused not guilty of assault for two reasons. First, the officers had no right to be in the store. They had no permission by law (e.g. a search warrant). Even though they had an implied permission from the accused to enter like any other members of the public, that permission was revoked when the accused requested them to leave. Second, the accused did not use excessive force in defending his possession of the store.

In *R. v. Montague*[29] the issue was whether the accused had used more force than was necessary in removing a person from his property. Atkinson, a member of the Jehovah's Witnesses, came to the door of the accused's home and asked him if he would be interested in a discussion of the Bible. The accused said he was not interested and told him to leave. Atkinson agreed to leave. At this point in the case, there was a conflict in the evidence. However, the accused admitted that he pushed Atkinson in order to get him to leave. He then followed Atkinson to a point on his property about twenty feet from the house and pushed him down in a snowbank. Atkinson got up and ran to the road with the accused chasing after him. The court concluded that, even if Atkinson was a trespasser, the accused had used more force than was necessary. The court said that Atkinson was actually leaving as requested when the accused proceeded to follow him out. There was nothing to suggest that Atkinson would not have continued leaving if the accused had simply closed the door and stayed in his house. His attack on Atkinson at the snowbank was an assault and was clearly not necessary for the defence of his property.

Under s.41(2) a trespasser who resists an attempt by the possessor of property to remove him from the property is guilty of an assault. However, in order to be guilty, the trespasser must do some overt act of resistance. Passive resistance is not suffi-cient to justify a conviction. In *R. v. Kellington,*[30] about twenty-five persons came to the offices of the Social Services Department of the city of Vancouver at about 5 p.m. They were there to get information about the Department's policy regarding funerals for indigent persons. The Director of the Department discussed the policy with them for about thirty minutes. Then disagreements arose between the Director and the group and he asked them to leave the building. They refused and the police were called to remove them. One member of the group simply remained seated in a chair until arrested. She was charged with assault under s.41(2). The court found her not guilty because she had done no overt act to resist her removal from the property.

J. MISTAKE OF FACT

If a person commits a prohibited act while believing that certain circumstances exist, but which do not actually exist, he may be able to rely on the defence of mistake of fact. A mistake of fact is an error as to some circumstance. For example, if A takes B's book, believing it to be his own, he is acting under a mistake of fact.

Except for strict liability offences, a mistake of fact will be a defence to a criminal charge if:
(1) the mistake was an honest one and
(2) no offence would have been committed if the circumstances had been as the accused believed them to be.

So, in the example above, A would not be guilty of theft if he had an honest belief that the book belonged to him. If the book did belong to him, no offence would have been committed.

Mistake of fact is a defence to most charges under the Code because if a person is acting under a mistaken belief in the facts, he does not have the *mens rea* or guilty mind required to commit the offence. In the example above, A did not have the *mens rea* to commit theft (i.e. the intent to deprive the owner) because he believed that he owned the book.

The Supreme Court of Canada has dealt with the defence of mistake of fact in *R. v. Rees* and *Beaver v. R.* In *Rees,* which was discussed in Chapter Three, the accused was found not guilty of contributing to juvenile delinquency because he made an honest mistake about the age of the juvenile with whom he had sexual intercourse.

In *Beaver*[31] the accused was charged with illegal possession of a narcotic drug. He had sold heroin to an undercover R.C.M.P. officer. His defence was that he honestly believed that he was selling sugar, not heroin, even though he had told the officer that he was selling a narcotic. The court found the accused not guilty because "[t]he essence of the crime is the possession of the forbidden substance and in a criminal case there is in law no possession without knowledge of the character of the forbidden substance." In short, to be guilty of illegal possession of a narcotic, the accused must know that he has a narcotic. If he has an honest, but mistaken, belief that the substance is sugar, then he does not have the knowledge required for possession. The mistaken belief must be honest, but it is not necessary that it be reasonable. Whether or not a reasonable person would have believed that the heroin was sugar is merely one factor to be considered by the jury in determining whether the accused's mistake was an honest mistake.

A mistake of fact will not be a defence if an offence would have been committed if the circumstances would have been as the accused believed them to be. For example, A's mistaken belief that he was trafficking in cocaine would be no defence to a charge of trafficking in heroin.

This general principle is expressly recognized in s.212(b) which states that murder is committed

> **where a person, meaning to cause death to a human being... by accident or mistake causes death to another human being, notwithstanding that he does not mean to cause death...to that human being.**

So, for example: A intends to kill B. He shoots a gun at a person who looks like B, but who is actually C, killing him. The mistake as to the identity of the victim is no defence because A had the intention *(mens rea)* to kill a human being. An offence would have been committed even if the facts were as A believed them to be.

On the other hand, if A were hunting and killed C believing that he was a bear in the distance, he would not be guilty of murder. He may be guilty of manslaughter if it is shown that he was criminally negligent. But, his mistake would be a defence to a murder charge because he did not have the intention to kill a human being.

K. MISTAKE OF LAW

The general rule that "ignorance of the law is no excuse" is contained in s.19:

> **19. Ignorance of the law by a person who commits an offence is not an excuse for committing that offence.**

In other words, everyone is presumed to know the criminal law. If a man is simply unaware that it is against the criminal law to have sexual intercourse with a female who is under the age of fourteen and who is not his wife [s.146(1)], he will still be guilty of the offence. Similarly, if he honestly believed that it was not a criminal offence to have sexual intercourse with the female if she gave her consent, he would still be guilty because the consent of a female under the age of fourteen is no defence (s.140). Unlike a mistake of fact, A's honest mistake about the criminal law will not excuse his conduct.

A mistake of fact is an error as to some circumstance or fact. A mistake of law is an error as to the legal status of the circumstance or fact. For example, in *Beaver v. R.,* discussed above, Beaver was found not guilty of possession of heroin because he honestly believed that the heroin was sugar. This was a mistake of fact. However, if Beaver knew that he had heroin, but honestly believed that it was legal to possess heroin, he would be making a mistake of law and would be guilty.

In some situations, a mistake of civil law may be a defence. A mistake of civil law occurs when a person has an honest belief that he has a legal right under the civil law, but in fact does not have the right. In *R. v. Harrison*[32] the accused, the operator of a car-towing service, was charged with theft. Haines had parked his car on private property. There were signs on the property stating that unauthorized cars would be towed away at the owner's expense. The owner of the private property asked the accused to remove the car. The accused towed it to a yard surrounded by a high fence and guarded by an attendant and a dog. When Haines arrived at the yard, the attendant told him that he could not have his car unless he paid $12.00 for the towing and storage. Haines did not get his car back until the next evening when he paid the towing and storage charges.

The offence of theft is committed if a person deprives a property owner of the property "without colour of right." The term "colour of right" refers to an honest mistake of fact or law which leads a person to believe that he has a legal justification for his actions. In this case, the accused had no legal right to refuse to release the car, but he honestly believed that he had the legal right to refuse until the money was paid. The court found the accused not guilty because he acted with colour of right. He made a mistake of law and thus acted without the *mens rea* required in the offence of theft. However, the court warned the accused that now that he was aware of his legal position he could not rely on the same mistake of law as a defence to any similar charges in the future.

QUESTIONS FOR REVIEW AND DISCUSSION

1. What is a defence to a crime?
2. Does the accused have to "prove" his defence? Explain.
3. What is a common law defence? Give an example.
4. What docs "everyone is presumed to be sane until the contrary is proven" mean?
5. What must be established on behalf of the accused if he is to be found not guilty by reason of insanity?
6. Define the defence of automatism.
7. What degree of intoxication must exist before an accused can rely on intoxication as a defence?
8. Could intoxication be used as a defence to common assault, a general intent crime? Why?
9. What sort of threat or force must have been exerted on an accused before he can successfully argue duress as a defence?
10. Can duress be used as a defence to a charge of murder? Why?
11. Can consent be used as a defence in a situation where the accused used excessive force during a fist fight in which the victim willingly took part? Why?
12. Who is entitled to use force in the defence of property? Does it matter whether the property is real or movable? How much force may be used?
13. Can provocation be used as a defence to a charge of assault causing bodily harm? Why?
14. What are the elements of the defence of provocation?
15. When can a person use the defence of self-defence?
16. What does mistake of fact mean when it is used as a defence?
17. Is mistake of law a defence to a crime? Explain.
18. How is mistake of fact different from mistake of law?

19.   A, a 13-year-old boy, is charged with theft and rape. Can he be convicted? If so, what must be established?

20.   What is the meaning of ''wrong'' as the word is used in the defence of insanity? What do you think the meaning of ''wrong'' should be?

21.   How is automatism different from insanity?

22.   A intends to kill B but he is afraid to carry out his intention. So, he drinks a large quantity of liquor in order to give himself the courage to do the killing. While in a highly intoxicated state, A succeeds in killing B. He is charged with murder and his defence is intoxication. Should A be convicted? Why?

23.   A is charged with the theft of one pound of butter from a grocery store. Theft requires the specific intent to deprive another person of his property. A's defence is that he was too intoxicated to form this specific intent. In making his decision, the magistrate considers the following points in favour of the accused's defence:

  (1) A drank 20 bottles of beer between 12 and 5 p.m. in a beer parlour.
  (2) While waiting for the police to arrive, A suddenly went to sleep or lost consciousness in the manager's office.
  (3) He did not need the butter since he had an ample supply in his apartment.
  (4) He did not remember what happened to the money given to him by his roommate an hour before the incident.
  (5) He had no lunch that day.
  (6) He had no memory of taking the butter.
  (7) He seemed to have taken the butter without caring whether anybody saw him or not.

The magistrate also considers the following points against the accused:

  (1) A caused no drunken disturbance either in the beer parlour or store or in the police station.
  (2) He had a perfectly lucid conversation with the store manager a few minutes before he took the butter.
  (3) Although his breath smelled of alcohol, there was no clinical evidence that the accused was drunk.
  (4) He walked perfectly steadily, even on an icy street without rubbers.
  (5) Neither the police nor the store manager recognized A as being drunk. He appeared normal to them except that his breath smelled of alcohol.

Should A be convicted? Why?

See *R. v. Regehr* (1952), 13 C.R. 53 (Sask.).

24.   C owes $500 to D, a well-known underworld figure. D threatens C by saying: ''If you don't pay me by 10:00 p.m. tonight, you'll be dead tomorrow morning''. C knows that D is serious and will carry out the threat if necessary. So, C breaks into a store, steals $500 and makes the payment to D. C is charged with break, enter and theft. C raises the defence of compulsion. Will his defence be successful? Why?

¹ *R. v. Craig* (1974), 22 C.C.C. (2d) 212 (Alta. S.C.).

² (1972), 10 C.C.C. (2d) 149 (Alta.S.C.)

³ quoted and adopted in *R. v. Leech, supra.* Reproduced by permission of the Minister of Supplies and Services Canada.

⁴ *Supra*, note 1.

⁵ (1953), 17 C.R. 373 (Alta.C.A.)

⁶ (1952), 104 C.C.C. 274 (Ont.C.A.)

⁷ But see *R. v. Borg* [1969] 4 C.C.C. 262 at p. 269 (S.C.C.).

⁸ (1934) 62 C.C.C. 172 (Ont.S.C.).

⁹ (1965) 1 C.C.C. 1, 44 C.R. 193 (S.C.C.).

¹⁰ (1962), 133 C.C.C. 1, 38 C.R. 52 (S.C.C.).

¹¹ The court in this case did not specifically mention automatism. However, as noticed in *R. v. Hartridge* (1967) 1 C.C.C. 346 (Sask.C.A.), automatism would be a defence in this situation.

¹² (1938) 70 C.C.C. 159(Ont.C.A.).

¹³ An unreported case discussed by N. Morris in "Somnambulistic Homicide: Ghosts, Spiders and North Koreans," (1951) 5 *Res Judicata* 29.

¹⁴ (1970), 3 C.C.C. (2d) 84 (Ont. H.Ct.).

¹⁵ (1960), 128 C.C.C. 289, 34 C.R. 1 (S.C.C.)

¹⁶ (1970) 5 C.C.C. 217 (S.C.C.)

¹⁷ (1954), 109 C.C.C. 26, 18 C.R., 326 (Ont.C.A.)

¹⁸ (1974), 17 C.C.C. (2d) 512 (N.S.)

¹⁹ (1967) 2 C.C.C. 190, 2 C.R.N.S. 16 (S.C.C.)

²⁰ See Chapter Twelve: Assault and Related Offences.

²¹ (1975), 22 C.C.C. (2d) 1. Affirmed 5 N.R.599 (S.C.C.)

²² (1955) 21 C.R. 192 (S.C.C.)

²³ (1966) 1 C.C.C. 380 (Sask.C.A.).

²⁴ (1972) 18 C.R.N.S. 127 (N.B.C.A.).

²⁵ (1931) 3 W.W.R. 52

²⁶ *Fowther v. R.* (1957) 26 C.R. 150 (Que.C.A.).

²⁷ (1960), 33 C.R. 174 (Ont.C.A.).

²⁸ (1956), 116 C.C.C. 239, 24 C.R. 214 (B.C.C.A.)

²⁹ (1949) 97 C.C.C. 29 (Ont.Cty.Ct.)

³⁰ (1972), 7 C.C.C. (2d) 564 (B.C.S.C.).

³¹ (1957) 118 C.C.C. 129, 26 C.R. 193 (S.C.C.)

³² (1966) 3 C.C.C. 348, 47 C.R. 322 (Ont.C.A.).

Chapter Five

Criminal Procedure

Criminal procedure is concerned with the legal machinery by which certain specified rights and duties, in the area of criminal responsibility, are enforced. It governs the rules for bringing a defendant into court as well as the proceedings that occur during the actual trial process. Generally criminal procedure can be separated into three distinct phases: pre-trial procedure, trial procedure, and post-trial procedure. This chapter will consider only the more important aspects of pre-trial procedure including the powers of arrest and search, pre-trial release, police interrogation, and rights of the accused before and after arrest.

A. POWERS OF ARREST

1. General

Everyone is aware that police officers are empowered to make arrests during the course of their duties. What is perhaps not as well known is that the Criminal Code also permits private citizens to make arrests provided certain conditions are fulfilled. Whether it is a police officer or a private citizen making the arrest the person arresting must notify the person being arrested that he is under arrest and, where it is feasible to do so, he must inform him of the reason for his arrest. This duty is imposed by s.29 of the Code:

> **29.(2) It is the duty of every one who arrests a person, whether with or without warrant, to give notice to that person, where it is feasible to do so; of**
> **(a) the process of warrant under which he makes the arrest, or**
> **(b) the reason for the arrest.**

An arrest can consist of the actual seizure or touching of the accused's body. It is sufficient for the arresting person to merely put a finger on the accused and to tell him that he is under arrest.

An arrest can also be made by words alone. The arresting person must use words such that the person being arrested is made aware his freedom is being restricted and that he is compelled to follow the instructions of the arresting person. Whether or not an arrest had been made in such circumstances was the question for determination in *Lebrun v. High-Low Foods Ltd.* [1] At the beginning of a visit to the supermarket, L picked up a carton of cigarettes. He subsequently made a trip to his car and returned. When he "checked out" the cigarettes were not among his purchases. The manager of the supermarket called Constable P, told him that several employees had seen L pick up the cigarettes, that they had not been returned and had not been paid for. The constable came to the store and stopped L's car as it was leaving the parking lot.

The constable told L: "There appears to be a mixup in your order. The store believes that you have something for which you have not paid." Constable P then asked L to move his car to where the police car was parked. The police officer asked L if he could search the vehicle. L replied, "Go ahead. I'd like to get this cleared up". The constable then proceeded to search the main area of the car, the glove compartment, the trunk and the back seat.

The police officer was polite and almost apologetic for the inconvenience he was causing. L was co-operative, polite, calm and was not visibly upset. L made no attempt to leave and made no request to be allowed to leave. L did not deny this but said that he *felt he had no alternative* but to submit to the search; that he unlocked the trunk of his car at the request of Constable P because he felt he would be arrested if he refused to do so.

The court decided that L, notwithstanding Constable P had neglected to inform him of the fact, had indeed been arrested. L *believed* that he was under total restraint and was *compelled* to do as directed by Constable P.

A. USE OF FORCE A private citizen or a police officer may, *if necessary,* use force in making an arrest. This power is granted by s.25. However, no more force than is reasonably necessary to make the arrest is justified. For example, in situations where merely grasping an arm would suffice, an "armlock" would be an unjustifiable use of force.

If a person "takes flight" from arrest a *police officer* may use, in extreme situations, a firearm in order to prevent the person's escape. This power is derived from s.25(4):

> **25.(4) A peace officer who is proceeding lawfully to arrest . . . any person . . . is justified, if the person to be arrested takes flight to avoid arrest, in using as much force as is necessary to prevent the escape by flight, unless the escape can be prevented by reasonable means in a less violent manner.**

Priestman v. Colangelo and Smythson[2] is a case in which a police officer used s.25(4) as a justification for his actions. Constables P and A were on patrol duty when they received a message on the radio telephone reporting the theft of a car. Almost immediately they saw a motor vehicle which they believed to be — and which later turned out to be — the stolen vehicle, driven by S. The police car pulled up alongside the stolen car and P ordered S to stop. Both officers were in uniform and S, no doubt, realized that they were police officers. Instead of stopping, he pulled around the corner quickly and drove away at a high rate of speed. The police car followed and on three occasions attempted to pass the stolen car in order to cut it off, but each time S pulled to the south side of the road and cut off the police car. On the third occasion the police car was forced over the south curb on to a boulevard and was compelled to slow down in order to avoid colliding with a hydro pole. Following this third attempt and as the police car went back on the road, P fired a warning shot into the air from his .38 calibre revolver. The stolen car increased its speed and when the police car was one and a half to two car lengths from the stolen car, P aimed at the left rear tire of the stolen car and fired. The bullet hit the bottom of the frame of the rear window, shattered the glass, ricocheted and struck S in the back of the neck, causing him to lose consciousness immediately. The stolen car went over the curb on the south side of the road, grazed a hydro pole, crossed a street and, coming to a stop, struck the verandah of a house. Before hitting the house the car ran into and killed two people waiting for a bus.

Constable P took the position that S's escape could not have been prevented by reasonable means in a less violent manner. In other words, P believed he was justified in firing his revolver. The court agreed with P. They found that his actions were justified by s.25(4). He used no more force than was *reasonably necessary* to prevent S's escape.

2. Police Officers

A. ARREST WITHOUT WARRANT A police officer has two powers of arrest conferred on him: the power to arrest without a warrant and the power to arrest with a warrant. A warrant is a document issued by a justice of the peace, or a judge, authorizing the police to arrest the person named in the warrant.

Section 450 of the Criminal Code defines the situations in which a police officer may make an arrest without a warrant. Section 450(1) provides:

> **450.(1) A peace officer may arrest without warrant**
> **(a) a person who has committed an indictable offence or who, on reasonable and probable grounds, he believes has committed or is about to commit an indictable offence,**
> **(b) a person whom he finds committing a criminal offence, or**
> **(c) a person for whose arrest he has reasonable and probable grounds to believe that a warrant is in force within the territorial jurisdiction in which the person is found.**

Section 450 speaks of "peace officers" rather than "police officers." Peace officers are listed in s.2 of the Code. They include a mayor, a warden, a sheriff, a prison guard, certain customs officials, a pilot in command of an aircraft while the aircraft is in flight, certain military personnel and, of course, police officers. However, a private security guard or official such as one employed by a department store or a business is *not* classified as a peace officer. He has only the same power of arrest that any other ordinary citizen possesses. For the purpose of discussion in this chapter, "police officer" will be used instead of "peace officer" although it must be remembered that what is to be said about police officers will also have application to those officials described in s.2.

Section 450(1) outlines five situations in which a police officer may make an arrest without a warrant.

Situation One: The arresting officer *knows* the accused has committed an indictable offence. The arresting officer need not have actually seen the accused in the act of committing the offence. He may rely on information stating that the accused has committed an indictable offence in the past.

Situation Two: The arresting officer *believes on reasonable and probable grounds* that the accused has committed an indictable offence. This situation demands that a "reasonable and probable" grounds test be used to determine if an arrest can be made. It is not necessary that an indictable offence has actually been committed. The arresting officer must have an honest belief that an indictable offence has been committed, and his honest belief must be based on reasonable and probable grounds.

Generally, reasonable and probable grounds are grounds which would lead any ordinary, prudent and cautious person to conclude that the person to be arrested is probably guilty of the crime imputed to him.

Whether or not police officers had reasonable and probable grounds to make an arrest was discussed in three recent cases, *Koechlin v. Waugh and Hamilton,*[3] *Scott v. R.*[4] and *Cheese v. Hardy.*[5]

In *Koechlin,* the neighbourhood in which the accused was arrested had been subject to a break-in a few nights earlier. The suspect involved in the break-in was reported to have been wearing rubber-soled shoes. The accused and a friend were stopped by the police at approximately eleven o'clock a few evenings later. At this time, the accused was observed to be wearing shoes that matched the shoes worn by the suspect. The accused explained that he was returning home from a show. The police decided to arrest him on *suspicion* of having committed the break-in. The court held that the above facts did not amount to reasonable and probable grounds for believing the accused had committed the break-in.

In *Scott,* the accused was arrested for possession of narcotics. At the time of his arrest the accused was drinking in a hotel known to be a center for drug trafficking. He was seated at a table with a number of prostitutes. Also sitting at the same table was a person who the arresting police officers thought was a "pusher." When the officers approached the table the accused quickly lifted his glass of beer and appeared to take a gulp from it. He was placed under arrest. The officers believed that the accused gulped at his beer in order to swallow narcotics which they thought he had hidden in his mouth. It was the first time the officers had seen the accused. The court held that, based on the above facts, the police officers involved did not have reasonable and probable grounds to believe the accused had possession of narcotics, and that, therefore, the arrest was unlawful.

In the *Cheese* case, the accused was also arrested for possession of narcotics. The accused was known to the arresting officers. He was unemployed yet was enjoying a high standard of living. He was also a good friend to several known drug traffickers and was in the habit of spending his evenings with them. These evenings were usually spent at night clubs which were known to be centers for drug trafficking. On the night of his arrest the accused had left such a club in the company of a known "pusher," and had been driving around the west end of Vancouver in a "purposeless and erratic" manner before he was stopped by the police.

The court held that the accused's arrest was justified on reasonable and probable grounds. The judge stated his conclusions as follows: "I find that the police officers were justified in detaining the accused on the reasonable suspicion that he was engaged in trafficking in narcotics. I do not say that mere association with known drug traffickers can justify an arrest . . . . I do say, however, that the courts would be blind to reality if known drug traffickers and their associates were permitted to drive around . . . . in the early morning hours in a purposeless, erratic and suspicious manner without being subject to temporary detention and search."

Why the arrest was held to be lawful in the *Cheese* case, while the arrest in the *Scott* case was found to be unlawful, is at first glance difficult to understand. There are, however, two points which should be noted when the cases are compared. In *Scott,* none of the arresting officers had seen the accused before. They had no idea about his past, his present employment, his character or his habits. In *Cheese,* the officers knew the accused was unemployed and yet seemed to have money to throw away. They also knew he had several friends who were known to be involved in drug trafficking. Secondly, in *Scott,* the accused's only suspicious behaviour at the time of his arrest amounted to taking a gulp from his beer. In *Cheese,* the accused's behaviour, driving erratically and as if he were under the influence of drugs, was more questionable.

If, in the *Scott* case, the police had had the same sort of information about the accused that the police in the *Cheese* case possessed about "their" accused, *and* they had observed him take a sudden gulp of his beer when approached, then it would have been more reasonable and probable to believe he was attempting to swallow drugs.

It would appear, from an analysis of the *Koechlin, Scott,* and *Cheese* cases, that all of the circumstances surrounding an accused's arrest are to be considered in determining if reasonable and probable grounds for the arrest existed. These include the accused's actions at the time of his arrest and any information about the accused available to the arresting officer. That is, information about the accused's life style, the people he associates with and the character of the places he frequents, etc. If all these facts, when *linked together,* add up to a reasonable belief that an accused has committed an indictable offence, then a police officer may make a lawful arrest.

Situation Three: The arresting officer has *reasonable and probable grounds* to believe an indictable offence is *about to be committed.* This situation also demands that the police use a reasonable and probable test in determining if an indictable offence is about to be committed. The definition of reasonable and probable in this situation is the same as for situation two. If a police officer has an honest belief based on reasonable and probable grounds that an individual is about to commit an indictable offence, even though that person has not yet made an attempt to commit the offence, then the police officer may make the arrest. For example, if a police officer observed a person stagger drunkenly out of a beverage room and stagger over to his car, he would be justified in arresting the person. He would have reasonable and probable grounds to believe the person was about to commit an indictable offence, that is, the offence of driving while impaired.

Situation Four: The arresting officer *finds* the accused committing any criminal offence. This situation allows a police officer to arrest any person whom he finds committing a criminal offence. Any criminal offence includes summary conviction offences as well as those that are indictable. It does not include provincial offences. Arrest powers for provincial offences are contained in the statutes (provincial) that create them.

The only power that a police officer has to arrest for a *summary conviction* offence, *without a warrant,* is that granted by situation four (as described in s.450) and by the power to arrest that everybody has as granted by s.449. Section 449 allows a person to make an arrest if, on reasonable and probable grounds, he believes the accused has committed a criminal offence, and is being "freshly pursued" by someone at the time of his arrest. The meaning of "freshly pursued" is considered later in this chapter.

Situation Five: The arresting officer believes on *reasonable and probable grounds* that the accused is the *subject of a warrant* which is in force within the jurisdiction in which the accused is found. This situation considers the circumstance where a police officer has reasonable and probable grounds to believe that there is a warrant in effect for the arrest of the accused. The warrant must be in force in the territorial jurisdiction in which the accused is found at the time of his arrest. In other words, if a warrant is in force in only one county or district of a province it cannot be used to arrest an accused who is found in a different county or district.

(i) limitations on power to arrest without a warrant

A police officer's right to arrest without a warrant is limited by ss.(2) of s.450:

> **450.(2) A peace officer shall not arrest a person without a warrant for**
> **(a) an indictable offence mentioned in section 483,**
> **(b) an offence for which the person may be prosecuted by indictment or for which he is punishable on summary conviction, or**
> **(c) an offence punishable on summary conviction.**

Indictable offences which are contained in s.483 include:
a) theft (other than theft of cattle) under $200;
b) obtaining or attempting to obtain money or property by false pretences where the value of the thing is under $200;
c) having in possession anything, knowing that it was obtained by the commission in Canada of an offence punishable by indictment, where the value of the thing is under $200;
d) attempted theft;
e) keeping a common gaming-house;
f) bookmaking and other related offences under s.186 and s.187;
g) offences in relation to lotteries;
h) driving while disqualified or prohibited.

Two examples of offences that can be prosecuted either as an indictable offence or as a summary conviction offence are driving while the ability to drive is impaired (s.234) and carrying a concealed weapon (s.85). Section 85 reads:

> **85. Every one who carries a weapon concealed, unless he is the holder of a permit under which he may lawfully so carry it:**
> **(a) Is guilty of an indictable offence and is liable to imprisonment for five years, or**
> **(b) Is guilty of an offence punishable on summary conviction.**

Examples of summary conviction only offences include nudity in a public place (s.170) and soliciting for the purpose of prostitution (s.195.1).

If a police officer finds himself confronted with one of the three categories of offences described in ss.(2) of s.450, then he may *not* make an arrest *without a warrant* unless he considers, on reasonable and probable grounds, that it is in the public interest to make the arrest. "In the public interest" is a general term which means the safety and well-being of the public is to be given priority.

In order to determine whether the public interest would be served by an arrest, the police officer must consider all the circumstances of the offence, including:
(a) the need to establish the identity of the person;
(b) the need to protect and/or keep evidence; or
(c) the need to prevent the continuation or repetition of the offence or the commission of another offence.

The arresting officer must also make up his mind as to whether there exist any good reasons for believing that the accused, if he is not arrested, will fail to show up on his court appearance date.

An example of when an arrest could be made for an offence such as theft under 200 dollars (an offence listed in s.483) would be if the arresting officer had good reasons for believing that the accused was giving him false information with respect to his identity and address. In such a situation, an arrest would be in the public interest.

If the police officer decides that an arrest is not needed, he may issue the accused with an "appearance notice" compelling his attendance in court at a specified date, time and place. Appearance notices will be explained in greater detail later in this chapter.

(ii) summary of power of arrest without warrant

The following briefly summarizes a police officer's power to arrest without a warrant:

(1) He must find himself presented with one of the five situations outlined in ss.(1) of s.450, or with that part of s.449 that entitles any person, on reasonable and probable grounds, to arrest, without warrant, an accused who has committed a criminal offence and is being "freshly pursued."

(2) If he finds that he is presented with such a situation, he must then consider whether or not the offence in question is one which falls within the three categories mentioned in ss.(2) of s.450. If it is not, then he may make an arrest without further deliberation.

(3) If the offence does fall within one of the three categories, then he must decide whether an arrest should be made on the basis of the public interest. If an arrest should not be made he must issue the accused with an appearance notice or have him served with a summons.

The Criminal Code provides in two specific sections additional police powers of arrest without a warrant. Section 31(1) reads:

> **31.(1) Every peace officer who witnesses a breach of the peace and every one who lawfully assists him is justified in arresting any person whom he finds committing the breach of the peace or who, on reasonable and probable grounds, he believes is about to join in or renew the breach of the peace.**

Breach of the peace is not defined in the Code. Generally, situations that may amount to a breach of peace involve threats of violence, such as when a group of people are loitering and a fight threatens to break out among them.

The second offence which specifically includes the power to arrest without a warrant is concerned with the keeping of gaming-houses. Section 181(2) allows a police officer to take into custody any person whom he finds in a gaming-house.

The situations that have been described in the preceding pages are the *only situations* in which a police officer has the power to make an arrest without a warrant. For all other arrest situations he must first obtain a warrant.

B. APPEARANCE NOTICE AND SUMMONS If a police officer decides not to make an arrest, he may issue an appearance notice pursuant to s.453. Such a notice must contain:

a) the name of the accused;
b) the substance of the charge;
c) the time and place when the accused is to attend court in order to answer the charge.

If the police officer does not issue an appearance notice, he may appear before a justice of the peace or judge and request that a summons be issued in the name of the accused. Section 455 governs the issuance of a summons. The summons contains essentially the same information as an appearance notice. A summons will normally be served personally on the accused.

It should be noted that police officers are not the only persons who may go before a justice of the peace with information. Anyone who has reasonable grounds to believe that another person has committed an indictable offence may swear out his information to a justice. The justice of the peace then has the power to issue a warrant or a summons, which the police will serve on the accused.

C. ARREST WITH WARRANT A justice of the peace or judge may issue a warrant pursuant to s.455 for the arrest of a person he reasonably suspects has committed a criminal offence. The justice or judge must also believe that an arrest is in the public interest before he issues the warrant. The procedure followed is for the person seeking the warrant to go before the justice and "make out a case" against the accused. In other words he will provide information for the justice such that the justice can determine whether or not there are reasonable grounds for believing a warrant is necessary.

An arrest warrant may also be issued if the accused disobeyed an appearance notice or a summons.

A police officer who executes a warrant has a duty to have the warrant with him and to produce it for the inspection of the accused if it is asked for.

3. Arrest by Any Person

As mentioned in the general remarks at the beginning of this chapter, the Criminal Code provides that in certain situations an ordinary citizen is empowered to make an arrest. Section 449 spells out three such situations:

> **449.(1) Any one may arrest without a warrant:**
> **(a) a person whom he finds committing an indictable offence, or**
> **(b) a person who, on reasonable and probable grounds, he believes**
>   **(i)   has committed a criminal offence, and**
>   **(ii) is escaping from and freshly pursued by persons who have lawful authority to arrest that person.**
> **(2) Any one who is**
> **(a) the owner or a person in lawful possession of property, or**
> **(b) a person authorized by the owner or by a person in lawful possession of property,**
> **may arrest without a warrant a person whom he finds committing a criminal offence on or in relation to that property.**

The first situation in which a power of arrest is granted by s.449 occurs when the arresting person *finds* the accused in the *act of committing an indictable offence.* If an offence is one which can be prosecuted as either an indictable offence or an offence punishable on summary conviction, for the purposes of s.449 it will be treated as an indictable offence. Thus, if a citizen arrested an accused he found carrying a concealed weapon (s.85), an offence which can be either indictable or summary, the arrest would be lawfully within s.449.

A person may "find" another committing an indictable offence without actually seeing the act committed. The person, however, must see some acts, before or after the commission of the offence, that are *so closely connected with the commission of the offence,* they can be said to be evidence of the offence itself. In *Frey v. Fedoruk,* [6] the arresting person, F, did not see R, the person he arrested, commit the offence. But his mother did. She screamed and within a fraction of a second, F saw R in the act of leaving F's property. F shouted and R immediately started to run. F gave chase and captured R. The judge decided that F had found R committing an offence. He stated: "I am of the opinion that in the circumstances when F apprehended R after he had seen him leave his property and ran when shouted at there was evidence which pointed so strongly to R having been the man at the mother's window that F can be said . . . .on the facts alone to have found R committing the offence . . . ."

The second situation described in s.449 occurs when a person believes on reasonable and probable grounds that the accused has *committed a criminal offence* and is *escaping* from and being *freshly pursued* by persons having *lawful authority* to arrest him. It should be remembered that "criminal offence" includes summary conviction offences as well as those that are indictable. It does not include provincial offences.

To be "freshly pursued" means that the accused must be followed in a manner that is *continuous* and conducted with *reasonable effort,* such that it can be said that the pursuit and capture of the accused, together with the actual commission of the crime, form a single transaction.

Consider an example. A robs a store. He is chased from the store by three customers plus the owner. They follow him for several blocks. A finally "loses" them by hiding in an alley. The pursuers search the area for a few minutes but can't find A. At this point A is still being "freshly pursued". After several more minutes of fruitless searching they decide to go to the police station, and then afterwards, to return to continue the hunt. At this point A is no longer being freshly pursued. The search is no longer continuous. However if only the owner went to see the police and the others maintained the search the pursuit would still be fresh.

A person who has "lawful authority" would include, of course, a police officer. It also would include any person who is granted the power to make an arrest by the Criminal Code. Thus, if, as described above in s.449, a citizen finds an accused committing the offence of robbery (an indictable offence) he is a person who has a lawful authority to arrest the accused.

The third situation in which anyone may make an arrest occurs when the owner of property, or a person such as a tenant lawfully in possession of property, *finds* an accused *committing a criminal offence on or in relation to that property.* Thus if A was renting a house he could arrest B if he saw B deliberately break a window in the house.

Section 30 provides an additional power of arrest to the private citizen. Anyone who sees a breach of the peace is justified in interfering to prevent the continuance or renewal of the breach and may detain any person involved in or about to join in the breach. Thus, if a person is in a bar and a brawl starts, he may grab a person who wants to join in, or who has already joined in, and hold him back until the police arrive.

There is one other power of arrest available to a private citizen that is not granted by the Criminal Code. If a police officer requests a citizen to assist him in making an arrest, the common law grants a power of arrest to the citizen.

4. Arrest by Persons in Charge of a Vehicle, Vessel or Aircraft

The Criminal Code grants additional powers of arrest to certain specified persons. Section 191 allows anyone who is in charge of any kind of vehicle, vessel or aircraft used for public transportation to arrest, without warrant, a person who he has good reason to believe has committed or attempted to commit or is attempting to commit an act of gambling. A person in charge of one of these means of public transportation may delegate his power of arrest to his subordinates.

5. Duties After Arrest

The Criminal Code imposes a duty on a private citizen who has made an arrest to deliver, as soon as is reasonably possible, the accused into the hands of a police officer.

A police officer who has made an arrest also has certain obligations imposed on him by the Code.

If the offence for which he has arrested the accused is one of the following:
a) an offence listed within s.483;
b) an offence which can be treated as an indictable offence or as a summary conviction offence; or
c) a summary conviction offence,
he must release the accused as soon as is practicable after his arrest. He may compel the accused's appearance in court by way of an appearance notice or by way of summons. Thus, where a police officer has *already arrested* an accused in order to confirm the accused's identity, once his identity is confirmed he must release him. The police officer would then issue the accused an appearance notice, or arrange for a summons to be delivered to him. The only circumstance in which he may continue to keep the accused in custody is if it is in the public interest.

If the police officer does not issue an appearance notice or a summons but keeps the accused in custody, then he *must*, whatever offence the accused is charged with, take the accused before a justice of the peace or judge without unreasonable delay. The justice or judge will then determine whether the accused shall be kept in custody, or, whether he shall be released upon a *promise to appear* at a court date to be set by him, or upon any other conditions of release which might be set.

If an accused has been released by the arresting officer and given an appearance notice, the officer must still go before a justice of the peace. He must give him all of the information concerning the offence the accused has been alleged to have committed. The justice is then empowered to either confirm the appearance notice or cancel it.

6. Civil and Criminal Responsibility of Arresting Person

Section 28 of the Criminal Code states that where a person who is authorized to execute an arrest warrant believes, in good faith and on reasonable and probable grounds, that the person arrested is the person named in the warrant, he is protected from criminal prosecution.

If the arrest is made without a warrant by either a police officer or a private citizen, the arresting individual must have an honest belief based on reasonable and probable grounds that the accused is guilty of the offence for which he is arrested. If, in fact, the accused can prove that the arresting person's belief was not based on reasonable and probable grounds then he may sue for damages for *false imprisonment*.

If the arrest of the accused was accompanied by more force than was necessary to make the arrest, the arresting person may be sued for damages based on an assault. In addition, the arresting person can be prosecuted in a criminal court for the offence of assault or one of the more serious criminal offences involving bodily harm.

7. Other Arrest Powers

In closing the section on arrest powers, it should be realized that certain provincial statutes, for example, those statutes that deal with highway traffic and liquor control offences, also confer on police officers wide powers of arrest with or without warrant. This chapter has only dealt with the powers of arrest that are granted by the Criminal Code.

B. POWERS OF SEARCH

1. General

As a general rule, it can be stated that the police cannot search a place without first going through the process of getting a search warrant approved. There are, however, powers of search granted to the police that allow them to conduct a search without seeking a warrant. Some of these powers are authorized by the Criminal Code and others are authorized by such federal acts as the Narcotic Control Act, the Food and Drugs Act and the Customs Act. In addition, there are search powers granted to police in certain provincial acts. Search powers contained within provincial Acts will not be discussed.

2. With a Warrant

A. THE CRIMINAL CODE Section 443 authorizes a justice of the peace or judge to issue a search warrant. Section 443, ss.(1) reads:

> **443.(1) A justice who is satisfied by information upon oath...**
> **that there is reasonable ground to believe that there is in a build-**
> **ing, receptacle or place**
> > **(a) anything upon or in respect of which any offence against**
> > **this Act has been or is suspected to have been committed,**
> > **(b) anything that there is reasonable ground to believe will**
> > **afford evidence with respect to the commission of an of-**
> > **fence against this Act, or**
> > **(c) anything that there is reasonable ground to believe is in-**
> > **tended to be used for the purpose of committing any of-**
> > **fence against the person for which a person may be ar-**
> > **rested without warrant,**
>
> **may at any time issue a warrant... authorizing... a peace**
> **officer to search the building, receptacle or place for any such**
> **thing, and to seize and carry it before the justice...**

It should be noted before proceeding with a discussion of s.443 that the courts have consistently held that a search warrant should *not* be lightly granted. A search warrant cannot authorize what in reality would amount to a "fishing expedition" for evidence. When the police request that a search warrant be issued they must convince the justice that there are reasonable grounds for him to believe that the conditions set forth in s.443 are satisfied.

A justice may issue a warrant in any of the three situations contemplated by s.443:

(1) If there is in a *building, place,* or *receptacle, anything relating to an offence* that has been, or is suspected to have been committed. The offence must be an offence that is described in the Criminal Code. Thus, if the offence is a provincial statute offence a search warrant cannot be issued under s.443.

(2) Anything that it is *reasonably* believed will afford *evidence of a crime* that is described in the Code.

(3) Anything that is reasonably believed to be *intended for use* in the *commission* of an offence against the person and for which an accused can be arrested without a warrant.

Offences for which an accused may be arrested without a warrant were discussed in the preceding section, on powers of arrest. Offences against the person are found in Part VI of the Code. These include offences such as murder (s.212), causing bodily harm with intent (s.228), and the offence of common assault (s.245).

A "building, place or receptacle" is given a very wide meaning. It includes, for example, boats, cars, backyards, safety deposit boxes in banks, furniture, household plumbing, dwelling-homes, business offices and summer cottages.

In a recent Quebec case,[7] the police sought a warrant to search in the body of the accused (he was still very much alive) for a bullet which was alleged to have been fired from police revolvers. To conduct the search a major operation would have been necessary because the bullet was deeply imbedded in the accused's shoulder. The Quebec court held that for the purposes of s.443, the body is not a "place or receptacle."

The search warrant must specify the "thing" or "things" being sought with some precision. In an unreported case, the police believed they would find obscene books on the accused's property. The search warrant included the power to search for "company records, including invoices". Because the warrant did not add the following qualification, "company records including invoices *pertaining to the distribution of obscene books*" the search warrant was quashed. It was considered to be too vague in its description of the evidence sought.

The place of search must be specified in the warrant. As well, the owner or occupier of the property must be identified, along with the name of the accused. In addition, the warrant must describe the offence for which the evidence is being sought.

A s.443 search warrant *cannot* be issued to search the person. In this context "search the person" means frisking or examining an accused. The power to search a person will be discussed shortly.

There are two more points to be noted with respect to a s.443 search warrant. According to s.445, with a warrant issued under s.443, police searchers may seize, in addition to the things mentioned in the warrant, anything that on reasonable grounds they believe has been obtained or used in the commission of an offence; also a s.443 warrant must be executed by day unless it is specifically authorized to be used at night.

There are other sections in the Criminal Code that grant the right of search to the police if certain specific offences are involved.

Section 181 allows a police officer to apply for a search warrant if he suspects, on reasonable grounds, that a gaming-house (s.186), bookmaking (s.186 and 187), a lottery (s.189 and 190) or a common bawdy-house (s.193) exists in any premises.

Section 182 authorizes the issue of a search warrant to look for a woman enticed to or concealed in a bawdy-house.

The following is an actual warrant that was issued by a justice:

> *To the Peace Officers in the said County or District of York:*
> *Whereas it appears on the oath of Detective-Sergeant S. of the Ontario Provincial Police in the County of York that there are reasonable grounds for believing that oil paintings, art books, artists' supplies, paints and restoration materials, records, correspondence and documents of all descriptions pertaining to these things will afford evidence to the police that the public in the Province of Ontario have been defrauded by the sale of fake oil paintings attributed to well*

known Canadian artists, are in the premises of Mr. W. at 5 Jean Street, Toronto, Ontario. This warrant is, therefore, to authorize and require you between the hours of 9:00 a.m. and 12:00 midnight to enter into the said premises and to search for the said things and to bring them before me or another justice.
Dated this 7th day of November, A.D. 1963, at Toronto, Ontario.

B. THE NARCOTIC CONTROL ACT It should be remembered that search warrants can be issued under other federal Acts such as The Customs Act and The Food and Drugs Act. As the powers of search under these other Acts are not any wider than they are under the Narcotic Control Act (N.C.A.), and because the search powers granted by the N.C.A. are the ones more frequently used, the other Acts will not be discussed.

The only place for which a search warrant is needed under the N.C.A. is if the place to be searched for narcotics is a dwelling-place. *Any other place may be searched without the aid of a warrant.*

Section 10(2) of the Act reads,

10.(2) A justice who is satisfied by information . . . . that there are reasonable grounds for believing that there is a narcotic, by means of or in respect of which an offence under this Act has been committed, in any dwelling-house may issue a warrant . . . authorizing a peace officer named therein at any time to enter the dwelling-house and search for narcotics.

Although it is not specifically mentioned, a search warrant under ss.(2) also allows the police to search *any person* that is *found in the dwelling-house* at the time of the search.

The police officer may only be granted a warrant if he reasonably believes there are narcotics to be found in the house. A warrant to search for anything other than narcotics cannot be issued under the Narcotic Control Act. If the thing sought is other than a narcotic, or a thing other than something that may be evidence of the possession of, or the trafficking of, a narcotic, the police would have to seek a warrant under s.443 of the Criminal Code.

A narcotic is defined as any substance, or anything that contains any substance, which is listed in the Act. The list is very long and includes the opium poppy and any drug that can be manufactured from it, including: opium itself, morphine, codeine, thebaine, and heroin. Also included are cocaine, methadone, and, as of the writing of this book, marihuana (see Appendix).

Unlike a warrant under s.443, a warrant under the N.C.A. can be used at any time without the need for a special endorsement to that effect. Also, the actual powers of search are extremely wide. Section 10(4) provides:

10.(4) For the purpose of exercising his authority under this section, a peace officer may, with such assistance as he deems

necessary, break open any door, window, lock, fastener, floor, wall, ceiling, compartment, plumbing fixture, box, container or any other thing.

3. Without a Warrant

A. THE CRIMINAL CODE The Code allows the police, in certain limited circumstances, to conduct a search without a search warrant. This power is only granted for specific offences. If the offence the police are investigating is not one which authorizes a search without a warrant then they must first seek a warrant.

A police officer under s.103 who has reasonable grounds to believe that an offence has been, or is being, committed with respect to any provisions in the Code that deal with prohibited or restricted weapons, (defined in s.82), may search, without a warrant, *a person* or a vehicle or any premises *other than a dwelling house*. The power to seize incriminating items, or those items suspected of being incriminating, is the same as if the search had been authorized by a warrant under s.443.

Section 299 allows a police officer who has reasonable grounds to suspect that registered timber is being kept without the consent of the owner to enter the place where the timber is, without a search warrant.

Section 405 authorizes police to enter any vehicle or boat without a search warrant to determine if any offences with respect to the transportation of cattle are being committed (s.404).

B. INCIDENT TO A LAWFUL ARREST Apart from the provisions in the Criminal Code (section 103) and Narcotic Control Act (and other federal Acts such as the Customs Act and the Food and Drugs Act), *the right to search the person exists only as an incident to arrest.* After the police have arrested an accused they are entitled to conduct a search of his person.

When a person has been arrested, either with or without a warrant, the right of search extends not only to the person of the accused, but also to the premises under his control, including a dwelling house, and to other things under the control of the accused including his car.

The power to search the person incident to a lawful arrest is not conferred by the Criminal Code. It comes from the Common Law, which is preserved in such matters by s.7 of the Code.

The power to search the person as an incident to arrest is very wide. Two cases, *R. v. Brezack,* [8] and *Reynen v. Antonenko et. al.,* [9] illustrate this fact.

In the *Brezack* case Constable M of the Royal Canadian Mounted Police, on special duty on the narcotic squad at Hamilton, and another constable established themselves in a position where they could keep a restaurant under observation. While so stationed, they saw the accused come around a street corner and proceed in the direction of the restaurant. At the same time, they observed certain persons known to them to be drug addicts also going into the restaurant. The accused had a prior conviction for having possession of narcotics, and from information the constables had, they believed the accused had drugs hidden on his person. Their information led them to believe they would find the narcotics in capsules hidden in the accused's mouth.

Acting on this information, the constables, as the accused approached the restaurant, left their place of hiding and, with two other constables (making a total of four officers all together), rushed him. One of them seized the accused by the arms, and Constable M caught him by the throat, to prevent him from swallowing anything that he might have in his mouth. The three of them fell to the ground and a considerable struggle ensued. Constable M persistently tried to insert his finger in the accused's mouth, to recover the drugs that he thought were hidden there, and each time he tried, the accused bit his finger. A good deal of force was applied by the constables, and Constable M at last succeeded in getting his fingers into the accused's mouth. He found that the accused did not have any drugs hidden in his mouth. The accused was allowed to stand and was taken away from the crowd that had gathered. The constables then searched his clothing but did not find any narcotics on him.

The constables then took the accused to the car which he had left parked around the corner. Upon searching the car, the police found five capsules containing narcotics. The accused started a court action claiming Constable M had illegally searched him.

The court concluded that the constable had reasonable and probable grounds upon which the accused could be arrested without a warrant. The court also decided that Constable M's efforts to search for the drug in the accused's mouth were reasonable in the circumstances. The Court made this point with respect to persons suspected of being involved in drug trafficking:

> Constables have a task of great difficulty in their efforts to check the illegal trafficking in drugs. Those who carry on the trafficking are cunning, crafty, and unscrupulous almost beyond belief. While, therefore, it is important that constables should be instructed that there are limits upon their right of search of the person, they are not to be encumbered by technicalities in handling the situations with which they often have to deal in narcotics cases, which permit them little time for deliberation.

In the *Reyen* case, the accused claimed that a search to which he had been subjected, as an incident to his arrest, was done without legal justification. He charged the searching officers with assault.

Constable G received information leading him to believe that the accused would be travelling from Edmonton to Vancouver to buy drugs, leaving and returning on the same day, and that the accused would be carrying the drugs on his person hidden in his rectum.

The accused was arrested at the airport and taken to the R.C.M.P. quarters in the air terminal where he was placed in a separate room under guard. He was asked to disrobe which he did. The police proceeded to search his clothing but found no drugs.

The accused was asked to bend over. His rectum was visually examined and it was noticed that the hair around his anal area appeared to have been "greased." The accused was asked to go to the bathroom and remove the drugs or otherwise he would be taken to the hospital where they would be removed. His reply was, "let's go to the hospital" or words to that effect.

The accused was taken to a hospital in Edmonton where Dr. A. was on duty as resident physician. Detective D and Constable H informed Dr. A that the accused was under arrest and that they had reasonable grounds to believe that he was carrying drugs internally and requested that he be examined.

The accused was then taken to an examining room. A nurse entered with a surgical or hospital gown, telling the accused to remove his clothes and put on the gown. This he did. Dr. A at this time or slightly earlier told the accused that he would have to do a rectal examination which would be uncomfortable. The accused did not respond to this information.

The doctor requested the accused to position himself on the examining table. The accused adopted the position requested. The doctor then performed a rectal examination by finger. He followed this by a further examination using a "sigmoidoscope," an instrument in the form of a hollow tube which was inserted in the anal canal to a depth of six inches. Examination showed two red rubber condoms in the rectum which were removed by the doctor. The doctor testified that such an examination as that performed requires the co-operation of the patient and that he would never try such an examination without the patient's full co-operation. The examination took less than five minutes' time.

The condoms removed from the plaintiff contained 25 capsules each which were found on later tests to contain heroin.

The judge, after concluding the arrest was lawful, stated that the police had every right, and, in fact, had the duty, to conduct the search as they did with the accused. He went on to add that the police are clearly authorized to use as much force as is reasonably proper and necessary to carry out their duties as long as no unnecessary violence is involved.

C. THE NARCOTIC CONTROL ACT

(i) without warrant

Section 10(1) of the Narcotic Control Act allows a police officer to, at any time:

> **10.(1)(a) without a warrant enter and search any place other than a dwelling-house, and under the authority of a writ of assistance or a warrant issued under this section, enter and search any dwelling-house in which he reasonably believes there is a narcotic by means or in respect of which an offence under this Act has been committed;**
> **(b) search any person found in such place.**

Writs of assistance are described in the next subsection.

Without a warrant the only place the police cannot enter, in a search for drugs, is a dwelling-house. As was mentioned previously, when s.10(2) of the Narcotic Control Act was discussed, a warrant allowing the search of a dwelling-house is available to a requesting officer.

The major offences described in the Act include possession of a narcotic (s.3), trafficking in a narcotic (s.4), importing and exporting a narcotic (s.5), and cultivation of opium poppy or marihuana (s.6), (see Appendix).

The police have the same power to search when they do so without a warrant as if, in fact, they had a search warrant.

(ii) with writ of assistance

A writ of assistance is a special document which gives extensive powers of search. The writ may only be granted under the power of four federal statutes: The Food and Drugs Act, the Excise Act, the Customs Act, and the Narcotic Control Act. Only the N.C.A. will be discussed.

The writ can only be issued by a federal court. In other words a magistrate, a provincial court judge (criminal division) and a justice of the peace cannot issue a writ of assistance.

The writ is issued, as a general rule, to a member of the R.C.M.P.. Only the officer to whom the writ is issued may use it, although this officer may take others with him to assist in search raids. The writ continues to operate for the entire career of the officer to whom it is issued, unless it is specifically cancelled. Therefore, if a member of the R.C.M.P. were issued the writ in 1954, and he is still in the "force" today, the writ remains valid.

A writ of assistance entitles the holder, without any further formality, to enter any place, including a dwelling house, at any time if he suspects narcotics are hidden in that place. He may also search any person he finds within the place.

There are not a great number of writs of assistance in circulation. In 1974, there were just over 200 of them in circulation. That is to say, approximately 200 R.C.M.P. officers were carrying writs of assistance.

4. Summary

The following briefly highlights the various powers of search that have been discussed:

1) *Criminal Code*
   a) *with a warrant:* may search any building, receptacle or place including a dwelling-house.
   b) *without a warrant:* cannot search a dwelling place, and cannot search a person (unless accused is suspected of possessing a prohibited or restricted weapon).
2) *Incident to a Lawful Arrest*
   a) may search any place, including a dwelling-house, under the accused's control, and may search the person.

3) *Narcotic Control Act (FOR DRUG OFFENCES ONLY)*
   a) *with a warrant:* may search any place, including a dwelling-house, and any person found within the place.
   b) *without a warrant:* may search any place except a dwelling-house, and may search any person found within the place.
   c) *with a writ of assistance:* may search any place, including a dwelling-house, and any person found in the place.

Any reasonable amount of force may be used in making the search. However, if an excess of force is used by the searching officers they will be liable in both a civil action for damages and a criminal action for assault.

C. WIRETAPPING AND ELECTRONIC SURVEILLANCE

Anyone who, by means of an electromagnetic, acoustic, mechanical or other device, deliberately intercepts a private communication is guilty of an indictable offence.

Anyone who owns, sells or buys such a device, or a part of such a device, knowing that it is primarily useful for secret interception of a private communication, is also guilty of an indictable offence.

All of these offences are contained in s.178.11.

However, a police officer may obtain permission to "bug" private communications if it is in the "best interests of justice" to do so (s.178). What is in the best interest of justice is decided by the following criteria:
(a) other investigative procedures have failed;
(b) other investigative procedures are unlikely to succeed; or
(c) the urgency of the matter is such that wiretapping is the only practical procedure.

An authorization for bugging is good for sixty days only. It must be renewed after that time.

D. RIGHTS OF THE ACCUSED AFTER ARREST

Police officers have no power to compel private citizens, whether or not they are suspects in a crime, to answer their questions. Obviously, they may ask questions but if the person does not wish to answer, *he may lawfully refuse to do so.* However, it should be remembered that under provincial highway traffic legislation, police are empowered to stop motor vehicles and they can lawfully demand to see a driver's licence, vehicle registration, and vehicle permit. This is all that the driver need show the police officer. He is under no obligation to provide any other information.

If an individual is placed under arrest by a police officer, he *must accompany him,* but once again, he *may remain silent* if he so wishes. The police may not use force in an attempt to get an accused to talk.

An accused person under arrest has the right to call and speak with a lawyer. This right would appear to be guaranteed by the Canadian Bill of Rights.

An accused person under arrest is required to have his photograph and finger prints taken. This requirement is dictated by the Identification of Criminals Act. However, if an accused is under arrest for a summary conviction offence, the police have no right to photograph or fingerprint him. An accused, again for a non-summary offence, may be required to appear in an identification line-up. Force may be used if an accused refuses to be either photographed or fingerprinted, or refuses to appear in a line-up.

Within 24 hours after his arrest, or as soon as possible thereafter, the accused *must be brought* before a justice of the peace or judge. At this appearance the prosecutor *must show cause* why the detention of the accused in custody is justified. The prosecutor may justify keeping the accused in custody by establishing that he is unlikely to appear in court for his hearing if he is released. Or the prosecutor may establish that the accused's detention in custody is necessary in the public interest, as for the protection of the safety of the public. If the prosecutor fails to establish one of these needs for keeping the accused in jail, the justice of the peace, or judge, must release him. The accused may be released, with or without bail, until the date of his hearing.

QUESTIONS

Arrest

1. List the situations or offences for which only a police officer has the power to arrest.
2. Constable Smith is patrolling town in his patrol car. A despatch comes over the radio informing him to be on the lookout for a Kawasaki motorcycle, colour red and silver, that has been reported stolen. Approximately ten minutes after the radio message, Smith pulls up behind a motorcycle. It is a Kawasaki and the colour matches that of the motorcycle reported stolen. He signals the rider to pull over. The driver pulls over to the curb immediately. Smith asks the driver who the owner of the bike is. The driver says that it belongs to him. Smith asks for a driving licence, the bike ownership and insurance papers. The driver gives him the operating licence but says he hasn't got the insurance or owner's permit with him. He says he must have forgotten them at home and volunteers to fetch them. Smith says that won't be necessary and puts the driver under arrest for the theft of a motorcycle. The driver protests that he hasn't done anything wrong and that he owns the bike. In the end, however, he gets into Smith's patrol car and is driven down to the police station.
   (i) What section did Smith rely on as authority to arrest the motorcycle driver?
   (ii) What specific situation in that section did he use or rely on?
   (iii) Given your understanding of the section in question, do you think Smith made the right decision when he arrested the driver? Explain your answer.
3. (i) If a police officer finds a person committing an offence under s.483, what must he first consider before he can lawfully make an arrest?

(ii) What might he do, if he doesn't arrest the person, to compel the person's appearance in court?

4. Sam is walking down the street. Behind him he hears a lady shriek "My purse! He's stolen my purse!" Sam turns around. He sees the lady who has had her purse stolen. She is standing still, staring at her empty hands. He can also see the head and shoulders of a man who appears to be running through the crowd on the sidewalk. A lot of people are staring at him but nobody is chasing him.

(i) Can Sam chase the man who is running and make an arrest?

(ii) If he did make an arrest, what section of the Code would he be relying on?

(iii) Given your understanding of the section in question, do you think Sam can lawfully make an arrest?

(iv) Suppose that Sam catches up with the man who is running, warns him to stop and when he doesn't, tackles the man and wrestles him to the ground. Would Sam be justified in using force in this manner?

5. If a person is placed under arrest by a police officer, what information must he give the officer?

Search

1. Constable Dust has been issued a search warrant in accordance with s.443 of the Criminal Code, empowering him to search Gerry's house. When he arrives at the house, he insists that the warrant also entitles him to search Gerry. Is he right?

2. Martin has been arrested by the police. They believe he is a drug pusher. When he was arrested Martin was observed to swallow something. The police took Martin to the hospital and asked the intern on duty to pump Martin's stomach.

(i) Can the police have Martin's stomach pumped to see if he did swallow any drugs?

3. Constable Armstrong arrests Blaine in a department store for theft. He asks Blaine the whereabouts of his car and is informed the car is outside in the parking lot. Constable Armstrong proceeds to the parking lot. He finds Tom and John sitting in the car. He orders them out and then searches them both. Was he legally entitled to search Tom and John?

4. Constable Orton of the R.C.M.P. is the holder of a Writ of Assistance. At 2 a.m. one morning, he knocks on the door of Sylvia's home. She opens the door and Constable Orton with five other police officers (not members of the R.C.M.P.) rush into the house and begin to search it. In the process they dismantle her stereo speakers. They do not find any drugs and, after an hour of searching, they leave.

(i) Could Constable Orton search without a warrant?

(ii) If he could, what was his authority to do so?

(iii) Was he allowed to take apart Sylvia's stereo speakers?

(iv) Was he allowed to search her house at night without getting special permission?

(v) If he had found other people in Sylvia's house could he have searched them?

(vi) Were the non-R.C.M.P. police officers allowed to take part in the search?

5. In what situations may a police officer search *a person* for something *other* than drugs:

(i) with a search warrant?

(ii) without a search warrant?

[1] (1970), 70 D.L.R. (2d) 718 (B.C.S.C.)
[2] (1959) 19 D.L.R. (2d) 1 (S.C.C.)
[3] (1957), 118 C.C.C. 24 (Ont.C.A.)
[4] (1975), 20 C.C.C. (2d) 65 (Fed.Ct.)
[5] (1975), 56 D.L.R. (3d) 113 (B.C.S.C.)
[6] (1950), 10 C.R. 26 (S.C.C.)
[7] *Laporte v. Laganiere* (1972), B.C.C.C. (2d) 343, 18 C.R.N.S. 357 (Que.Q.B.)
[8] (1949), 93 C.C.C. 97; 9 C.R. 73 (Ont.C.A.)
[9] (1975), 20 C.C.C. (2d) 342 (Alta.S.C.)

PART B

CRIMINAL
CODE
OFFENCES

Chapter Six

Offences Against
The Administration of
Justice and
Public Order

A. BRIBERY

In general, bribery is the accepting or offering of an undue reward or "payoff" in order to influence a public official's behaviour in office. There are several Code sections involving bribery. These sections mention various types of *rewards, public officials* and *behaviours.*

1. An Example: Section 108

An example of a Code section involving bribery is s.108:

> 108.(1) Every one who
> (a) being the holder of a judicial office, or being a member of the Parliament of Canada or of a legislature, corruptly
>   (i)   accepts or obtains,
>   (ii) agrees to accept, or
>   (iii) attempts to obtain,
>   any money, valuable consideration, office, place or employment for himself or another person in respect of anything done or omitted or to be done or omitted by him in his official capacity, or
> (b) gives or offers corruptly to a person who holds a judicial office, or is a member of the Parliament of Canada or of a legislature, any money, valuable consideration, office, place

or employment in respect of anything done or omitted or to be done or omitted by him in his official capacity for himself or another person,
is guilty of an indictable offence....

In this bribery offence, it is clear that the public official could be a judge, a member of Parliament or a member of a provincial legislature. The reward could be money, a job, or practically anything of value. The behaviour involved could be any act or omission by the official in carrying out his public duties.

Bribery involves two parties: the public official and any other person. Offences may be committed by one or both of them. Paragraph (a) refers to three separate offences which may be committed by the public official: (i) actually accepting a bribe; (ii) simply agreeing to accept a bribe; and (iii) soliciting or trying to obtain a bribe. Paragraph (b) refers to two offences which may be committed by the other person: (i) actually giving a bribe to the official and (ii) simply offering a bribe to the official.

If a person offers a bribe to an official, it is no defence that the official refused it. In other words, the offence is complete when the offer is made.

It is also necessary that the offering, giving or accepting, be done "corruptly." The word "corruptly" means with the intention to accomplish the purpose forbidden by the Code.[1] So, under s.108, it must be shown that the offering, accepting, etc. was done with the intention of having the official do or omit to do some act in his official capacity.

In *R. v. Bruneau*,[2] the accused was charged with agreeing to accept $10,000 for the use of his influence in his official capacity as a member of Parliament. Bruneau had agreed to accept the money from B, one of his constituents, to use his influence to have the Federal Government buy B's property as the site for a post office. The usual practice, which was followed in this case, was that after a number of possible sites were examined by Federal officials, the local member of Parliament was consulted for his recommendation. B's property was purchased and Bruneau accepted $10,000 from B. Bruneau's lawyer argued that Bruneau had not been acting "in his official capacity" because that phrase refers to the power of a member of Parliament to take part in legislation and matters directly related to it in the House of Commons. The court rejected this argument and found Bruneau guilty. The court felt that since the accused had been consulted because of his membership in Parliament, any action taken by him would be "in his official capacity."

2. Other Bribery Offences

Section 109 prohibits the bribery of other public officials including peace officers, justices of the peace, police commissioners and, generally, persons employed in the administration of criminal law. The offences are basically the same as in s.108 except that the bribe must be offered with the intent

109.(a)(iv)   to interfere with the administration of justice,
     (v)   to procure or facilitate the commission of an offence, or
    (vi)   to protect from detection or punishment a person who has committed or who intends to commit an offence.

A person can not be convicted under s.109 of offering a bribe to a peace officer with intent to interfere with the administration of justice unless he knew that the person to whom the offer was made was a police officer.[3]

The meaning of "administration of justice" was discussed in *R. v. Kalick*.[4] In that case, the accused gave a bribe of $1,000 to a police officer in order to persuade him not to charge him with an offence which he had committed. Kalick argued that there could be no intent to interfere with the administration of justice until after some proceeding, such as the formal charging of the accused, had taken place. The Supreme Court of Canada decided that "administration of justice" must be given a wider meaning which "includes the taking of necessary steps to have a person who has committed an offence brought before the proper tribunal and punished for his offence. It is a very wide term covering the detection, prosecution and punishment of offenders." Because of this broad definition, Kalick was convicted.

Section 110 makes it an offence to bribe government officials. "Official" is broadly defined in s.107 as "a person who (a) holds an office or (b) is appointed to discharge a public duty."

Section 112 makes it an offence to bribe a "municipal official" which refers to a member of a municipal council or a person who holds an office under a municipal government. The term includes persons such as the chief building inspector for a city.[5]

B. OBSTRUCTING A PEACE OFFICER

118.   Every one who
(a)   resists or wilfully obstructs a public officer or peace officer in the execution of his duty or any person lawfully acting in aid of such an officer,
(b)   omits, without reasonable excuse, to assist a public officer or peace officer in the execution of his duty in arresting a person or in preserving the peace, after having reasonable notice that he is required to do so, or
(c)   resists or wilfully obstructs any person in the lawful execution of a process against lands or goods or in making a lawful distress or seizure,
is guilty of
(d)   an indictable offence . . ., or
(e)   an offence punishable on summary conviction.

Subsection (b) is fairly straightforward. It makes it an offence to fail to help a peace officer or public officer in arresting a person or in keeping the peace, unless there is a reasonable excuse for not helping. The terms ''peace officer'' and ''public officer'' are discussed below.

Subsection (c) prohibits interfering with a person who has the legal authority to seize or hold land or goods. For example, a sheriff's bailiff may be under a court order to take possession of a house. If the person living in the house refuses to allow the bailiff to take possession, then he would be violating subsection (c).

Subsection (a) requires more elaboration and it will be discussed in detail. The essential elements of a charge under s.118(a) are that (1) the accused obstructed; (2) the obstruction was wilful; (3) the person obstructed was a public officer or peace officer; and (4) the officer was in the execution of his duty.

1. Obstruction

The ordinary meaning of the term ''obstruct'' is to hinder, block or stop up.[6]

The obstruction may involve physical force such as assaulting a police officer. For example, in *Bain v. R.,*[7] the accused resisted being lawfully arrested by kicking and breaking the leg of one of the officers.

The obstruction may occur without the use of physical force. In *R. v. Matheson,*[8] the accused refused to permit officers to make a lawful search of his house. The accused used no physical force or threats, did not shut a door in the officers' faces or block an entrance with his body. He simply said that he did not want the officers in his house and that he refused to allow them to search. The court held that the accused had obstructed the officers in the execution of their duty. The court said that physical acts of obstruction are not necessary. All that is necessary is for the accused to do an act which leads the officer to think that there would be violence if he proceeded. The accused in this case had obstructed by preventing the officer from proceeding to search the house, unless the officer chose to do so by force.

In *R. v. D'entremont,*[9] the accused was held to be obstructing by refusing to stop his car when ordered to do so by officers in the execution of their duties under the law. It was also established that the accused knew that he was being ordered to stop by an officer.

2. Wilfully

The term ''wilfully'' as used in this section means deliberately or intentionally. It refers to a deliberate purpose to accomplish something forbidden, a determination to carry out one's own will in defiance of the law.[10]

3. Peace Officer or Public Officer

The term ''peace officer'' is defined in s.2 and was discussed in Chapter Five. In most situations it refers to a police officer.

The term ''public officer'' is also defined in s.2:

"public officer" includes
(a) an officer of customs or excise,
(b) an officer of the Canadian Forces,
(c) an officer of the Royal Canadian Mounted Police, and
(d) any officer while he is engaged in enforcing the laws of Canada relating to revenue, customs, excise, trade or navigation.

In general, "peace officer" and "public officer" refer to persons who have the duty of enforcing the law.

4. Execution of Duty

The requirement that the officer must be in the execution of his duty when he is obstructed means he must be carrying out some duty or obligation imposed on him by law. If he is not carrying out such a duty, then there is no offence under s.118.[11]

Following are some cases which involve the question of whether or not the officer who was obstructed was in the execution of his duty: In *R. v. Westlie*[12] two plain-clothed police officers were working in the skid row area of Vancouver. The accused knew that they were police officers and he starting shouting "undercover pigs, undercover fuzz, watch out for the pigs." Many people in the area were attracted by the shouting. One of the officers told the accused that he was on duty in the area and warned him to stop. The accused then began stopping people on the street pointing at the two police officers and referring to them as "undercover pigs" and "undercover fuzz." The accused was charged with wilfully obstructing a peace officer in the execution of his duty. There were three main issues in the case: (1) at the time of the incident was the police officer in the execution of his duty? (2) was there obstruction of the police officer? and (3) was the obstruction wilful? The court held that (1) the officer was in the execution of his general duty as a policeman to take all steps necessary to ensure that the public peace would be kept, to prevent and detect crime, to bring offenders to justice and to protect property from criminal damage. (2) The accused did all he could to identify the officers to the public and thus completely frustrate the officers in the execution of their duty. This amounted to obstruction. (3) There was no question that the conduct of the accused was intentional and deliberate. But if he had a lawful excuse for his conduct then he would not be guilty of the offence. However, the court felt that it was clear that the accused was trying to warn law-violators in the area that the two men were police officers and to stop breaking the law until the officers had left the area. Therefore, the accused was convicted.

In *R. v. Potvin*,[13] the accused was charged with resisting a peace officer contrary to s.118(a). The accused and a friend had gone to a park in Montreal. He had placed his kayak on a lake in the park when a police officer told him that boating was not permitted on the lake and warned him that he would be arrested if he did go boating. The accused went for a boat ride and was arrested. He resisted the arrest and two police officers had to push him into a patrol car. The Crown argued that the accused had violated a city by-law which prohibited, among other things, throwing anything in city lakes and playing unauthorized games. The Crown also argued that the arrest was lawful. The court disagreed, saying that the accused had the right to resist the arrest because he had not violated the by-law and, even if he had, it was not an offence which allows an arrest without a warrant. The police officers were acting without authority and thus were not in the execution of their duty. Therefore, the accused had a lawful excuse for resisting the arrest and he was not guilty under s.118(a).

Knowlton v. R.[14] involved the following facts. In 1971, Premier Kosygin of the U.S.S.R. was to visit Edmonton as a part of his official visit to Canada. He was going to make a short stop at the Chateau Lacombe Hotel. A few days before the visit Kosygin had been assaulted in Ottawa by a man who had grabbed the Premier and tried to drag him to the ground. To prevent another such incident, twenty-six police officers cordoned off an area in front of the entrance of the hotel. The accused wanted to get in the cordoned-off area to take pictures. A police officer told him that he could not enter the area and warned him that if he did, he would be arrested. The accused ignored the warning. He began to go into the restricted area, pushing his way through two constables. He was arrested and charged with wilfully obstructing a peace officer in the execution of his duty. The incident took place at about the time Kosygin was scheduled to arrive. The Supreme Court of Canada said that the police had interfered with Knowlton's right to move freely in a public street. Such an interference could only be justified if the police were carrying out some duty imposed on them by law. The court held that the police were acting in the execution of their general duty to preserve peace, order, and public safety. They had a duty to prevent another criminal assault on Kosygin and the accused was obstructing them in carrying out that duty.

C. PERJURY

120. Every one commits perjury who, being a witness in a judicial proceeding, with intent to mislead gives false evidence, knowing that the evidence is false.

A judicial proceeding is defined in section 107:

107. ..."judicial proceeding" means a proceeding
  (a) in or under the authority of a court of justice or before a grand jury,
  (b) before the Senate or House of Commons of Canada or a committee of the Senate or House of Commons, or before a legislative council, legislative assembly or house of assembly or a committee thereof that is authorized by law to administer an oath,
  (c) before a court, judge, justice, magistrate or coroner,
  (d) before an arbitrator or umpire, or a person or body of

**persons authorized by law to make an inquiry and take
evidence therein under oath, or**
   **(e) before a tribunal by which a legal right or legal liability
may be established,**
**whether or not the proceeding is invalid for want of jurisdiction
or for any other reason.**

In order to be convicted of perjury, it must be proved beyond a reasonable doubt
that (1) evidence given by the witness was false; (2) the witness knew when he
gave the evidence that it was false, and (3) he gave it with the intent to mislead.
These requirements were considered by the Supreme Court of Canada in *Calder v.
R.* [15] The accused was a witness in a divorce case. He made a false statement at the
divorce trial regarding the length of time a woman had been living in a trailer on his
business premises. At the perjury trial, he claimed that his evidence had been an
honest statement of what he could remember. The court held that he was not guilty
of perjury because, even though he had made a false statement, there was no proof
that he knew the evidence was false or that he intended to mislead the court. In
short, an honest error made by a witness does not amount to perjury.

In *R. v. Regnier,* [16] the Ontario Court of Appeal held that to constitute perjury, it
is not necessary that a false statement mislead the court. It is enough if the witness
knows that his statement is false and he intends to mislead.

In *R. v. Hayford,* [17] the Saskatchewan Court of Appeal held that if a witness
makes a statement which is true in one sense and false in another, the Crown must
prove that the statement was false in the sense that the witness used it. The accused
had been a witness at a preliminary hearing on a charge of assault. He stated at the
hearing that he had not agreed to sell to R certain furniture. A month before he had
said to a police officer that he had made an agreement with R to sell the furniture. It
was decided at the assault trial that the agreement was void (i.e. it had no legal
effect). At the perjury trial the court said that there was an agreement in the sense
that the accused and R had gone through the form of an agreement. But, there was
no agreement in the sense that it was not legally binding. The Crown failed to prove
in which sense the accused had stated that there was no agreement. Thus, the
accused could not be convicted of perjury.

D. OBSTRUCTING JUSTICE

1. Professional Bondsmen

**127.(1) Every one who wilfully attempts in any manner to
obstruct, pervert or defeat the course of justice in a judicial
proceeding,**
   **(a) by indemnifying or agreeing to indemnify a surety, in any
way either in whole or in part, or**
   **(b) where he is a surety, by accepting or agreeing to accept a
fee or any form of indemnity whether in whole or in part**

> from or in respect of a person who is released or is to be
> released from custody,
> is guilty of
> > (c) an indictable offence and is liable to imprisonment for two
> > years, or
> > (d) an offence punishable on summary conviction.

This subsection outlaws professional bondsmen. A acts as a surety for B by posting bond or giving money to the court to release B from custody on the understanding that B will appear for trial. The idea behind allowing A to post bond for B is that A will have a real interest in seeing that B appears for his trial. If B appears, then A gets his money back. If B does not appear, then A does not get his money back. Under s.127(1), it is an offence for A and B to attempt to defeat the course of justice by making an agreement that when released from custody, B would pay back ("indemnify") A the amount of the bond or the amount of the bond plus a fee. Under such an agreement, A would have no interest in seeing that B appeared for trial because he would get his money back regardless of whether or not B appeared. Thus, B would be released from custody, A could get his money back, B could avoid standing trial, and the course of justice would be defeated.

2. Other Ways of Obstructing Justice

> 127....
> (2) Every one who wilfully attempts in any manner other than
> a manner described in subsection (1) to obstruct, pervert or
> defeat the course of justice is guilty of an indictable offence and is
> liable to imprisonment for ten years.

The phrase "course of justice" has been given a broad meaning and is not limited to proceedings which follow the laying of a charge. In *R. v. Morin*[18] the Quebec Court of Appeal held that "course of justice" should be given the same meaning as "administration of justice," which has been interpreted by the Supreme Court of Canada as a very wide term covering the detection, prosecution and punishment of offenders.[19] In *Morin,* the accused was charged with attempting to obstruct the course of justice by offering a bribe to a peace officer. While being driven to the police station, he offered money to the officers in the hope of avoiding arrest. He was convicted of attempting to obstruct the course of justice. It would seem that Morin could have been charged either with attempting to obstruct justice or with offering a bribe to a peace officer, contrary to s.109.

If something is said or done which obstructs justice, but the person did not have the *mens rea* to obstruct justice, then no offence is committed. In *R. v. Savinkoff,*[20] the accused was charged with attempting to obstruct justice by trying to induce two men to give false evidence at their trial. The Crown failed to prove that the accused knew that the evidence was false. Without this guilty knowledge, the accused had no *mens rea* and was acquitted of the charge.

3. Bribes and Threats

The use of bribes and threats is mentioned in s.127(3) as a specific way of obstructing the course of justice in a judicial proceeding:

127.(3) Without restricting the generality of subsection (2), every one shall be deemed wilfully to attempt to obstruct, pervert or defeat the course of justice who in a judicial proceeding, existing or proposed,
(a) dissuades or attempts to dissuade a person by threats, bribes or other corrupt means from giving evidence;
(b) influences or attempts to influence by threats, bribes or other corrupt means, a person in his conduct as a juror; or
(c) accepts or obtains, agrees to accept or attempts to obtain a bribe or other corrupt consideration to abstain from giving evidence, or to do or to refrain from doing anything as a juror.

In short, it is obstruction of justice to use bribes or threats to try to corrupt witnesses and jurors. It is also obstruction of justice for a witness or juror to accept a bribe. Note that the section refers to judicial proceedings that are already in progress and those that are not yet in progress but are proposed.

Under paragraph (a), it is no defence that the accused believed that the evidence to be given by a witness was false. In *R. v. Silverman,*[21] the accused offered a bribe to a witness to persuade him not to give certain evidence at a trial. His purpose was to get the witness to tell what the accused believed to be a true version of the facts. The court found him guilty because the offence was complete when he made the offer of a bribe not to give evidence. It made no difference that the accused honestly believed that the witness was going to give an untrue version of the facts.

E. TREASON

46.(1) Every one commits high treason who, in Canada,
(a) kills or attempts to kill Her Majesty, or does her any bodily harm tending to death or destruction, maims or wounds her, or imprisons or restrains her;
(b) levies war against Canada or does any act preparatory thereto;
(c) assists an enemy at war with Canada, or any armed forces against whom Canadian Forces are engaged in hostilities whether or not a state of war exists between Canada and the country whose forces they are;
(2) Every one commits treason who, in Canada,
(a) uses force or violence for the purpose of overthrowing the government of Canada or a province;
(b) without lawful authority, communicates or makes available

to an agent of a state other than Canada, military or scientific information or any sketch, plan, model, article, note or document of a military or scientific character that he knows or ought to know may be used by that state for a purpose prejudicial to the safety or defence of Canada;

(c) conspires with any person to commit high treason or to do anything mentioned in paragraph (a);

(d) forms an intention to do anything that is high treason or that is mentioned in paragraph (a) and manifests that intention by an overt act; or

(e) conspires with any person to do anything mentioned in paragraph (b) or forms an intention to do anything mentioned in paragraph (b) and manifests that intention by an overt act.

(3) Notwithstanding subsection (1) or (2), a Canadian citizen or a person who owes allegiance to Her Majesty in right of Canada,

(a) commits high treason if, while in or out of Canada, he does anything mentioned in subsection (1); or

(b) commits treason if, while in or out of Canada, he does anything mentioned in subsection (2).

(4) Where it is treason to conspire with any person, the act of conspiring is an overt act of treason.

This is a rarely used section of the Code and one which is largely self-explanatory. Its general purpose is to prohibit acts which threaten the security of Canada.

A distinction is made between high treason and treason. High treason includes killing or attempting to kill the Queen, levying war against Canada and assisting an enemy at war with Canada. The minimum punishment for high treason is life imprisonment.

Treason includes using force or violence to overthrow the government and providing to an agent of another country military or scientific information which might threaten the safety of Canada. Treason also includes conspiring with another person to commit high treason or treason and forming the intention to commit high treason or treason and demonstrating that intention by some overt act. The case of *R. v. Bleiler*[22] provides an example of an overt act which demonstrated an intention to commit treason: the accused wrote letters advising the German Emporer during World War One to purchase a certain device or invention which would be of assistance to the German army.

There is no minimum punishment for treason. However, the maximum punishment for treason is life imprisonment unless the offence is under paragraph 46(2)(b) or (e) and is committed while no state of war exists between Canada and another country. In such a case, the maximum punishment is imprisonment for fourteen years.

If the acts of treason or high treason are committed in Canada, any person, whether or not he is a citizen of Canada, may be convicted. If the acts of treason or high treason are committed outside Canada, only Canadian citizens and persons owing allegiance to Canada may be convicted.

There are very few reported Canadian cases on treason or high treason. One such case, *Lampel v. Berger,*[23] involved the meaning of the phrase "assisting an enemy at war with Canada" [s.46.(1)(c)]. Berger had agreed to sell to Lampel a piece of property in Sarnia, Ontario in 1917 (during World War One). Berger was a Hungarian citizen who was living in the United States. Hungary was at war with Canada and the United States was a neutral country at the time of the contract. Therefore, Berger was an alien enemy subject living in neutral territory. Before paying for the property, Lampel (a Canadian citizen) learned that Berger regularly sent money to his wife and children in Hungary. Lampel was in doubt as to whether he could lawfully pay the purchase money to Berger because this might be construed as assisting an enemy at war with Canada. So, he started a civil action to have a court determine the matter. The first issue in the case was whether the contract regarding the property was valid. The court said that it was unlawful for a resident of Canada to trade with "the enemy", but for the purposes of contract law, Berger was not considered an enemy because he was not residing or carrying on business in an enemy country. Therefore, the contract was valid. The second issue was whether Lampel could pay the purchase money to Berger, knowing that Berger would be sending some of the money to Hungary. The court said that money sent to Hungary would become part of the financial resources of that enemy country and thus would aid the enemy by contributing to its capacity to prolong the war. Lampel knew of Berger's intention to send the money and if he enabled Berger to carry out his intention by paying to him the purchase money, he would be assisting an enemy at war with Canada, contrary to the Criminal Code. The court concluded that it was its duty to intervene by impounding the money and keeping it in court to the credit of Berger until after the war.

F. SEDITION

62. Every one who
(a) speaks seditious words,
(b) publishes a seditious libel, or
(c) is a party to a seditious conspiracy,
is guilty of an indictable offence and is liable to imprisonment for fourteen years.

Section 62 contains three separate crimes of sedition. With each offence it is necessary that a seditious intention be involved. That is, spoken words or a published libel (e.g. written words) are seditious only if they express a seditious intention. Similarly, a seditious conspiracy is an agreement between two or more persons to carry out a seditious intention.

"Seditious intention" is not exhaustively defined in the Code but the following provision is helpful:

60.(4) Without limiting the generality of the expression "seditious intention," every one shall be presumed to have a seditious intention who
   (a) teaches or advocates, or
   (b) publishes or circulates any writing that advocates,
the use, without the authority of law, of force as a means of accomplishing a governmental change within Canada.

In *Boucher v. R.*[24] the Supreme Court of Canada clarified the meaning of seditious intention by deciding that seditious intention involves an intention to incite to violence or to create public disturbance or disorder against the Queen or the institutions of the government of the country. The court noted that English textbooks define seditious intention as including an intention "to promote feelings of ill-will and hostility between different classes of [Her Majesty's] subjects" or an intention to bring the administration of justice into hatred or contempt. The court held that these types of intention were not seditious unless they were accompanied by the intention to incite people to violence or resistance for the purpose of disturbing constituted governmental authority.

The *Boucher* case involved a member of Jehovah's Witnesses who was charged with seditious libel for publishing in Quebec a pamphlet entitled "Quebec's Burning Hate for God and Christ and Freedom." The pamphlet described many instances of persecution of members of Jehovah's Witnesses including the destruction of Bibles and violent attacks unrestrained by the police who, instead of arresting the attackers, arrested the unoffending Witnesses who were distributing Bibles or Bible leaflets. The pamphlet also contained allegations that Roman Catholic priests and public officials were behind the criminal prosecutions brought against members of Jehovah's Witnesses and that the Roman Catholic Church influenced the Courts and the administration of justice in Quebec. The pamphlet called for an end to these injustices and for people to study the Bible. The court held that although the accused's intention may have been to stir up ill-will between classes of people or to bring the administration of justice into contempt, there was no evidence of an intention to incite to violence or resistance for the purpose of disturbing constituted governmental authority. Therefore, the court concluded that there was no basis for convicting the accused.

The meaning of seditious intention is further clarified by s.61:

61. Notwithstanding subsection 60(4), no person shall be deemed to have a seditious intention by reason only that he intends, in good faith,
   (a) to show that Her Majesty has been misled or mistaken in her measures;
   (b) to point out errors or defects in
      (i) the government or constitution of Canada or a province,
      (ii) the Parliament of Canada or the legislature of a province, or
      (iii) the administration of justice in Canada;

    (c) **to procure, by lawful means, the alteration of any matter of government in Canada; or**

    (d) **to point out, for the purpose of removal, matters that produce or tend to produce feelings of hostility and ill-will between different classes of persons in Canada.**

This provision recognizes that free criticism is a basic element of modern democratic government. The purpose of s.61 is to protect the widest range of public discussion and controversy, so long as it is done in good faith and for the purposes mentioned. However, this section does not protect a person from criminal liability if, in addition to his good faith, he intends to incite violence or public disorder.

G. UNLAWFUL ASSEMBLIES AND RIOTS

64.(1) An unlawful assembly is an assembly of three or more persons who, with intent to carry out any common purpose, assemble in such a manner or so conduct themselves when they are assembled as to cause persons in the neighbourhood of the assembly to fear, on reasonable grounds, that they

(a) will disturb the peace tumultuously, or

(b) will by that assembly needlessly and without reasonable cause provoke other persons to disturb the peace tumultuously.

(2) Persons who are lawfully assembled may become an unlawful assembly if they conduct themselves with a common purpose in a manner that would have made the assembly unlawful if they had assembled in that manner for that purpose.

(3) Persons are not unlawfully assembled by reason only that they are assembled to protect the dwelling-house of any one of them against persons who are threatening to break and enter it for the purpose of committing an indictable offence therein.

65. A riot is an unlawful assembly that has begun to disturb the peace tumultuously.

66. Every one who takes part in a riot is guilty of an indictable offence and is liable to imprisonment for two years.

67. Every one who is a member of an unlawful assembly is guilty of an offence punishable on summary conviction.

The elements of an unlawful assembly are: (1) three or more persons, (2) the intent to carry out a common purpose and (3) the causing of persons in the neighbourhood to fear that there will be a tumultuous disturbance of the peace.

A riot occurs when the unlawful assembly actually begins to disturb the peace tumultuously. The term ''tumultuous'' is not defined in the Code but it means marked by a great commotion and uproar.

There may be an unlawful assembly even though the common purpose of the persons involved is lawful. The important point is the manner in which the purpose is, or is likely to be, carried out. If the manner causes persons in the neighbourhood to fear that there will be a riot, an offence is committed regardless of the lawfulness of the common purpose. Of course, the fear must be based on reasonable grounds.

Under s.64(1)(b) the assembly will be considered unlawful if it causes neighbours to reasonably fear that it will needlessly and without reasonable cause provoke other persons to disturb the peace tumultuously. In the English case of *Beatty v. Gillbanks*,[25] a Salvation Army band intended to parade through the streets as it had done on several previous occasions. On these previous occasions, the band had been assaulted and stoned by a group called the Skeleton Army which was opposed to the Salvation Army. As the parade began, the police arrested its leaders and charged them with being members of an unlawful assembly. The court held that the leaders were not guilty. They had no intention to use force and they conducted themselves in a peaceful manner. The court felt that it was unjust to hold law-abiding persons guilty because of the likelihood that others would disturb the peace. However, the court went on to say that the leaders could have been convicted if their intention, or the necessary result of their parade, had been that the Skeleton Army would cause a disturbance. It is not clear whether this same reasoning would be applied to s.64(1)(b) by Canadian courts.[26]

In *R. v. Beattie*,[27] the accused addressed a quiet and orderly group of about 500 unemployed persons. After a short speech, the accused and two other representatives of the unemployed persons went to city hall to meet with the mayor. A police officer informed them that the mayor was unable to see them at that time but would probably see them later. The three representatives returned to the crowd and the accused said: "They will not let us get into the city hall. Are there any red-blooded men among you who will follow us into the city hall?" Shouts and applause came from the crowd and about 300 men led by the accused rushed forward, yelling and swearing, to the city hall, where they were opposed by eight police officers. An affray with the police resulted. The accused was charged with being a member of an unlawful assembly and was found guilty. In its reasons for judgment, the court said:

> *[T]here was here an unlawful assembly from the moment that two or three hundred unemployed, appealed to as "red-blooded men" to go and enter the city hall which they knew would be opposed by the peace officers, began making their way across King Street in the manner described. That, by itself, made it an unlawful assembly, because the conduct of the crowd at that moment was already such as to cause persons in the neighbourhood to fear on reasonable grounds that the peace would thereby be tumultuously disturbed, as to which there was evidence given by persons present that the scene did arouse in them such a feeling of fear ....*

H. EXPLOSIVE SUBSTANCES

77. Every one who has an explosive substance in his possession or under his care or control is under a legal duty to use reasonable care to prevent bodily harm or death to persons or damage to property by that explosive substance.

78. Every one who, being under a legal duty within the meaning of section 77, fails without lawful excuse to perform that duty, is guilty of an indictable offence and if as a result an explosion of an explosive substance occurs that

(a) causes death or is likely to cause death to any person, is liable to imprisonment for life, or

(b) causes bodily harm or damage to property or is likely to cause bodily harm or damage to property, is liable to imprisonment for fourteen years.

Section 77 establishes a legal duty of care regarding explosive substances. Any person in possession of such substances must use reasonable care to prevent injury to persons or damage to property.

An "explosive substance" includes a bomb, grenade, dynamite or other substances used in blasting operations. The term also includes anything intended to be used to make an explosive substance and anything used or intended to be used to cause an explosion with an explosive substance.[28]

Section 78 makes it an indictable offence to fail, without lawful excuse, to perform the duty regarding explosives. If an explosion resulted from the breach of the duty and a person was killed (or was likely to have been killed), the punishment is life imprisonment. If the explosion caused (or was likely to have caused) bodily harm or property damage, the punishment is imprisonment for 14 years. If no such explosion resulted but there was a failure to use reasonable care to prevent injury, death or property damage, the offender is liable under s.658 to imprisonment for five years.

Under s.79 it is an indictable offence (1) to do anything with the intent to cause an explosion that is likely to cause serious bodily harm, death or serious property damage; (2) to cause an explosion with the intent to do bodily harm; (3) to throw or place an explosive anywhere with the intent to damage property without lawful excuse and (4) to make or possess an explosive with the intent to endanger life or cause serious property damage. These and other offences in s.79 require proof of the specific intents mentioned, unlike s.78 offences which simply require proof of a failure to exercise reasonable care (i.e. negligence).

A separate offence of possession of an explosive is contained in s.80. Neither intent nor negligence is necessary for a conviction under this section. Simply being in possession is sufficient, unless the accused can prove that he had some lawful excuse for possessing the explosive.

I. OFFENSIVE WEAPONS

The term "offensive weapon" (or simply "weapon") is defined in s.2 as anything that is designed to be used as a weapon, or anything that a person uses or intends to use as a weapon regardless of whether it was designed for that use. For example, a rifle is designed to be used as a weapon. A beer bottle is not designed to be used as a weapon; it is designed to be used as a container for beer. However, it could be a weapon if a person used it or intended to use it as a weapon in assaulting another person. In other words, almost any object could be a weapon, depending on the intention of the possessor.

Under s.83, it is an indictable offence to possess a weapon or an imitation of a weapon for a purpose dangerous to the public peace or for the purpose of committing an offence. For a conviction under this section, the prosecution must prove (1) possession and (2) intention.

The fact that a person was carrying a weapon for a defensive purpose is not necessarily a defence. In *R. v. Nelson,*[29] the accused feared being attacked by two men, the Bougie brothers, with whom he had had some previous trouble. Before going to a club where he expected that they would be, he armed himself with a double bladed home-made knife having an 18-inch blade. After drinking some beer at the club, the accused got into a fight with one of the Bougies and the two of them were required to leave the club. Outside the club, the accused was confronted by the Bougie brothers and he began swinging his knife at them, causing some injury to each. The accused was convicted of carrying a weapon for a purpose dangerous to the public peace. The court noted that even though the weapon was intended for defence purposes, it was necessary to consider other factors such as the nature of the weapon, how it was acquired, the manner of its use, the time, the place and relevant statements or actions of the accused. The court concluded: "In this instance the character of the weapon and the reasons for its acquisition as well as the clear intention of the [accused] to make use of what was, under the circumstances, a clearly illegal method of defence make it clear that the weapon was being carried for a purpose dangerous to the public peace."

Other related offences include: carrying a concealed weapon (s.84), dangerous use of a firearm (s.86), and delivering a firearm to a person under 16 years of age (s.87).

Weapons are classified as prohibited weapons and restricted weapons. These terms are defined in s.82(1):

> **"prohibited weapon" means**
> (a) **any device or contrivance designed or intended to muffle or stop the sound or report of a firearm,**
> (b) **any knife that has a blade that opens automatically by gravity or centrifugal force or by hand pressure applied to a button, spring or other device in or attached to the handle of the knife, or**
> (c) **a weapon of any kind, not being a restricted weapon or a**

shotgun or rifle of a kind commonly used in Canada for
hunting or sporting purposes, that is declared by order of the
Governor in Council to be a prohibited weapon.
"restricted weapon" means
(a) any firearm designed, altered or intended to be aimed and
fired by the action of one hand,
(b) any firearm that is capable of firing bullets in rapid
succession during one pressure of the trigger,
(c) any firearm that is less than twenty-six inches in length or
that is designed or adapted to be fired when reduced to a
length of less than twenty-six inches by folding, telescoping
or otherwise, or
(d) a weapon of any kind, not being a shotgun or rifle of a kind
commonly used in Canada for hunting or sporting purposes,
that is declared by order of the Governor in Council to be a
restricted weapon.

Under s.89, it is an offence to possess a prohibited weapon. Under s.91, it is an
offence to possess a restricted weapon unless the person in possession has a permit.
No permits are given for prohibited weapons.

QUESTIONS FOR REVIEW AND DISCUSSION

1. Define the offence of bribery.
2. What is the meaning of "administration of justice" in s.109 (bribery)?
3. What are the essential elements of the offence of obstructing a peace officer
    [s.118(a)]? Is it necessary for a conviction that the accused employed physical
    force? Why?
4. Give an example of a police officer not acting in the execution of his duty.
5. What are the essential elements of the offence of perjury?
6. Questions on s.127(1): What is a surety? What does it mean to indemnify a
    surety? What is the purpose behind enacting s.127(1)? What are the essential
    elements of the offence?
7. Questions on s.127(2) and (3): When does the "course of justice" begin?
    When does the "course of justice" end? Which of the following would be
    considered an attempt to obstruct, pervert or defeat the course of justice:
    (a) Destroying documents to be used in a trial.
    (b) Denying that the person named in a summons is living in the house when
        a policeman attempts to execute it.
    (c) Denying that you are the person named in a summons when you are. See
        R. v. Balsdon, [1968] 2 C.C.C. 164.
    (d) Telling a policeman you were the driver of a car involved in an accident
        when in fact Y was driving. See *R. v. Snider,* 106 C.C.C. 175.
    (e) Attempting to persuade X not to testify in an upcoming trial.

(f) Attempting to persuade Y not to testify even before charges are laid or a date of trial is established.

(g) Trying to suppress evidence you know is false.

(h) Leaving the country knowing that you may be a witness in a trial.

(i) Taking jurors out to dinner during a trial in which you are the accused.

(j) Telling a policeman investigating a crime lies which the policeman ignores because he knows they are lies.

8. Which of the following would be offences under s.118?

(a) Speeding up an automobile as a policeman makes efforts by signalling and using his siren to have it pull over to the side of the road.

(b) Resisting arrest for (i) disorderly conduct, (ii) theft.

(c) Refusing to open the glove compartment of a car for inspection upon request of a police officer who suspects liquor violations.

(d) Refusing to give one's name and address to a police officer on request.

(e) Resisting arrest for theft when the arrest is made by a police officer who is in the course of his part-time job with a factory. See *R. v. Johnston*, [1966] 1 C.C.C. 226.

(f) Rubbing the chalk off the tires of automobiles after the marks were put on by the police to help indicate when a parking violation had occurred. See *R. v. Brunetti*, 131 C.C.C. 171.

(g) Verbally protesting the excessive force used by the police in lawfully arresting a friend.

9. Explain the difference between treason and sedition.

10. What are the essential elements of an unlawful assembly? How is a riot different from an unlawful assembly?

11. What would be a lawful excuse for being in possession of an explosive substance? Would this lawful excuse protect the possessor from criminal liability for an injury caused by the explosion of the explosive substance? Explain.

12. What is a "weapon"? Give two examples. What is the main effect of classifying a weapon as restricted rather than as prohibited?

---

[1] *R. v. Gross* (1946), 86 C.C.C. 68 (Ont.C.A.).
[2] (1964) 1 C.C.C. 97, 42 C.R. 93 (Ont.C.A.).
[3] *R. v. Smith* (1921), 38 C.C.C. 21 (Ont.C.A.).
[4] (1920), 35 C.C.C. 159 (S.C.C.).
[5] *R. v. Belzberg* (1962), 131 C.C.C. 281, 36 C.R. 368 (S.C.C.).
[6] *R. v. Matheson* (1913), 21 C.C.C. 312 (N.B.C.A.).
[7] (1955), 11 C.C.C. 281, 21 C.R. 144 (Man.C.A.).
[8] See note 6.
[9] (1932) 57 C.C.C. 174 (N.S.C.A.).
[10] *R. v. Griffin* (1935), 63 C.C.C. 286 (N.B.C.A.).
[11] See Chapter Twelve under the offence of assaulting a police officer for further discussion of the phrase "execution of his duty."

[12] (1971), 2 C.C.C. (2d) 315 (B.C.C.A.).

[13] (1973), 15 C.C.C. (2d) 85 (Que.C.A.).

[14] (1973), 10 C.C.C. (2d) 377, 21 C.R.N.S. 344 (S.C.C.)

[15] (1960), 129 C.C.C. 220 (S.C.C.).

[16] (1955), 112 C.C.C. 79, 21 C.R. 374 (Ont.C.A.).

[17] (1921), 35 C.C.C. 293 (Sask.C.A.).

[18] (1968), 5 C.R.N.S. 297 (Que.C.A.)

[19] *R. v. Kalick,* see note 4.

[20] (1962), 39 C.R. 306 (B.C.C.A.).

[21] (1908), 14 C.C.C. 79 (Ont.C.A.).

[22] (1917), 28 C.C.C. 9 (Alta.C.A.)

[23] (1917), 38 D.L.R. 47 (Ont.S.Ct.).

[24] (1951), 99 C.C.C. 1 (S.C.C.).

[25] (1882), 9 Q.B.D. 308.

[26] See *R. v. Patterson* (1931), 55 C.C.C. 218 (Ont.C.A.)

[27] (1931), 55 C.C.C. 380 (Man.C.A.)

[28] s.2(16).

[29] (1972) 8 C.C.C. (2d) 29 (Ont.C.A.)

Chapter Seven

Sexual Offences, Obscenity, And Disorderly Conduct

A. SEXUAL OFFENCES

1. Rape

143. A male person commits rape when he has sexual intercourse with a female person who is not his wife,
(a) without her consent or
(b) with her consent if the consent
   (i)   is extorted by threats of fear of bodily harm,
   (ii) is obtained by personating her husband, or
   (iii) is obtained by false and fraudulent representations as to the nature and quality of the act.

144. Every one who commits rape is guilty of an indictable offence and is liable to imprisonment for life.

The essential elements of the offence of rape are (a) a male person (b) has sexual intercourse (c) with a female person who is not his wife (d) without her real or valid consent.

A. MALE PERSON Rape can be committed only by a male. However, a female can be a party to the offence by aiding a male to commit rape on another female. According to s.147, the male must be at least 14 years of age. So, even if a 13-year-old boy satisfies all the other requirements of rape, he will not be guilty of the offence. This minimum age rule also applies to sexual offences in s.146 and s.150 discussed below.

B. SEXUAL INTERCOURSE Under s.3(6) of the Code, sexual intercourse is complete when there is penetration to even the slightest degree of the female's sexual organs. It is not necessary that semen be emitted.

C. FEMALE PERSON NOT WIFE The section simply refers to female person and there is no minimum age requirement. A male can not be a victim of the offence of rape. A man can not be convicted of raping his wife. However, he could be convicted of assaulting his wife. Once the marriage is dissolved by divorce, a man could be convicted of raping his former wife. A man could also aid and abet another man to rape his wife. He would then be a party to the offence and could be charged and convicted of rape.

D. LACK OF VALID CONSENT For the offence of rape to occur, the female must not consent to the act of sexual intercourse. It is not real or valid consent if the consent is obtained by threats or fear of bodily harm, by personating the victim's husband or by fraud as to the nature and quality of the act. But a female may be persuaded or induced in other ways to give her consent. In *R. v. Arnold,* [1] the accused gave a ride to a woman who was waiting for a street car. During the course of their conversation, the accused offered the woman a job in his cartage business. He also said that in addition to her regular wages, she would receive extra money if, from time to time, she would consent to have sexual intercourse with him. Then the accused drove to a secluded area of the city and there, according to the woman, he attempted to rape her. It was up to the jury to decide whether or not the woman gave her consent. The Ontario Court of Appeal held that if the jury found that the accused had persuaded her to consent by the offer of a job and additional money, then he could not be convicted of rape. In short, consent obtained by such means is a defence to a rape charge.

In *R. v. Landry,* [2] the accused was charged with attempting to rape a 14-year-old girl. The important issue in this case was: "if a man without the use of force works on the passions of a girl until such passions overcome the girls's unwillingness and she becomes willing for intercourse, would this consent be considered as having been given under force or as having been given freely?" The New Brunswick Court of Appeal held that such consent would have to be considered to have been given freely. Thus, it would be real consent and the accused could not be found guilty.

(i) Consent by threats or fear of bodily harm

If a man extorts a woman's consent to sexual intercourse by threats or a genuine fear of bodily harm, then there is no real consent and he can be convicted of rape. In *R. v. Bursey,* [3] the accused took the woman complainant to a secluded area and had sexual intercourse with her in his car. One of the questions in the case was whether or not the accused said or did anything which amounted to extortion by threats or fear of bodily harm in order to obtain the consent of the woman to have sexual intercourse with him. The woman testified that the accused made the statement that she might never get home unless she did what he wanted. When she was asked in court what effect this statement had on her, she said that she "started crying"; she was "very nervous"; she felt as if she was going to be sick and she was "very frightened." When she was asked what frightened her, she said: "I thought he was going to attack me and then just leave me in the ditch. I thought he wouldn't take me home now because he would be afraid of getting someone after him. I didn't think this man would take me home after he had done this." The court held that the accused had not extorted her consent to sexual intercourse by threats or fear of bodily harm. The court felt that the woman's testimony showed that her nervousness and fright were caused mainly by what might happen to her *after* the accused had intercourse with her. In other words, the nervousness and fright were not caused by what might happen to her if she did not give her consent. Thus, because there was no proof of extorted consent, the accused was found not guilty.

(ii) Consent by fraud

If a man obtains a woman's consent to sexual intercourse by false and fraudulent representations as to the nature and quality of the act, then there is no real consent and he can be convicted of rape. In *R. v. Harms*,[4] the accused was charged with raping a 20-year-old woman. The woman had been suffering from a pain in her chest. Her father suggested that she see the accused, whom the father knew as "Doctor Harms." When the accused met with the woman in his room at a boarding house, he asked her how her periods were. The woman replied that they were irregular and scanty. The accused then told her that he could correct her periods by a treatment if she could come back later. The woman returned later and the accused had her drink some yellow liquid. The liquid made her dizzy and the accused suggested that she should lie down on his bed. Later, the accused took out two pills and he told her that he was going to insert them in her private parts. After removing her underwear, he inserted the pills. Then, after removing his own underwear, the accused got on her and tried to excite her for the purpose of having sexual intercourse. He told the woman that he was doing it to make the pills work properly. She objected and pushed him away, while he continued to claim that it was necessary in order to cure her. After some other efforts to get her to have sexual intercourse, he stopped and said that if she insisted on being so uncooperative, she would have to take the consequences. Finally, she gave in and the accused had intercourse with her. Afterwards, he assured the woman that she would now be all right and that her periods would occur regularly. The "treatment" did not work. She became pregnant and the accused was charged with rape. His defence was that the woman had consented to having sexual intercourse. The issue in the case was whether or not the consent had been obtained by false and fraudulent representations as to the nature and quality of the act. The lawyer for the accused argued that there was no such fraud because the woman clearly understood that she was being asked to consent to sexual intercourse. In other words, she was not deceived as to what the act was. The court disagreed with this narrow view and said that the purpose or reason for her consent had to be considered. She consented because the accused, by false and fraudulent representations, led her to believe that it was part of a treatment which would correct her physical ailment. The court concluded that the principle involved was that a man will be guilty of rape if he overcomes the woman's resistance by fraud, just as he would be guilty if he overcame the resistance by force. Thus, the accused was found guilty of rape.

E. THE REQUIRED INTENT There is disagreement in the cases as to whether rape is a general intent offence or a specific intent offence. The main importance of the issue is that if rape requires only a general intent, then intoxication will not be a defence. If rape requires a specific intent, then intoxication will be a defence.

In *R. v. Vandervoort,*[5] the Ontario Court of Appeal held that the prosecution must prove that the accused had the specific intent to have intercourse without the woman's consent. The court concluded that intoxication is a defence to a rape charge. An intoxicated person may have the general intent to have sexual intercourse. But he may be too intoxicated to form the specific intent to force the intercourse upon the woman. In other words, he may be too intoxicated to realize that she is not consenting.

In *R. v. Boucher,*[6] the B.C. Court of Appeal made an opposite decision. The court held that rape is a general intent offence. It compared rape to assault: "Each requires proof of the doing of a physical act without consent. In assault (a general intent offence), the physical act is a simple bodily attack; in rape it is enforced coition (i.e. intercourse). In either case consent is a defence." Once the bodily attack is proved, the general intent to assault is presumed. Once forcible intercourse is proved, the general intent to rape is presumed. Thus, in British Columbia, intoxication is not a defence to a rape charge.

2. Sexual Intercourse With a Female Under the Age of 14

> **s.146(1) Every male person who has sexual intercourse with a female person who**
> **(a) is not his wife, and**
> **(b) is under the age of fourteen years, whether or not he believes that she is fourteen years of age or more, is guilty of an indictable offence and is liable to imprisonment for life.**

This offence is similar to rape except in two respects: (1) the female must be under 14 at the time of the sexual intercourse; (2) lack of consent is not required.

Consent by a girl under the age of 14 is no defence to this charge.[7] The law will not recognize her consent as a real consent to sexual intercourse.

It is not a defence that the accused honestly believed that the girl was over 14. For example: A is a very mature-looking girl of 13. Most people think that she looks about 18 years of age. B, an 18-year-old male, meets A in a bar. B knows that a person must be at least 18 to be admitted to the bar. So, he assumes that A is at least 18. When he talks with A, she says that she is 18 and she suggests that they go to B's apartment to have sexual intercourse. They arrive at the apartment and A not only consents to having sexual intercourse, but is the one who initiates the sexual activity. B could be convicted under s.146(1).

3. Sexual Intercourse With a Female Between the Ages of 14 and 16

146.(2) Every male person who has sexual intercourse with a female person who
> **(a) is not his wife,**
> **(b) is of previously chaste character, and**
> **(c) is fourteen years of age or more and is under the age of sixteen years,**

whether or not he believes that she is sixteen years of age or more, is guilty of an indictable offence and is liable to imprisonment for five years.

(3) Where an accused is charged with an offence under subsection (2), the court may find the accused not guilty if it is of the opinion that the evidence does not show that, as between the accused and the female person, the accused is more to blame than the female person.

This offence is different from the preceding one in three respects: (1) the female must be at least 14 and under 16 years of age, (2) the female must be of previously chaste character, (3) it must be shown that the accused was more to blame than the female person.

The meaning of "previously chaste character" was discussed in *R. v. Johnston.* [8] In that case, the accused was charged with having sexual intercourse with a female under the age of 16 and over the age of 14. The court said that chaste character refers to "moral cleanliness." A female is of chaste character if she is "decent and clean in thought and conduct."

Chaste character and virginity are not necessarily the same thing. A virgin would be of unchaste character if she were not "decent and clean in thought and conduct." Also, a female may lose her chastity and later regain it. An extreme example might be a prostitute becoming a nun.

The burden of proving that the female was *not* of previously chaste character is on the accused. [9] In other words, it will be assumed that the female was previously chaste unless the accused can prove otherwise. Also, the fact that the accused had, prior to the time of the offence, sexual intercourse with the female is not evidence that she was not of previously chaste character. [10]

On the other hand, the prosecution must prove, under s.146(3), that the accused was more to blame than the female. If there is a reasonable doubt about whether he was more to blame, then he should be acquitted. [11]

4. Indecent Assault

A. INDECENT ASSAULT ON A FEMALE

149.(1) Every one who indecently assaults a female person is guilty of an indictable offence and is liable to imprisonment for five years.

> **(2) An accused who is charged with an offence under
> subsection (1) may be convicted if the evidence establishes that
> the accused did anything to the female person with her consent
> that, but for her consent, would have been an indecent assault, if
> her consent was obtained by false and fraudulent representations
> as to the nature and quality of the act.**

An indecent assault on a female involves two elements: (1) an assault (see Chapter Twelve) and (2) circumstances of indecency. If either of these elements is missing, the offence is not committed.

Indecency is not defined in the Code. It is a question of fact in each case whether indecency was involved. In general, an indecent act is one which violates community standards of decency.

An assault may be indecent in itself, such as the touching of the sexual organs of a female. Or, the assault may not be indecent in itself, but because of surrounding circumstances, it will constitute an indecent assault.

In *R. v. Louie Chong,*[12] the accused followed a 15-year-old girl on her way home at a late hour of the night. At an isolated spot, he grabbed her and offered her $5.00 to go with him for an "immoral purpose." The girl screamed and threatened to have him arrested. The accused fled and the girl ran home and told her father what had happened. The accused was charged with indecent assault. The lawyer for the accused argued that he should not be convicted because although he assaulted the girl by grabbing her, there was nothing indecent in the way he grabbed her. The court disagreed. The surrounding circumstances, including the words spoken at the time, made what would otherwise be a common assault an indecent assault.

In general, the consent of the female will be a defence to a charge of indecent assault. However, the consent of a girl under 14 years of age is no defence. Also, as in rape, consent obtained by fraud is no defence.

In *Bolduc and Bird v. R.,*[13] a medical doctor and a friend were charged with indecently assaulting a female patient. The patient had come to Dr. Bolduc's office for a vaginal examination. Before the examination began, Bolduc introduced a lay friend of his to the patient as "Dr. Bird." Bolduc told the patient that Bird was a medical intern and asked her if she would mind if Bird observed the examination. In fact, Bird was a night club musician who wanted to observe for his own pleasure. The woman patient consented to Bird's presence and Bolduc conducted his examination. During the examination, Bolduc touched the patient's private parts and inserted an instrument in the vaginal canal. Bird stood next to Bolduc, looking on, but did not touch the patient. The issue in the case was whether or not the patient's consent to the examination was obtained by false and fraudulent representations as to the nature and quality of the act. The Supreme Court of Canada decided that there was no false and fraudulent representation as to the nature and quality of the act to be performed by the doctor. He did exactly what the patient understood that he would do, namely, conduct a vaginal examination. There was no fraud on his part as to what he was supposed to do and in what he actually did. The patient knew that Bird was present and consented to his presence. The fraud was not as to the nature and quality of what was to be done. Rather, the fraud was as to Bird's identity as a medical intern. Bird did not touch the patient and his observing could not constitute an assault. Both Bolduc and Bird were found not guilty of indecent assault.

B. INDECENT ASSAULT ON A MALE

> **156. Every male person who assaults another person with intent to commit buggery or who indecently assaults another male person is guilty of an indictable offence and is liable to imprisonment for ten years.**

Unlike s.149, this offence can be committed only by males. There is no minimum age for the male offender. In other words, a boy under the age of 14 could be found guilty of indecently assaulting a male.

If the male victim is under the age of 14, his consent will not be a defence.

In this section, there is no specific mention of consent obtained by fraud. But, it would seem that such consent would not be real consent and thus would not be a defence.

The offence of buggery is discussed below.

5. Seduction

Seduction refers to sexual intercourse with a female which is made possible by obtaining her consent through persuasion, promises, bribes or other means without the use of force.[14] The main difference between seduction and rape is that in seduction the female consents to the intercourse.

A. SEDUCTION OF FEMALE BETWEEN 16 AND 18.

> **151. Every male person who, being eighteen years of age or more, seduces a female person of previously chaste character who is sixteen years of age or more but less than eighteen years of age is guilty of an indictable offence and is liable to imprisonment for two years.**

This offence can only be committed (1) by a male who is at least 18 years old, (2) with a female who is between 16 and 18, and (3) who is of previously chaste character. Again, the accused has the burden of proving that the female was previously unchaste.

B. SEDUCTION UNDER PROMISE OF MARRIAGE

> **152. Every male person, being twenty-one years of age or more, who, under promise of marriage, seduces an unmarried female person of previously chaste character who is less than twenty-one years of age is guilty of an indictable offence and is liable to imprisonment for two years.**

In this offence, the male must be at least 21 and the female must be under 21. She must be of previously chaste character and unmarried at the time of the offence. It also must be shown that she consented to sexual intercourse because the male promised to marry her. A man will not be convicted of this offence if he can prove that he subsequently married the female.

6. Buggery and Gross Indecency

155. Every one who commits buggery or bestiality is guilty of an indictable offence and is liable to imprisonment for fourteen years.

This section prohibits anal intercourse between humans (buggery). It also prohibits sexual intercourse with an animal (bestiality).

157. Every one who commits an act of gross indecency with another person is guilty of an indictable offence and is liable to imprisonment for five years.

Gross indecency is not defined in the Code, but it refers to indecency of a very great degree. Fellatio may be an act of gross indecency depending on the time, place and circumstances.[15] In *R. v. Davis,*[16] the accused woman and a man committed fellatio, cunnilingus and buggery. The court felt that a conviction for gross indecency was justified because of the following circumstances: the acts were done in the presence of a 16-year-old girl under the influence of L.S.D. who photographed them committing the acts.

Certain exceptions are mentioned in s.158:

158.(1) Sections 155 and 157 do not apply to any act committed in private between
  (a) a husband and his wife, or
  (b) any two persons, each of whom is twenty-one years or more of age, both of whom consent to the commission of the act.

An act is not done in private if it is committed in a "public place." Public place includes any place to which the public have access as of right or by invitation. In *R. v. Hogg,*[17] the accused was charged with committing a gross indecency in a cubicle of a subway washroom. The cubicle was locked but members of the general public could see into it. The court held that the cubicle was a public place and convicted the accused. In *R. v. Lavoie,*[18] a car parked on a side road frequented by the public was considered a public place.

An act is also not done in private if more than two persons take part or are present.

The two persons must be at least 21 years old.

The consent of the two persons is also required. Consent obtained by fraud is not considered real consent; nor is consent given by a feeble-minded or insane person considered real, if the other person knows or has good reason to believe that the person is feeble-minded or insane.

7. Procuring and Soliciting

The crime of procuring is commonly called "pimping." Generally, it consists of a person providing a female for the purpose of prostitution.[19] Section 195(1) contains several provisions intended to prohibit this practice. Three of the main provisions are:

> **195.(1) Every one who**
> **(a) procures, attempts to procure or solicits a female person to have illicit sexual intercourse with another person, whether in or out of Canada,**
>   ....
> **(d) procures or attempts to procure a female person to become, whether in or out of Canada, a common prostitute, [or]**
>   ....
> **(j) lives wholly or in part on the avails of prostitution of another person**
> **is guilty of an indictable offence and is liable to imprisonment for ten years.**

Section 195(1) makes it an offence to solicit (or accost) any person in a public place for the purpose of prostitution:

> **195(1) Every person who solicits any person in a public place for the purpose of prostitution is guilty of an offence punishable on summary conviction.**

There is a conflict in the cases as to whether a male person can "solicit". In *R. v. Patterson*,[20] the court held that a male could not be guilty of soliciting because, the court concluded, only females can be prostitutes. However, in *R. v. Obey*[21] it was held that regardless of whether a male can be a prostitute, a male falls within the meaning of "person" and can be convicted of soliciting. In *R. v. Gallant*,[22] a man impersonating a woman accosted a plain-clothed officer, indicating his availability for prostitution and was convicted of soliciting under s.195.1.

B. CORRUPTION OF MORALS

1. Obscene Materials

159.(1) Every one commits an offence who
(a) makes, prints, publishes, distributes, circulates or has in his possession for the purpose of publication, distribution or circulation any obscene written matter, picture, model, phonograph record or other thing whatsoever ....
(2) Every one commits an offence who knowingly, without lawful justification or excuse,
(a) sells, exposes to public view or has in his possession for such a purpose any obscene written matter, picture, model, phonograph record or other thing whatsoever ....

In s.159, subsection (1)(a) is directed toward *publishers* and *distributors* of obscene material. Subsection (2)(a) is directed toward *sellers* of obscene material (e.g. the operator of a bookstore) and those who expose obscene material (e.g. manager of an art gallery).

A. "KNOWINGLY" An important difference between the two subsections is:
   (1) On a charge of publishing or distributing obscene material [s.159(1)(a)] the fact that the accused was not aware of the nature or presence of the obscene material is no defence.
   (2) On a charge of selling obscene material [s.159(2)(a)] the prosecution must show that the selling was done "knowingly". Thus, it is a defence that the accused was not aware of the nature or presence of the obscene material.

In *R. v. Britnell*,[23] the accused was the operator of a bookstore who was charged with selling obscene books. The court pointed out that the prosecution must prove that the accused "knowingly" sold obscene books. The court said that "knowingly" meant (1) that the books were sold with knowledge; and (2) that he knew of their obscene character. Neither of these requirements were satisfied in the case. The accused carried a stock of nearly 250,000 books in his store. The ordering of the few copies of obscene books was done by a clerk, not the accused. There was no evidence that the accused was aware of the presence of the books in his store or that he had knowledge of their obscene character. Also, there was no evidence that he was present when any of the obscene books were sold. Thus, he was found not guilty.

In *R. v. Cameron*,[24] it was held that "knowingly" does not require that the accused should have the legal knowledge of whether or not the material is obscene. It is enough if he has knowledge of the subject-matter and sells the material or exposes it to public view. In this case, the accused was the manager of an art gallery. She was charged with exposing to public view seven obscene drawings in her gallery. The court held that she must have had the necessary knowledge of the subject-matter because: (1) she collected the drawings through other galleries and from the artists themselves; and (2) she arranged for the display of the drawings in her gallery. It was not necessary that she knew that the drawings met the legal definition of obscenity. It was only necessary that she was aware of the subject-matter or what was depicted in the drawings.

B. THE MEANING OF OBSCENITY Although it has been the subject of much discussion and case law, the meaning of obscenity is unclear. A definition of obscenity is contained in s.159(8):

> **159.(8) For the purposes of this Act, any publication a dominant characteristic of which is the undue exploitation of sex or of sex and any one or more of the following subjects, namely crime, horror, cruelty and violence, shall be deemed to be obscene.**

Several issues are raised by this definition:

(i) Is this definition the only test of obscenity?

In other words, is it possible for material to be legally obscene and yet not fall within s.159(8)? Strictly speaking, this question has not been decided. Some cases have said that the common law test of obscenity may also be applied. The common law test is whether the material tends "to deprave and corrupt those [whose] minds are open to such immoral influences and into whose hands a publication of this sort may fall."[25] Despite this uncertainty, the cases since 1962 seem to indicate that the definition in s.159(8) is the only test of obscenity in Canada.

(ii) Does the definition apply only to "publications"?

If so, what things can be considered publications? This is another unclear area. Books and magazines are publications, but the definition has also been applied by the courts to paintings, pictures, and motion picture films. It is unsettled whether or not the definition of obscenity in s.159(8) can also be applied to other things, such as phonograph records.

(iii) What is the meaning of "dominant characteristic"?

Again, this is not entirely clear. "Dominant characteristic" seems to refer to a main or distinctive feature or pecularity of the material. But can there be more than one dominant characteristic? And, how is it decided that a characteristic, such as undue exploitation of sex, is dominant? In *Brodie v. R.,*[26] four judges (not a majority) of the Supreme Court of Canada suggested answers to these questions: First, material (in this case, a book) may have more than one dominant characteristic. Second, in searching for a dominant characteristic, it is necessary to read the whole book, not merely isolated passages and isolated words. Third, it is relevant to consider the purpose of the author and the literary or artistic merit of the book.

(iv) What is "undue exploitation of sex"?

The four judges in the *Brodie* case, mentioned above, suggested that this phrase means that some exploitation of a sexual theme is permitted. In determining whether there is "undue" (excessive) exploitation, the judges said that it depends on (1) the author's purpose, (2) the artistic or literary merit and (3) whether the material violates the community standards of decency.

It should be noted that the *Brodie* principles, discussed above, were suggested by a minority of Supreme Court judges and, therefore, are not binding law. However, these principles have been adopted in several later lower court decisions, although there is still confusion and disagreement as to exactly how the principles should be applied.[27]

Despite the general uncertainty of this area of the law, it is clear that the community standard of decency is probably the most important factor in deciding whether material is obscene. The meaning of "community standards of decency" was discussed in *Dominion News and Gifts v. R..*[28] In that case, the Supreme Court of Canada was asked to decide whether certain issues of "Dude" magazine and "Escapade" magazine had a dominant characteristic of undue or excessive exploitation of sex. The court relied on the judgment of one of the lower court judges,[29] who said that one factor, but not the only one, in determining "community standards", is the number of people who read the magazine. He went on to say:

> *Those (community) standards are not set by those of lowest taste. Nor are they set exclusively by those of rigid, austere, conservative or puritan taste and habit of mind. Something approaching a general average of community thinking and feeling has to be discovered.*

The judge also noted that the community standards must be Canadian and they must be contemporary (i.e. in keeping with the attitudes of the times):

> *Times change, and ideas change with them. Compared with the Victorian era, this is a liberal age in which we live. One manifestation of it is the relative freedom with which the whole question of sex is discussed. In books, magazines, movies, television and sometimes even in parlour conversation, various aspects of sex are made the subject of comment, with a candour that in an earlier day would have been regarded as indecent and intolerable. We cannot and should not ignore these present-day attitudes when we face the question of whether "Dude" and "Escapade" are obscene according to our criminal law.*

(v) application of the s.159(8) definition of obscenity

The judges who have used s.159(8) are often not clear as to how the facts of a case fit (or do not fit) the definition of obscenity. This should be kept in mind when considering cases in which the s.159(8) definition has been applied.

In *Brodie v. R.,*[30] the Supreme Court of Canada held that *Lady Chatterly's Lover* was not obscene. The book included very detailed and explicit descriptions of the sexual relations between a man and a woman. The court said that sex could be described as a dominant characteristic of the book; however, the book, as a whole, did not unduly or excessively exploit sex.

In the *Dominion News*[31] case, certain issues of "Dude" magazine and "Escapade" magazine were held to be not obscene. The issue of "Dude" consisted of 80 pages and contained five main categories of material: (a) advertisements, correspondence and comments, 17 pages, (b) blatantly sexual cartoons, 4 pages, (c) photographs of nude or semi-nude female models, which included exposure of female breasts, 13 pages (d) fiction, 9 pages and (e) articles of various types, 37 pages.

The fiction consisted of two short stories, one of which was about a young executive on holiday who spent a night with the wife of his firm's most important client.

The articles included (1) a humorous satire by a well-known author; (2) a satire of television commercials; (3) a criticism of the idea of unrestricted freedom of speech; (4) a comment on the interest of movie addicts in certain dead actors; (5) a satire on psychiatrists, illustrated by a drawing of a nude woman; (6) a poem about a wife having a sexual affair with her next door neighbour; and (7) a long and detailed account of one man's "techniques of seduction" as applied to the wife of his employer, his landlady's daughter, a teenager and a servant girl.

Basically, the same type and pattern of material were in the issue of "Escapade."

After discussing the meaning of community standards, the court went on to say that in cases close to the border line of obscenity, it is better to be tolerant of the material than to suppress it: "Unless it is confined to clear cases, suppression may tend to inhibit those creative impulses and endeavours which ought to be encouraged in a free society."

The court concluded that the magazines were not obscene when viewed as a whole. They were "flippant and saucy" and when they dealt with sex they treated it in a normal and not perverted way. The magazines were risqué but they were not obscene.

In *R. v. Cameron*,[32] seven drawings on display in an art gallery were held to be obscene. Four of the drawings portrayed at least two female figures in the nude. One showed a single, nude female "in an attitude of sexual invitation." Three portrayed acts of lesbianism. One showed a male nude figure and a female nude figure with the female grasping the male's genitalia with her right hand. One drawing portrayed a female and a male in the nude in a position, or in the act, of sexual intercourse. The court concluded that the artistic merit of the drawings would be an important factor only if there were doubt about whether the community standards were offended. In this case, the court felt that there was no doubt that the drawings offended community standards. That is, the exploitation of sex was undue or excessive.

In *R. v. Great West News*,[33] the magazines "Film and Figure" and "Nude Living" were considered. The photographs in the magazines were mainly of nude females "deliberately posed to reveal their genitalia — often with the pubic hair shaved so as to permit an unobstructed view not only of the exterior portion of the female organ but also to some degree of its internal apparatus. . . .'' The court felt that the magazines had no literary or artistic merit and that the exploitation of sex offended community standards.

C. DEFENCE OF PUBLIC GOOD A defence to charges under s.159 is the defence of the public good in s.159(3):

> **159.(3) No person shall be convicted of an offence under this section if he establishes that the public good was served by the acts that are alleged to constitute the offence and that the acts alleged did not extend beyond what served the public good.**

There are two parts to this defence which must be proved by the accused: (1) that the public good was served and (2) that the acts (e.g. publishing or selling of obscene books) did not go beyond what served the public good. Material that otherwise would be obscene will not be considered obscene if this defence is established.

Something serves the public good if it is necessary or advantageous to objects of general interest, such as religion, science, literature or art.[34]

In the *Cameron* case, discussed above, the court found that the exposure of the obscene drawings to the public did not serve the public good. The lawyer for the accused had argued that the drawings could benefit art students and could assist in the education of the public in an appreciation of art. The court said this argument failed because to accomplish these benefits the exposure of obscene drawings was unnecessary.

2. Immoral, Indecent, or Obscene Theatrical Performance

> **163.(1) Every one commits an offence who, being the lessee, manager, agent or person in charge of a theatre, presents or gives or allows to be presented or given therein an immoral, indecent or obscene performance, entertainment or representation.**
>
> **(2) Every one commits an offence who takes part or appears as an actor, performer, or assistant in any capacity, in an immoral, indecent or obscene performance, entertainment or representation in a theatre.**

Subsection (1) is directed against the person in charge of the theatre in which the immoral, indecent or obscene performance takes place. Subsection (2) is directed at those who participate in the performance.

A. INDECENT PERFORMANCE As mentioned earlier, ''indecent'' is not defined in the Code and the courts have not developed a clear test. However, in general, something is indecent if it offends against community standards of decency or good taste.

B. IMMORAL PERFORMANCE Immoral is another term not defined in the Code. In general, it refers to not conforming with accepted patterns of conduct.

The meaning of immoral was clarified somewhat by the Supreme Court of Canada in *Johnson v. R.*.[35] In that case, the issue was "whether the performance of a dance in a theatre before a public audience, which would have been unexceptional if performed when fully or partly clad, becomes 'immoral' on the sole ground that it is performed 'in the nude.'" The accused woman appeared on stage in a cabaret in front of about seventeen people. She danced five dances. Three dances were "topless" and one was completely in the nude. At the time of the nude dance, she was alone on the stage. She did nothing offensive by way of words or gestures while she danced. The court held that the performance was not immoral. There was nothing immoral about displaying a naked human body and there was no evidence that the dance was "immoral" in any other way. The court noted that s.170 makes it an offence to be unclothed in a public place. But the simple fact that Parliament makes it an offence does not mean that it is a breach of moral standards. The result was that the dancer was not guilty of performing in an immoral performance.

C. OBSCENE PERFORMANCE It appears that the s.159(8) test of obscenity (whether a dominant characteristic is the undue exploitation of sex) is at least relevant in deciding whether a theatrical performance is obscene. In *R. v. Small*,[36] the B.C. Court of Appeal held that a judge is not bound or required to apply the test to theatrical performances. However, the court said that the test is one of several factors which may be considered by a judge in deciding whether a performance is obscene. The other factors mentioned were: dictionary definitions of obscenity; the common law test of whether there is a tendency "to deprave and corrupt"; the community standards of decency; the time, place, and circumstances of the performance; and the idea that a performance before paying adults may be less "dangerous" than a book or magazine which may fall into the hands of children.

C. DISORDERLY CONDUCT

1. Indecent Acts

> **169. Every one who wilfully does an indecent act**
> **(a) in a public place in the presence of one or more persons, or**
> **(b) in any place, with intent thereby to insult or offend any person,**
> **is guilty of an offence punishable on summary conviction.**

The essential elements of this section are as follows.

A. "INDECENT" ACT As mentioned earlier, indecency is not defined in the Code. Generally, it refers to a violation of community standards of decency or good taste. A common example of an indecent act is the exposure of the "private parts" of a person (i.e. indecent exposure). But, simply being nude in public, such as lying nude on a public beach, is not an indecent act, although the person could be charged under s.170 (see below).

B. "WILFULLY" The term ''wilfully'' has the same meaning that it has in most other sections of the Code: to do an act purposely and with a criminal intention.

C. PLACE OF THE ACT The act may occur in a public place (any place to which the public may go) but it must be in the presence of one or more persons [s.169(a)]. In *R. v. Hastings,*[37] the court held that urinating on a public street at night, with no exposure to any person other than a police officer, is not an offence.

If an indecent act is done with the specific intent to insult or offend any person, it makes no difference where the act occurs [s.169(b)]. In other words, the indecent act may occur in any place, public or private, but it must be shown that the accused did the act in order to insult or offend someone.

2. Nudity

> **170. Every one who, without lawful excuse,**
> **(a) is nude in a public place, or**
> **(b) is nude and exposed to public view while on private property, whether or not the property is his own,**
> **is guilty of an offence punishable on summary conviction.**

No act is required to commit this offence. Simply being nude is enough. Subsection (2) states that ''a person is nude who is so clad as to offend against public decency or order.''

It is an offence to be nude in a public place. Thus, it is an offence to be nude on a public beach. It also seems that it would be an offence to be nude in a public theatre or bar.

Under s.170(b), it is an offence for a person to be nude on private property if he is exposed to public view. So, if a person sunbathes in the nude on his front lawn in a typical residential area of a city, then he would be guilty of an offence.

3. Causing a Disturbance

> **171. Every one who**
> **(a) not being in a dwelling-house causes a disturbance in or near a public place**
> **(i) by fighting, screaming, shouting, swearing, singing or using insulting or obscene language,**
> **(ii) by being drunk, or**
> **(iii) by impeding or molesting other persons, . . .**
> **is guilty of an offence punishable on summary conviction.**

The essential elements of this offence are: (1) that the accused was not in a dwelling-house; (2) that he caused a disturbance; (3) that the disturbance occurred in a public place or near a public place; and (4) that the disturbance was caused by his fighting, screaming, etc. or by his being drunk or by his impeding or molesting other persons.

A. "DWELLING-HOUSE" Dwelling-house is defined in s.2 as

> **... the whole or any part of a building or structure that is kept or occupied as a permanent or temporary residence and includes**
>
> **(a) a building within the curtilage of a dwelling-house that is connected to it by a doorway or by a covered enclosed passageway, and**
>
> **(b) a unit that is designed to be mobile and to be used as a permanent or temporary residence and that is being used as such a residence.**

In *R. v. Jones,*[38] one issue was whether or not the administrative office of a university was a dwelling-house. Students of Simon Fraser University conducted a "sit-in" at the university. They occupied the administrative office and prevented officials and administrators from entering the office. They were charged with causing a disturbance by impeding other persons [s.171(a)(iii)]. The lawyer for the students argued that the sit-in occurred in a dwelling-house within the meaning of the definition in s.2 and therefore, no offence was committed. First, the lawyer argued that for legal purposes such as being sued, the "residence" of a university is its administrative office. The court agreed that for certain legal purposes, the administrative office is the residence of the university but not for the purpose of s.171. Second, the lawyer argued that because the students brought and used sleeping bags and food they used the premises as their temporary residence within the meaning of the definition in s.2. The court disagreed again by deciding that trespassers cannot by wrongfully occupying university property convert it into their residence and thereby make it a dwelling-house.

B. DISTURBANCE The meaning of "disturbance" was discussed in *R. v. C.D.*.[39] The accused was charged with causing a disturbance by using insulting language [s.171(a)(i)]. While standing in a public street, the accused shouted at Mr. and Mrs. Smith to "get your fucking car out of this fucking parking lot or I'll hit your fucking car." Then, the accused got in his car and drove it into the rear of the Smith car. This caused the child of the Smiths to be thrown to the floor of the car and it caused Mrs. Smith and the child to cry. There was no person other than the Smiths present when the shouting occurred. The court felt that the language used by the accused was insulting and that it occurred in a public place. But, there was no disturbance. Each of the three judges of the New Brunswick Court of Appeal gave his own interpretation of the meaning of disturbance. One judge said:

> *While it is difficult, if not impossible, to define with any degree of precision what is meant by a "disturbance" as used in s.171(a)(i), it is obvious it involves activities constituting a distraction to persons in or near public places who are pursuing their ordinary peaceable pursuits and includes a breach of the peace, a tumult, an uproar, a commotion and any other disorder. Where the acts specified in the*

> *section produce only annoyance or emotional upset not accompanied*
> *by activities in the nature of a disorder, there is not, in my opinion, a*
> *disturbance of the kind contemplated by the section.*

A second judge said that for there to be a disturbance, it is not necessary that there be a riot but there must be "something more than mere interruption of tranquility or peace of some person's mind." He concluded that no act caused by the insulting language was done which could be considered a disturbance.

The third judge said that disturbance referred to a "disorder or agitation" of the public or interference "with the ordinary and customary use by the public of the public place."

In short, all three judges agreed that although the language was insulting and emotionally upsetting to the Smith family, it did not cause a disturbance. Therefore, the accused was found not guilty. On the other hand, he probably could have been convicted of intimidation, mischief or assault.

4. Trespassing at Night

> **173. Every one who, without lawful excuse, the proof of which lies upon him, loiters or prowls at night upon the property of another person near a dwelling-house situated on that property is guilty of an offence punishable on summary conviction.**

This section is sometimes referred to as the "peeping tom" section. For the offence to be committed, (1) a person must "loiter or prowl"; (2) the loitering or prowling must occur at "night"; (3) it must be on another person's property; (4) it must be near a dwelling-house on that property. If the person has some lawful excuse for his actions, then it is up to him to prove it.

A. "NIGHT" The term "night" is defined in s.2 as the period between 9 p.m. and 6 a.m. If the loitering or prowling occurs before 9 p.m. or after 6 a.m., even if it is dark outside, the offence is not committed.

B. "LOITERS OR PROWLS" The meaning of "loiters" was considered in *R. v. Andsten and Petrie*.[40] The accused in the case were private detectives who had been hired by a man to investigate the conduct of his estranged wife. They kept the wife's house under surveillance from about 11:30 p.m. to about 2:30 a.m. "by lingering on the property, hanging around the house, listening at the windows and finally demanding admission to speak to a man whom they believed to be there." The court held that the meaning of "loiters" as used in s.173 is "hanging around" and that the detectives were loitering near the wife's house. The detectives argued that they had a lawful excuse for their actions. They said that they were on the wife's property for the lawful purpose of investigating her conduct. The court agreed that this was a lawful purpose; however, this purpose did not justify or excuse the civil wrong of trespass which they committed by their invasion of the wife's property. Therefore, the detectives were found guilty.

In the only reported case on the meaning of "prowls," the court decided that the term was meant to cover behaviour which is more overt than mere loitering. It refers to hunting in a stealthy manner for an opportunity to carry out an unlawful purpose. The court explained that a person who walks quickly through another person's property would not be loitering. But, if it could be proven that he was looking for a chance to break into the house or steal something, then he would be prowling.

QUESTIONS FOR REVIEW AND DISCUSSION

1. Questions on s.143, Rape:
   a. What are the essential elements of the crime of rape?
   b. Must physical or mental harm be done to the female for rape to occur?
   c. Can only men be convicted on a charge of rape?
   d. Can a husband rape his wife?
   e. Can a husband ever be convicted on a charge of raping his wife?
   f. What does s.143(b)(iii) mean?
2. Questions on s.146(1), Sexual intercourse with females under the age of 14:
   a. What are the essential elements of this offence?
   b. Which, if any, of the following are defences?
      (1) the female consents to the act.
      (2) the female's parents consent.
      (3) the female claims she was over 14 and she looked over 14.
      (4) the female was not of chaste character.
      (5) the female seduces the man.
3. Questions on s.146(2), Sexual intercourse with females between the ages of 14 and 16:
   a. What are the essential elements of this offence?
   b. Which, if any, of the following are defences?
      (1) the female consents.
      (2) the female looks and says she is older than 16.
      (3) the girl seduces the man.
      (4) the accused is under 14 years of age.
   c. Could a woman be convicted under this section or s.146(1)?
4. Questions on s.149, Indecent Assault:
   a. What are the essential elements of this offence?
   b. Is it a specific intent crime? See *R. v. Schmidt and Gole* (1972) 9 C.C.C. (2d) 101.
   c. Can a woman be convicted under this section?
   d. Problem: A man passes himself off as a doctor and performs an intimate physical examination of a woman who consented to the examination thinking the man was a doctor. The examination consists of nothing more than what a doctor would ordinarily do. Is this indecent assault?
   e. Problem: A man grabs a girl walking down the street and offers her $45.00 if she will have sexual intercourse with him. Is this indecent assault?

5. Questions on s.151, Seduction of a female between the ages of 16 and 18:
   a. What are the essential elements of this offence?
   b. Is it a defence that:
      1. the accused later marries the female?
      2. the female is married at the time of the seduction?
   c. Who has the onus of showing the male is older than 18?
   d. How is seduction different from rape?
6. Questions on s.152, Seduction on promise of marriage:
   a. What are the essential elements of this offence?
   b. Problem: X promises to marry a girl, 17, if she becomes pregnant. Because of this promise, the girl has sexual intercourse with X. Does s.152 apply? See *R. v. Seymour* (1931) 57 C.C.C. 95 (Sask).
   c. Is it a defence that the accused later married the victim?
7. Questions on s.157, Gross Indecency:
   a. What are the essential elements of this offence?
   b. What is a public place?
   c. Problem: A man sends notes to another man suggesting that they perform a grossly indecent act. The two of them agreed to meet to commit the act in one of their homes. Both men were over 21. Can they be charged with gross indecency? See *R. v. Bishop* (1970) 5 C.C.C. 387.
8. Why is it easier to convict a publisher of obscene material than a seller of obscene material?
9. What is the definition of obscenity? Do you think the definition is a good one? Explain.
10. What is the defence of the public good?
11. What is an indecent performance? an immoral performance?
12. What are the essential elements of the offence of causing a disturbance? What is a disturbance?
13. For a charge under s.171(a)(i) involving shouting, does it matter what words are shouted?
14. What is the difference between loitering and prowling in s.173?

---

[1] (1947) 87 C.C.C. 236, 3 C.R. 31 (Ont.C.A.).
[2] (1935) 64 C.C.C. 104 (N.B.C.A.).
[3] (1957) 118 C.C.C. 219, 26 C.R. 167 (Ont.C.A.).
[4] (1944) 81 C.C.C. 4 (Sask.C.A.).
[5] (1961) 130 C.C.C. 158, 34 C.R. 380 (Ont.C.A.).
[6] (1962) 39 C.R. 242 (B.C.C.A.).
[7] s.140
[8] (1948), 91 C.C.C. 59, 5 C.R. 320 (Ont.C.A.).
[9] s.139(3).
[10] s.139(4).
[11] *R. v. Royal,* (1970) 1 C.C.C. 272 (Ont.C.A.).
[12] (1914), 23 C.C.C. 250 (Ont.C.A.).
[13] (1967) 3 C.C.C. 294, 2 C.R.N.S. 40 (S.C.C.).
[14] *R. v. Gaselle,* (1934), 62 C.C.C. 295 (Sask.C.A.).
[15] *R. v. P.* (1968) 3 C.R.N.S. 302 (Man.C.A.).

[16] (1970) 3 C.C.C. 260 (Alta.C.A.).
[17] (1970), 15 C.R.N.S. 106 (Ont.C.A.).
[18] (1968) 1 C.C.C. 265 (N.B.C.A.).
[19] For a discussion of what constitutes prostitution, see Chapter Eight.
[20] (1972) 19 C.R.N.S. 289 (Ont.)
[21] (1973) 11 C.C.C. (2d) 28, 21 C.R.N.S. 121 (B.C.)
[22] (1974) 17 C.C.C. (2d) 555 (B.C.).
[23] (1912) 20 C.C.C. 85 (Ont.C.A.).
[24] (1966) 4 C.C.C. 273, 49 C.R. 49 (Ont.C.A.); Aff'd (1967) 2 C.C.C. 195, 1 C.R.N. S227 (S.C.C.).
[25] *R. v. Hicklin* (1868), L.R. 3 Q.B. 360 (Eng.).
[26] (1962) 37 C.R. 120 (S.C.C.).
[27] See Fox, R.G., "Obscenity", (1974) 12 Alberta Law Review 1972 and Barnett, C.S., "Obscenity and s.150(8) of the Criminal Code", (1969) 12 Criminal Law Quarterly 10.
[28] (1964) 3 C.C.C. 1, 42 C.R. 209 (S.C.C.).
[29] (1963) 2 C.C.C. 103, 40 C.R. 109 (Man.C.A.).
[30] *Supra,* note 25.
[31] *Supra,* note 27.
[32] *Supra,* note 23.
[33] (1970) 10 C.R.N.S. 42 (Man.C.A.).
[34] *R. v. American News Co. Ltd.* (1957), 118 C.C.C. 152 (Ont.C.A.).
[35] (1973), 23 C.R.N.S. 273 (S.C.C.).
[36] (1973), 12 C.C.C. (2d) 145 (B.C.C.A.).
[37] (1947) 4 D.L.R. 748 (N.B.C.A.).
[38] (1970), 1 C.C.C. (2d) 232 (B.C.C.A.).
[39] (1973), 13 C.C.C. (2d) 206, 22 C.R.N.S. 326 (N.B.C.A.).
[40] (1960), 33 C.R. 213 (B.C.C.A.).

Chapter Eight

Disorderly Houses, Betting And Lotteries

A. DISORDERLY HOUSES

"Disorderly house" is a general term which refers to a common bawdy-house, a common gaming house or a common betting house. It is an offence to "keep" a disorderly house, to be "found in" a disorderly house or to "knowingly permit" a place to be used as a disorderly house. A keeper is defined in s.179:

> **179. "Keeper" includes a person who:**
> **(a) is an owner or occupier of a place,**
> **(b) assists or acts on behalf of an owner or occupier of a place,**
> **(c) appears to be, or to assist or act on behalf of an owner or occupier of a place,**
> **(d) has the care or management of a place, or**
> **(e) uses a place permanently or temporarily, with or without the consent of the owner or occupier.**

The Supreme Court of Canada has held that simply falling within the definition above is not enough to be convicted of "keeping" a disorderly house. In general, a person must participate in the wrongful use of the disorderly house to be a keeper. There must be something more than simply being the owner or manager of a place which someone else uses as a disorderly house.[1]

If a person is "found in" a disorderly house, then it is up to him to show some evidence that he had a lawful excuse for being there. For example, a furnace repairman would have a lawful excuse if he were repairing the furnace in the house.

If the owner or someone else having charge or control of a place is charged with "knowingly permitting" the place to be used as a disorderly house, he will be found guilty only if he had knowledge of how the place was being used. For example, a landlord may not know that one of his apartments is being used for illegal betting.

Each of the types of disorderly houses will be discussed separately.

1. Common Bawdy-House

A common bawdy-house is defined in s.179(1):

> **179.(1) "common bawdy-house" means a place that is**
> **(a) kept or occupied, or**
> **(b) resorted to by one or more persons for the purpose of prostitution or the practice of acts of indecency.**

Offences regarding bawdy-houses are stated in s.193:

> **193.(1) Every one who keeps a common bawdy-house is guilty of an indictable offence and is liable to imprisonment for two years.**
> **(2) Every one who**
> **(a) is an inmate of a common bawdy-house,**
> **(b) is found, without lawful excuse, in a common bawdy-house, or**
> **(c) as owner, landlord, lessor, tenant, occupier, agent or otherwise having charge or control of any place, knowingly permits the place or any part thereof to be let or used for the purposes of a common bawdy-house,**
> **is guilty of an offence punishable on summary conviction.**

One isolated act of prostitution is not enough to make a place a bawdy-house. There must be frequent resort to, or habitual use of, the place for purposes of prostitution or indecent acts.

In *Paterson v. R.*[2] two women went with three plain-clothed police officers to a suburban home for the purpose of prostitution. After their arrival, the two women went to another part of the house and later returned wearing nothing but their underwear. At this point, the officers disclosed their identity and charged them with keeping a common bawdy-house. The Supreme Court of Canada held that to be convicted of "keeping," it is necessary that there be a frequent or habitual use of the premises for the purposes of prostitution. The court found the women not guilty because there was no evidence that the home had been used for prostitution on any other occasion.

A similar decision was reached in *R. v. Evans, Lee and Woodhouse,*[3] which involved a house being used for a stag party. Three women had sexual intercourse with a number of men at the party and were paid for their services. The house had never been used before for prostitution. The issue was whether the large number of acts of intercourse which occurred in one evening were enough to convict the women and two male occupants of keeping a common bawdy-house. The court held that they were not guilty because the use of the house on one evening did not amount to frequent or habitual use of the premises for prostitution.

It is also necessary that for a place to be a bawdy-house, the acts of prostitution or indecency must be physically performed there. In *R. v. Equigaray,*[4] a prostitute received telephone calls at her apartment from customers but she always met them on the street. Then, she and the customers would go to a hotel. The prostitute was charged with keeping her residence as a common bawdy-house. She was found not guilty because the acts of prostitution did not take place there.

The meaning of "acts of indecency" was considered in *R. v. Laliberte.*[5] The court defined an indecent act as one that offends the general standards that decency permits. In this case, masturbation performed by a masseuse on the customers of a massage parlour was considered an act of indecency. Thus, the massage parlour was a common bawdy-house.

"Prostitution" is not defined in the Code but it has been given a wide meaning by the courts. In *R. v. Lantay,*[6] the Ontario Court of Appeal held that prostitution is not limited to sexual intercourse. It includes a woman offering herself for money as a participant in physical acts of indecency for the sexual gratification of men. This case also involved masturbation performed on customers of a massage parlour. The court held that the operator of the massage parlour was guilty of keeping a common bawdy-house because it was being resorted to for the purpose of prostitution.

Other cases have decided that it is not necessary that there be monetary payment for prostitution to take place. In *R. v. Turkiewich*[7] a hotel registration clerk was charged with knowingly permitting the hotel premises to be used for purposes of a common bawdy-house [s.193(2)(c)]. The clerk argued that because there was no evidence that money had been paid to any woman, prostitution was not proven. The court disagreed and said that prostitution must be interpreted to include illicit or promiscuous sexual relations whether these relations take place for payment or not.

2. Common Gaming House

> **185.(1) Everyone who keeps a common gaming house or common betting house is guilty of an indictable offence and liable to imprisonment for two years.**
> **(2) Everyone who**
> **(a) is found, without lawful excuse, in a common gaming house or common betting house, or,**
> **(b) as owner, landlord, lessor, tenant, occupier or agent, knowingly permits a place to be let or used for the purposes of a common gaming house or common betting house,**
> **is guilty of an offence punishable on summary conviction.**

"Common gaming house" is defined in s.179(1):

> **179.(1) Common gaming house means a place that is**

(a) **kept for gain to which persons resort for the purpose of playing games, or**
(b) **kept or used for the purpose of playing games**
  (i) **in which a bank is kept by one or more but not all of the players,**
  (ii) **in which all or any portion of the bets on or proceeds from a game is paid, directly or indirectly, to the keeper of the place,**
  (iii) **in which, directly or indirectly, a fee is charged to or paid by the players for the privilege of playing or participating in a game or using gaming equipment, or**
  (iv) **in which the chances of winning are not equally favourable to all persons who play the game, including the person, if any, who conducts the game.**

A. "GAME" "Game" means a game of chance or mixed chance and skill [s.179(1)]. A game of chance is one in which luck entirely determines the winner. A game of mixed chance and skill is one in which the element of luck prevails despite the skill of the players.[8] In *R. v. Ross,*[9] it was decided that the card game of bridge is a game of mixed chance and skill. Even though the main ingredients of the game involve the use of skill, the players can only use their skill after the cards have been dealt. The court decided that the chance involved in the dealing of the cards was so important to the game that bridge would have to be considered a game of mixed chance and skill. In *R. v. Lebansky,*[10] target shooting at a miniature shooting range was considered to be a game of skill and not a game of chance. Although some element of chance was involved, it was too small to justify classifying the game as one of mixed chance and skill. In *R. v. McGee,*[11] the game of bingo was held to be a game of chance.

B. TYPES OF GAMING HOUSES There are two types of gaming houses mentioned in the definition of "common gaming house." In part (a) the important feature is that the house is kept for a profit. If a place is used for the playing of games involving chance and the place is kept for a profit, then it is a common gaming house. Under part (a), it does not matter that the games may be harmless and that money may not be wagered. On the other hand in part (b), the important feature is the type of game involved. If the game includes one of the elements mention in (i) – (iv), then the place is a common gaming house, even if the keeper of the house makes no profit.[12]

C. "KEPT FOR GAIN" Under paragraph (a) of the definition of common gaming house, it is necessary that the place is "kept for gain" (or profit). In *R. v. James,*[13] the accused was the manager of a cigar shop. In the rear of the shop was a room in which poker games were played. Out of the stakes which were bet during the games, a small amount of money was set aside to cover the cigars and refreshments consumed by the players. The court decided that the increased profits of the business derived from the sale of cigars and refreshments were a "gain" and the accused was guilty of keeping a common gaming house. A similar case, *R. v. Forder,*[14] involved the players in a poker game paying a small sum each half hour to the accused for a new pack of cards. The accused made a large profit in this way and the court held that he was guilty of keeping a common gaming house. It seems that these two cases would also fit within paragraph (b)(ii) of the definition of common gaming house because a portion of the bets was paid to the keeper of the place in each of the cases.

D. "BANK" A place is also a gaming house if it is kept or used for the purpose of playing games in which a "bank" is kept by one or more but not all of the players. In *R. v. Rubenstein,*[15] the accused was charged with keeping a common gaming house in that he was a banker in a game of blackjack played on a picnic table in a public park. A "bank" was defined as the sum of money which the dealer or banker has as a fund from which to draw the stakes and pay his losses, or the pile of money which the player who plays against all the other players has before him. The accused claimed that, at the time the police interfered, he was only taking his turn at the bank and so did not come within the terms of the definition of a common gaming house. However, during the time that the police watched, the deal went completely around three times and the bank did not change hands. The court found that the accused was running a bank which was "kept by one or more but not all of the players." The court also felt that if the bank had been passed around, the offence would not have been committed.

E. "PLACE" In *Rubenstein,* the accused also argued that he should not be convicted because the "place" where the game was played was a picnic table in a public park. The court held that he should be convicted because the table fell within the definition of "place" in s.179(1). It was not necessary that it be a room or building because the definition includes places which are not "covered or enclosed" and which are used by persons who do not have "an exclusive right of use." The accused also fell within the definition of "keeper" because he was a person using the place "temporarily with or without the consent of the owner or occupier."

F. "BONA FIDE SOCIAL CLUB" An exception to the definition of common gaming house is found in s.179(2):

> **179.(2) A place is not a common gaming house within the meaning of paragraph (a) or subparagraph (b)(ii) or (iii) of the definition "common gaming house" in subsection (1) while it is occupied and used by an incorporated *bona fide* social club or branch thereof, if**
>
> **(a) the whole or any portion of the bets on or proceeds from games played therein is not directly or indirectly paid to the keeper thereof, and,**
>
> **(b) no fee is charged to persons for the right or privilege of participating in the games played therein other than under the authority of and in accordance with the terms of a licence issued by the Attorney General of the province in which the place is situated or by such other person or authority in the province as may be specified by the Attorney General thereof.**

In general, a social club is a group of people who get together for a social purpose (e.g. playing games), not for the purpose of making a profit. In *R. v. MacDonald et al.*,[16] a secretary-manager of the Royal Canadian Legion was charged with keeping a common gaming house. The defence was that the Legion was a *bona fide* (real or legitimate) social club and fell within the exception in s.179(2). Members of the public wishing to play bingo were admitted upon payment of a 50-cent admission fee. In order to participate in prize money, an additional 50 cents was paid. The Legion kept only the admission fees and the other money was returned as prizes to the winning players. The Supreme Court of Canada decided that admission of the public, for a fee, was not occupation and use by a *bona fide* social club. The court went on to say: "It is unnecessary to go into the objects (or purposes) of the Canadian Legion . . . . The use of these premises on such a widespread scale contradicts any possible inference of the use as a *bona fide* social club."

There does not seem to be one single test for determining whether or not a place is being used by a *bona fide* social club. In the *MacDonald* case above, the admission of the general public for a fee on a widespread scale was an important factor in the court's decision that it was not being used by a *bona fide* social club. In *R. v. Tatti*,[17] the Ontario Court of Appeal referred to a *bona fide* social club as a club which is owned and controlled by all members equally. In that case, the accused was the manager of a recreation club which was used for playing card games, ping-pong and billiards. The court held that the exception for social clubs did not apply in the case because the club was owned and controlled completely by the accused. Other courts have taken into account whether or not the social objects or purposes of the club are really being carried out and whether or not non-members are allowed to play the games. However, in *Re Mow Chong Social Club*,[18] the Ontario Court of Appeal decided that the mere fact that a non-member was able to enter the club and that only some of the purposes of the club were being carried out, did not necessarily mean that a club was not a *bona fide* social club.

Even if a place is being used by an incorporated *bona fide* social club, it may still be considered a common gaming house if there is a violation of s.179(2)(a) or (b) which prohibit payments to the keeper from bets on or proceeds from the games and unauthorized fees charged to the players of the games.

3. Common Betting House

Section 179(1) contains the following definitions:

> **179.(1) "Common betting house" means a place that is opened, kept or used for the purpose of:**
> **(a) enabling, encouraging or assisting persons who resort thereto to bet between themselves or with the keeper, or**
> **(b) enabling any person to receive, record, register, transmit or pay bets or to announce the results of betting.**
> **"Bet" means a bet that is placed on any contingency or event that is to take place in or out of Canada, and . . .includes a bet that is placed on any contingency relating to a horse-race, fight, match or sporting event that is to take place in or out of Canada.**

It should be remembered that s.185, mentioned earlier, applies to both gaming houses and betting houses. Therefore, it is an offence to "keep", be "found in", or "knowingly permit" a place to be used as, a common betting house.

The recording of one bet is not enough in itself to make a place a common betting house. In *R. v. Weidman,* [19] the accused was the operator of a small store which sold newspapers, magazines and cigarettes. There was proof that one or two bets had been made at the store. The B.C. Court of Appeal held that there must be proof that the place is opened, kept, or used for the purpose of betting. This could be proved by one bet if there were other surrounding circumstances which showed that the place was kept for that purpose. In this case, these other circumstances did not exist and the accused was found not guilty of keeping a common betting house.

In *R. v. Woodward and Willcocks,* [20] a newspaper office was held to be a common betting house and the editor and business manager of the paper were convicted of "keeping." The newspaper operated a guessing contest in which the contestants paid a fee and tried to guess the results of football games. Prizes were awarded to the top three contestants. The prize money was taken from the fees paid by the contestants. This type of contest falls within the definition of "bet" because the contestants were betting among themselves "on a contingency relating to a sporting event."

There have been some interesting, but unsuccessful, attempts to evade the law against betting houses. In *R. v. Johnston,* [21] the accused was a barber who would step outside his barber shop and into the street to accept bets. The court held that the street was a "place" used for betting and, thus, was a common betting house. In *R. v. Osborne,* [22] a betting scheme was used which involved a bank, a telegraph office and an office where bets were paid. The person betting deposited his money in the bank and got a receipt. He then took the receipt to the telegraph office and a message placing his money on a certain horse was sent to a person in the United States who placed the bet on a race in that country. The race results were announced at the telegraph office and if the bettor won, he went to a third place where he was paid. The accused was the telegraph operator and he was convicted of keeping a common betting house because the telegraph office was used for the purpose of betting.

Operators of off-track betting shops have been charged with keeping common betting houses. These shops, other betting offences and certain types of legal betting will be discussed in part B of this chapter.

4. Presumptions

Section 180 creates certain presumptions in regard to disorderly houses:

A. OBSTRUCTION OF A PEACE OFFICER

    180.(1) In proceedings under this Part
    (a) evidence that a peace officer who was authorized to enter a place was wilfully prevented from entering or was wilfully

obstructed or delayed in entering is, in the absence of any
evidence to the contrary, proof that the place is a disorderly
house;

For example, in *Ewaschuk v. R.*,[23] a police officer came to the door of a house
with a search warrant. A woman opened the door slightly and, realizing that it was a
police officer, slammed and locked the door. By this action, she was wilfully
obstructing and delaying the officer, who was authorized to enter the house.
Because there was no evidence to show that the place was not a disorderly house,
the woman's action was enough for the court to decide that it was such a house.

B. GAMING EQUIPMENT

**180.(1)(b) evidence that a place was found to be equipped
with gaming equipment [anything that may be used for playing
games of chance or betting] or any device for concealing,
removing or destroying gaming equipment is, in the absence of
any evidence to the contrary, proof that the place is a common
gaming house or a common betting house, as the case may be;**
  **(c) evidence that gaming equipment was found in a place
entered under a warrant issued pursuant to this Part, or on or
about the person of anyone found therein, is, in the absence of
any evidence to the contrary, proof that the place is a common
gaming house and that the persons found therein were playing
games, whether or not any person acting under the warrant
observed any person playing games therein.**

For example, in *R. v. Achilles*,[24] there was evidence that a place was set up with
forty-eight chairs and eight card tables and other tables on which were cards, score
sheets and pencils. The court said that these items were gaming equipment and were
there for the purpose of playing a game of chance or mixed chance and skill. This
was enough evidence for the court to presume that the place was a common
gaming house. The accused did not testify and no evidence was given on their
behalf. In other words, the presumption was not rebutted and, thus, evidence of the
gaming equipment was considered proof that the place was a common gaming
house.

C. EVIDENCE OF CONVICTION

**180.(1)(d) evidence that a person was convicted of keeping a
disorderly house is, for the purpose of proceedings against
anyone who is alleged to have been an inmate or to have been
found in that house at the time the person committed the offence
of which he was convicted, in the absence of any evidence to the
contrary, proof that the house was, at that time, a disorderly
house.**

For example, John is convicted of keeping a common betting house. Jim was found in John's place during the time John was keeping it as a betting house. Jim is later charged with the offence of being "found in" a common betting house. At Jim's trial, John's conviction will be proof that the place was a common betting house unless there is some evidence at the trial to show that it was not.

D. SLOT MACHINES

> **180.(2) For the purpose of proceedings under this Part, a place that is found to be equipped with a slot machine shall be conclusively presumed to be a common gaming house.**

In general, a slot machine refers to a machine which provides goods or amusement and which involves some element of chance. However, pinball machines are not considered slot machines if the only prize that can be won is one or more free games [s.180(3)].

B. OTHER BETTING OFFENCES

Section 186(1) creates several betting offences which do not require the existence of a common gaming house or common betting house. These include: (a) knowingly allowing a place to be used for recording or registering bets or selling a pool; (b) keeping a gambling or betting machine; (c) being the custodian of a wager; (d) recording or registering bets; (e) engaging in bookmaking or in the business of betting; (f) printing or providing bookmaking information; (g) importing bookmaking information; (h) advertising an offer to bet on a contest; (i) wilfully and knowingly sending betting or bookmaking information; (j) aiding or assisting in committing any of these offences.

Section 188(1) states that the above offences and the offences pertaining to common gaming houses and common betting houses do *not* apply to the holder of any money which is to be paid to: (i) the winner of a lawful race, sport, game or exercise, (ii) the owner of a horse engaged in a lawful race, or (iii) the winner of any bets between not more than ten individuals. Also exempted are private bets between individuals not engaged in the business of betting and bets made through the agency of the pari-mutuel system at a horse-race course if the betting system and the race course are operated according to the provisions in s.188. Briefly, in a pari-mutuel system winners divide the total amount bet on a race between themselves in proportion to their wagers.

1. Betting as a Business

To be engaged in the business of betting [s.186(1)(e)] there must be more than a single or isolated act of betting. There must be a repetition or series of acts of betting. Also, it is not necessary that the accused receives a fee or makes a profit. In *R. v. Hynes,*[25] the accused made bets for a friend with a book-maker. He also collected any winnings from the bets and took them to his friend. He performed this service on a regular basis for at least six months. There was no evidence that the accused received payment from either the friend or the book-maker. The court convicted him of engaging in the business of betting.

2. Off-Track Betting Shops

Under s.187, it is a specific offence to place even a single or isolated bet on behalf of another person, if it is done for a fee. In addition, off-track betting shops are made illegal:

> **187. Every one who**
> **(a) places or offers or agrees to place a bet on behalf of another person for a consideration paid or to be paid by or on behalf of that other person,**
> **(b) engages in the business or practice of placing or agreeing to place bets on behalf of other persons, whether for a consideration or otherwise, or,**
> **(c) holds himself out or allows himself to be held out as engaging in the business or practice of placing or agreeing to place bets on behalf of other persons, whether for a consideration or otherwise, is guilty of an indictable offence ....**

The offences in s.187 are basically similar to the offence of engaging in the business of betting [s.186(1)(e)]. The main difference is that s.187 specifically prohibits off-track betting shops. These shops receive money from customers and, for a fee, wager the money for them at the race track. This practice does not constitute engaging in the business of betting, contrary to s.186(1)(e), because it falls within s.188(1)(c) which says that s.186 offences do not apply to bets made through a pari-mutuel system at a race track (see above).

In order to stop the operation of these shops, Parliament, in 1969, enacted part (a) of s.187. Part (a) prohibits any person from placing a bet for another person for a fee (i.e. consideration). This is outside the exception of s.188(1)(c), so it includes fees for placing bets for others at the race track. However, under part (a) there remained the possibility that off-track betting shops still might legally evade the restriction if they could collect a fee indirectly, so that it did not appear to be a fee for placing bets. By enacting s.187(b) and (c) in 1976, Parliament removed this possibility by making it an offence to be in the business or practice of placing bets, regardless of whether or not a fee is paid. Thus, it is now clear that off-track betting shops are illegal. However, under s.187, it seems that it is still legal for an individual to place a bet at the race track for someone else, as long as he does not receive a fee or make a business or practice of placing bets for others.

C. LOTTERIES AND OTHER SCHEMES

1. Lotteries

A lottery is a scheme for giving a prize by some method of chance, such as drawing numbered tickets from a container. In s.189, a lottery is referred to as "any proposal, scheme or plan for advancing, lending, giving, selling or in any way disposing of any property by lots, cards, tickets, or any mode of chance whatever." Section 189(1) covers several offences involving lotteries, including: (a) advertising or publishing a lottery; (b) selling or otherwise disposing of lottery tickets; (c) knowingly sending articles which are intended for use in a lottery; and (d) conducting or managing a lottery.

For a lottery to exist, it is essential that the prize ("property") be disposed of by some method of chance. If any skill is involved, then there is no lottery. Because of this rule, many contests include a "skill-testing question" which must be answered before the prize is awarded. However, some lotteries are permitted. In general, s.190(1) provides that a lottery scheme may be conducted and managed by: (a) the government of Canada or (b) the government of a province. Also, if licenced by the provincial government, lotteries may be conducted and managed by: (a) a charitable or religious organization, (b) an agricultural fair or exhibition, and (c) any person at a public place of amusement.

2. Other Schemes

Section 189(1)(e) covers other schemes and games which are not lotteries because they do not involve giving a prize by some method of chance. In brief, it prohibits the conduct or management of any scheme by which a person upon paying an amount of money becomes entitled to receive something of greater monetary value because of the contributions of others to the scheme. In *Dream Home Contests Ltd. v. R.,*[26] the accused were charged with operating such a scheme. They built a house called a "Dream Home" which was put on display to the public. Contestants had to buy a one-dollar ticket and had to estimate the total retail value of the Dream Home. The contestant who most closely estimated the total retail value of the home would win the home. In other words, the winning contestant became entitled to a home which was of much greater value than the amount he paid ($1.00). Giving away such a valuable prize was only made possible by the fact that so many other contestants "contributed to the scheme" (i.e. bought tickets). Therefore, the requirements of the offence were present and the accused were found guilty. The accused were also charged with advertising a lottery, contrary to s.189(1)(a). However, the accused were not guilty of this offence because the contest was not a lottery since it did not involve giving a prize by some method of chance. In other words, estimating the value of the house was considered to involve skill.

Section 189(1)(e) also covers pyramid selling schemes which operate like chain letters. In *R. v. Cote,*[27] the accused was an officer of the company known as Dare To Be Great of Canada Ltd. The Company's operation involved selling a course to persons at a cost of $1,500. The Company claimed that the objective of the course was to strengthen the personality of the subscriber (or "member"), to improve his self-confidence and to make him more successful in his occupation. The subscriber also received a suitcase containing a tape recorder, cassettes and other materials which had a total value of $100. After completing the course, the subscriber became a sales agent (or "motivator") and received a commission of $900 for every sale of the course to a new subscriber. Each of these new subscribers also had to pay $1,500 for the course. In turn, these new subscribers became sales agents after completing the course. The court held that this scheme fell within s.189(1)(e) because it was a means by which a person, upon paying $1,500, became entitled to receive from the Dare To Be Great company a larger sum of money than that which he paid himself by recruiting new members who, in turn, paid a certain amount of money.

The remaining paragraphs of s.189(1) are reasonably clear:

> **189.(1) Every one is guilty of an indictable offence and is liable to imprisonment for two years who ...**
>
> **(f) disposes of any goods, wares or merchandise by any game of chance or any game of mixed chance and skill in which the contestant or competitor pays money or other valuable consideration;**
>
> **(g) induces any person to stake or hazard any money or other valuable property or thing on the result of any dice game, three-card monte, punch board, coin table or on the operation of a wheel of fortune;**
>
> **(h) for valuable consideration carries on or plays or offers to carry on or to play, or employs any person to carry on or play in a public place or a place to which the public have access, the game of three-card monte;**
>
> **(i) receives bets of any kind on the outcome of a game of three-card monte; or**
>
> **(j) being the owner of a place, permits any person to play the game of three-card monte therein.**

Three-card monte is a card game in which a person tries to guess the location of one playing card among a total of three.

QUESTIONS FOR REVIEW AND DISCUSSION

1. Name the three types of disorderly houses.
2. Name three offences which can be committed in relation to a disorderly house.

3. Explain the meaning of "prostitution" and "acts of indecency" in the definition of common bawdy-house.
4. What are the two types of common gaming houses?
5. What is the meaning of "game"?
6. What is a *"bona fide* social club"?
7. What is a common betting house?
8. Give two examples of legal betting.
9. What are the essential elements of a lottery?
10. As part of a grand scheme for making money, D rents three houses and hires several prostitutes. The Red House is rented from A and is to be used for "group sex orgies" among customers and prostitutes. A agrees to let D use the house for this purpose. The Pink House is rented from B and is to be used for "private sex". The plan is for each room in the house to be used by one prostitute and one customer. B has no knowledge that the place is to be used for this purpose. The Purple House is rented from C and is to be used as a meeting place for prostitutes and "cautious" customers. After meeting at the house, the plan is for D to take the customer and the prostitute in C's car to a secluded location for the purpose of having sexual intercourse in the back seat. D and C agree to split the proceeds from this operation.

    The Purple House and the Pink House operate for several weeks before the opening of the Red House and prove to be very profitable. On the opening night of the Red House, all three houses are raided by the police and D, a customer, and a prostitute are arrested in C's car. The following charges result: (1) D is charged with keeping four common bawdy-houses: the three houses and the car; (2) A, B, and C are charged with permitting their places to be used as common bawdy-houses; (3) the prostitutes and customers are charged with being found in a common bawdy-house. On which charges should there be convictions? Why?
11. A operates a shooting range and charges a $2.00 admission fee. The most accurate shooter on any day wins a free admission. Is A guilty of keeping a common gaming house? Why?
12. A is charged with keeping a common betting house. The only evidence presented at the trial is that a slot machine was found in A's basement. Should A be convicted? Why?
13. A, B, C and D enjoy betting on horse races. Because C lives near the track, he places bets for himself, A, B and D each week during the racing season. Is C guilty of an offence? Why? Does it matter that C received no fee for placing the bets? Why?

[1] *R. v. Kerin,* (1963) 1 C.C.C. 233, 39 C.R. 390 (S.C.C.)
[2] (1968) 2 C.C.C. 247, 3 C.R.N.S. 23 (S.C.C.)
[3] (1973), 11 C.C.C. (2d) 130, 22 C.R.N.S. 32 (Ont.C.A.)
[4] (1971), 15 C.R.N.S. 58 (Que.C.A.)
[5] (1973), 12 C.C.C. (2d) 109 (Que.C.A.).
[6] (1965) 3 C.C.C. 170 (Ont.C.A.).
[7] (1962), 113 C.C.C. 301, 38 C.R. 220 (Man.C.A.)
[8] *R. v. Fortier* (1903), 7 C.C.C. 417 (Que.C.A.).
[9] (1968) 1 C.C.C. 261, 2 C.R.N.S. 185 (Ont.C.A.).
[10] (1941), 75 C.C.C. 348 (Man.C.A.).
[11] (1942), 77 C.C.C., 302 (Man.C.A.).
[12] *R. v. Hing Hoy* (1917), 28 C.C.C. 299 (Alta.C.A.).
[13] (1903), 7 C.C.C. 196 (Ont.C.A.).
[14] (1930), 54 C.C.C. 388 (Ont.C.A.).
[15] (1960), 32 C.R. 20 (Ont.C.A.).
[16] (1966), 47 C.R. 37 (S.C.C.).
[17] (1965) 4 C.C.C. 268, 47 C.R. 59 (Ont.C.A.).
[18] (1964), 47 C.R. 295 (Ont.C.A.)
[19] (1954), 108 C.C.C. 89, 18 C.R. 164 (B.C.C.A.).
[20] (1922), 38 C.C.C. 154 (Man.C.A.).
[21] (1910), 16 C.C.C. 379 (Ont.C.A.).
[22] (1895), 27 OR 185 (C.A.).
[23] (1955), 111 C.C.C. 377, (Man.C.A.).
[24] (1972), 6 C.C.C. (2d) 274 (Ont.C.A.).
[25] (1919), 31 C.C.C. 293 (Ont.C.A.)
[26] (1960), 33 C.R. 47 (S.C.C.).
[27] (1973), 11 C.C.C. (2d) 443 (Que.C.A.).

Chapter Nine

Homicide and The Offences of Murder, Manslaughter And Infanticide

A. HOMICIDE

Homicide is defined in s.205 of the Code as follows:

> **205.(1) A person commits homicide when, directly or indirectly, by any means, he causes the death of a human being.**
>
> **(2) Homicide is culpable or not culpable.**
>
> **(3) Homicide that is not culpable is not an offence.**
>
> **(4) Culpable homicide is murder or manslaughter, or infanticide.**
>
> **(5) A person commits culpable homicide when he causes the death of a human being,**
>
> **(a) by means of an unlawful act,**
>
> **(b) by criminal negligence,**
>
> **(c) by causing that human being, by threats or fear of violence or by deception, to do anything that causes his death, or**
>
> **(d) by wilfully frightening that human being, in the case of a child or sick person.**

Whenever a person causes the death of another person, he commits homicide. There are, however, two types of homicide, *culpable* and *non-culpable*. Only culpable homicide is a criminal offence.

Culpable homicide consists of three offences: murder, manslaughter and infanticide. Murder is the most serious type of culpable homicide. Generally speaking, the difference between murder and manslaughter is that murder requires a specific intent (e.g. to cause a person's death), while manslaughter is a general intent crime. So, for example, A is angry at his child B and beats the child severely. B dies from the beating. If it is clear that A did not specifically intend to cause B's death but only had the general intention to do the act of beating, he will probably be charged with manslaughter and not with murder. In contrast to murder and manslaughter, infanticide is a rarely used offence which only applies to certain situations involving newborn children.

Before deciding whether a death involves murder, manslaughter or infanticide, it is first necessary to decide whether the homicide is culpable or non-culpable.

1. Non-Culpable Homicide

Non-culpable homicide can be divided into two types, *justifiable* and *excusable*. Homicide is justifiable if it is authorized or ordered by the law. Examples of justifiable homicide are: a soldier killing an enemy during wartime, the execution of a person sentenced to death, a police officer shooting a person in the course of duty. In these situations, the law may either require the killing as when a death penalty is imposed or it may permit a killing as when a police officer finds it necessary to kill someone.

A homicide may be excusable where a person is forced to defend himself, those under his protection, or his property. Some of these excuses are discussed in Chapter Four on Defences. It is pointed out in that chapter that to rely on an excuse such as self-defence, the force used must be no more than that necessary to repel the attack. Homicide may also be excusable where it is caused accidentally. So, for example, where a person is doing a lawful act and unintentionally and without negligence kills another person, the death is considered accidental and no criminal liability will be attached. However, as will be discussed more fully later, if a person is doing an unlawful act and accidentally causes a death, the homicide will be culpable.

2. Culpable Homicide

Section 205(5) lists the methods by which culpable homicide can be committed:

205.(5)(a) by means of an unlawful act.
(b) by criminal negligence,
(c) by causing that human being, by threats or fear of violence or by deception, to do anything that causes his death, or
(d) by wilfully frightening that human being, in the case of a child or a sick person.

A. BY AN UNLAWFUL ACT One question which arises under s.205(5)(a) is, what is meant by an "unlawful act"? Does it refer only to criminal acts or does it include the breaking of any law, provincial, municipal or otherwise?

The law distinguishes two types of unlawful acts; those which are *malum in se,* or wrong in themselves, such as assault and murder, and those which are *malum prohibitum,* or wrong only because they are prohibited by law, such as parking regulations or laws passed for the purpose of raising revenue, (e.g. certain licensing laws). Unlawful acts which are *malum in se* are considered morally wrong while an act which is only *malum prohibitum* does not have this aspect of moral wrongness. For example, when a person forgets to put a coin in a parking meter and receives a ticket, although he has broken the law, it is unlikely his conscience will be bothered since he has only violated a rule that is *malum prohibitum.*

Courts have held that where the unlawful act is merely *malum prohibitum* and is not designed to prevent injury to a person, the violation of the law cannot be the foundation for a charge of culpable homicide. For example, in *R. v. D'Angelo,* [1] the accused was a bootlegger who sold alcohol to two persons. The accused believed that he had sold grain alcohol, but, in fact, it was wood alcohol. Both purchasers died and the bootlegger was charged with manslaughter. The court held that although the accused had violated the *Ontario Temperance Act,* he had not committed an unlawful act of the type required for a charge of manslaughter. One judge who heard the case stated: "I am of the opinion that the *Ontario Temperance Act* is not in pith and substance an act designed and intended to prevent injury to the person by prohibiting the supplying or consumption of intoxicating liquor but is rather an Act designed and intended only to regulate or limit the consumption of intoxicating liquor by prohibiting its sale for beverage purposes . . . ." In other words, the unlawful act committed by the accused was only *malum prohibitum* and not designed to protect persons.

Another case which considered the issue of what the Code means by unlawful act is *R. v. Lawson.* [2] In this case, the accused and others were hunting illegally in a National Park, not dressed properly and using illegal soft-nosed bullets. The accused accidentally shot one of his companions and was charged with manslaughter. The court held that the purpose of the law that the accused had violated was to protect game, and that he had not violated a type of law which the Code would consider an unlawful act. The court stated:

> *. . .I think the proper conclusion is that 'unlawful act' within the meaning of the above section does not include acts which are merely* malum prohibita. *The act must itself be of a criminal nature, or prohibition must be for the protection of the public from a dangerous act or conduct or the act must be dangerous or wrong in itself. Acts which are not wrong or dangerous in themselves, and are merely regulations or passed for revenue purposes, or for the protection of game, are not within that class.*

B. CRIMINAL NEGLIGENCE Culpable homicide may also occur where a person's death has been caused by criminal negligence. The offences of criminal negligence were discussed in Chapter Ten. The definition of criminal negligence, which is set out in s.202, applies to criminal negligence under s.205(5)(b). It might be noticed that the offence of *causing death by criminal negligence* would cover the same facts as culpable homicide by criminal negligence (the offence would be manslaughter). This is a situation where two sections of the Code overlap.

C. THREATS OR FEAR OF VIOLENCE Another way of committing culpable homicide is by causing a person to do something, through threats, fear of violence or deception, which causes his death. An example of a case where the court said that there were facts from which a jury could find that the deceased acted through fear of violence is *R. v. Graves*.[3] In this case, the accused, along with others, and while intoxicated, trespassed on the victim's front lawn. The accused and his friends were using grossly offensive language and refused to leave when asked. The victim, his wife and others who had been sitting on the front porch eventually went into the house. After a time, the victim loaded his gun, went to the front of the house and asked the accused and his friends to leave. Instead of leaving, they rushed upon the victim. The victim used the gun as a club to ward off the attackers. The gun went off, killing the victim. The accused was charged with manslaughter.

D. FRIGHTENING A CHILD OR SICK PERSON It is also culpable homicide to cause a person's death, where he is a child or sick person, by wilfully frightening him. This provision should be read along with s.211.

> **211. No person commits culpable homicide where he causes the death of a human being:**
> **(a) by any influence on the mind alone, or**
> **(b) by any disorder or disease resulting from influence on the mind alone,**
> **but this section does not apply where a person causes the death of a child or sick person by wilfully frightening him.**

An example of a case where the court found that the death was caused by influence on the mind is *R. v. Howard*.[4] In this case, the accused and victim were travelling on a streetcar. The accused was trying to get off and the victim was in his way. The men began to argue and blows were exchanged. A few moments later, the victim became unconscious and then died. The medical evidence showed that the deceased had been an elderly man in poor physical condition. His arteries were weak and death was caused by a brain hemorrhage. The court found that the blows had not caused the hemorrhage but that death was a result of the anger and excitement which caused the artery to burst. In this situation, death was actually caused by influence on the mind. The charges against the accused were dismissed.

3. Special Provisions Regarding the Causing of Death

Sections 206 – 211 deal with special or unusual situations which may be relevant to determining whether a person has caused another person's death.

A. SECTION 206 Since homicide is the causing of the death of a *human being* it is important to know when, in the eyes of the criminal law, a human being comes into existence.

Section 206 states:

> **206.(1) A child becomes a human being within the meaning of this Act when it has completely proceeded, in a living state, from the body of its mother whether or not**
> **(a) it has breathed,**
> **(b) it has an independent circulation, or**
> **(c) the navel string is severed.**

Thus, according to the criminal law, a fetus (i.e. an unborn child) is not a human being. The section then goes on to state:

> **206.(2) A person commits homicide when he causes injury to a child before or during its birth as a result of which the child dies after becoming a human being.**

So, if a woman takes a drug for the purpose of producing a miscarriage and the child is born alive but later dies because of its premature birth, the woman would have committed not only attempted abortion but also homicide. If, however, the miscarriage produces a child who dies before it becomes a human being, the woman would have only committed the offence of abortion.

Section 221 should be considered along with s.206 since it covers certain situations where the child dies before becoming a human being.

> **221.(1) Every one who causes the death, in the act of birth, of any child that has not become a human being, in such a manner that, if the child were a human being, he would be guilty of murder, is guilty of an indictable offence and is liable to imprisonment for life.**
> **(2) This section does not apply to a person who, by means that, in good faith, he considers necessary to preserve the life of the mother of a child, causes the death of such child.**

This section is often included in discussions with the Code provisions on abortion. It is, however, a distinct offence from abortion which refers only to the producing of miscarriages. Under s.221 it is essential that the death of the child occur while in the act of birth, and in such a way that it would be murder if the child had been a human being (as defined in the Code). This means that the causing of the death must fall within either s.212 or s.213. The exception provided in s.221(2) is to allow for situations where it is necessary to cause the death of the unborn child to save the mother.

B. SECTION 207

207. Where a person, by an act or omission, does anything that results in the death of a human being, he causes the death of that human being, notwithstanding that death from that cause might have been prevented by resorting to proper means.

This section would apply to the following type of situation: A inflicts a minor wound on B. B fails to get proper medical treatment for the injury. The wound becomes infected, causing B's death. A has caused the death of B even though the death could have been prevented if the wound had been given proper treatment.

C. SECTION 208 This section deals with a situation similar to s.207.

208. Where a person causes to a human being a bodily injury that is of itself of a dangerous nature and from which death results, he causes the death of that human being notwithstanding that the immediate cause of death is proper or improper treatment that is applied in good faith.

A case which involved the operation of s.208 is *R. v. Emkeit and 12 Others.*[5] Emkeit and the other twelve men were members of a motorcycle gang. During a fight with a rival gang, one of its members was hit on the side of the head with a chain by Emkeit. He died while being driven to the hospital. The victim's injuries consisted of several serious head lacerations. Doctors testified that the causes of death were pulmonary edema caused by the head injuries, and tracheobronchial aspiration which in effect meant that the victim had drowned in his own vomit. This had resulted from the injured man being laid on his back without his tongue being depressed while he was being taken to the hospital by his friends.

Emkeit argued that the jury could have found him not guilty if the jury found that the victim's life could have been saved if proper treatment had been given. The court held, however, that the jury did not need to consider this argument. In giving his reasons for rejecting Emkeit's appeal, the judge adopted the following example taken from an English case as an analogous situation to which s.208 would apply:

> ... *A man is stabbed in the back, his lung is pierced and hemorrhage results; two hours later he dies of hemorrhage from that wound; in the interval there is no time for a careful examination and the treatment given turns out in the light of subsequent knowledge to have been inappropriate and, indeed, harmful. In those circumstances no reasonable jury or court could, properly directed, in our view come to any other conclusion than that the death resulted from the original wound.*

The case from which the example was taken was *R. v. Smith*.[6] The facts were that during a fight at a military barracks, the accused stabbed the deceased in the back and arm. Unknown to anyone, the deceased's lung had been pierced and the wound was hemorrhaging. A fellow member of the company tried to carry him to the medical station. On the way he tripped twice and dropped the injured man on the ground. At the medical station, no one appreciated the seriousness of his injuries and the treatment he was given turned out to have been wrong and probably harmful. The man died about one hour after arriving at the station. If he had been given proper treatment his chances of recovery were as high as 75%. The court held that if at the time of death the original wound is still an *operating* and *substantial* cause then the death can be properly said to be the result of the wound, even though some other cause of death is also operating.

In sum, the *Emkeit* and *Smith* cases demonstrate that a person will not be able to escape criminal responsibility where he causes a serious injury but where the death is actually caused by proper or improper treatment. Notice however that the treatment must be given in "good faith." Presumably, if a person were seriously injured, taken to a doctor who turns out to be his worst enemy and who decides to kill him by giving him the wrong medication, the person who caused the original injury would possibly escape responsibility for the death.[7]

D. SECTION 209

> **209. Where a person causes bodily injury to a human being that results in death, he causes the death of that human being notwithstanding that the effect of the bodily injury is only to accelerate his death from a disease or disorder arising from some other cause.**

The effect of this section is that even though a person causes injury to another that by itself has not caused the death, if the injury has accelerated the death from other causes the person has still committed homicide. A case which relied on s.209 is *R. v. Nicholson*.[8] In this case, the accused and the deceased argued one evening at a school house meeting. The accused struck the deceased twice. At that point they were pushed outside the building. The deceased's body was found some hours later. Medical evidence indicated that the deceased was a man in poor physical condition, whose heart was abnormally small, and who suffered from Bright's disease. He had also been indulging freely in alcoholic beverages. The doctor who testified at the trial said that the blows struck by the accused were one cause of death, others being the man's bad health and drinking. A jury found the accused guilty of manslaughter since the blows contributed to the causing of the death.

E. SECTION 210

> **210. No person commits culpable homicide or the offence of causing the death of a human being by criminal negligence unless the death occurs within one year and one day commencing with**

the time of the occurrence of the last event by means of which he caused or contributed to the cause of death.

The rule in this section originated during medieval times when it was very difficult, if not impossible, to accurately identify as the cause of death an event that occurred over a year ago. In modern times there has been some criticism of this rule. The criticism points out that medical science has advanced to a stage where first, it is not difficult to trace a cause of death to an event which happened long ago and second, because medical science is so advanced, persons who would have previously died immediately now may linger for months before finally dying.[9]

B. OFFENCES OF CULPABLE HOMICIDE

Once it is established that the homicide is culpable, the next step is determining whether the homicide is murder, manslaughter or infanticide.

1. Murder

Culpable homicide is murder where certain additional factors, other than the culpable causing of death, are present. Under the common law, murder was defined as unlawful killing with "malice aforethought"; in other words, where the person intended to cause someone's death. Today the offence of murder covers not only those situations where the death has been specifically intended but also where certain surrounding circumstances exist. Although murder, in general, always requires a specific intent, it may not be an intent to cause a person's death. For example, persons who, while committing certain offences, unintentionally cause death may be charged with murder.

Sections 212 and 213 set out the situations in which culpable homicide is murder.

A. SECTION 212

212. Culpable homicide is murder
(a) where the person who causes the death of a human being
    (i) means to cause his death, or
    (ii) means to cause him bodily harm that he knows is likely to cause his death, and is reckless whether death ensues or not;
(b) where a person, meaning to cause death to a human being or meaning to cause him bodily harm that he knows is likely to cause his death, and being reckless whether death ensues or not, by accident or mistake causes death to another human being, notwithstanding that he does not mean to cause death or bodily harm to that human being; or
(c) where a person, for an unlawful object, does anything that he knows or ought to know is likely to cause death, and thereby causes death to a human being, notwithstanding that he desires to effect his object without causing death or bodily harm to any human being.

(i) s.212(a)

Murder under s.212(a)(i) is the simplest form of the offence. All that must be shown is that the accused by his voluntary act caused a person's death and that he intended to cause that person's death. Since it may be impossible to produce evidence that shows a person actually had the mental intention to cause another person's death, (unless, of course, he confesses), courts have long taken the position that it may be presumed that a person intends the natural consequences of his acts. As one judge stated: "If a man is aware that certain consequences will probably follow the act which he contemplates doing and yet deliberately proceeds to do that act, he must be taken to have intended those consequences to follow even though he may have hoped they would not.[10]

For example, A wants to kill B. A puts a bomb in B's car. A knows that C always travels with B and although A does not want C to die, he knows that C probably will die from the explosion. If B and C die, A can be charged with murder for both their deaths.

Murder under s.212(a)(ii) differs from that under s.212(a)(i) in that the specific intent necessary is to cause bodily harm that the accused knows is likely to cause death, rather than a specific intent to cause death. Before convicting a person of murder under s.212(a)(ii), it must be shown that the accused *intentionally* inflicted bodily harm that he *knew* was likely to cause death and that the accused was *reckless* as to whether death would result. All of these elements must be present, i.e. the intent, knowledge and recklessness. Thus a homicide will not fall within this section if the accused did not actually know that the death was a likely result of the bodily harm or if the accused caused the bodily harm recklessly rather than intentionally. Likewise, the homicide does not fall within this section unless the accused was reckless as to whether or not death would ensue. This means that the accused, who knew death was likely, without justification or without caring, did the act which caused the death. For example, A commits an apparently minor assault on B without meaning to cause serious injury and without realizing that it was likely to cause death. However, unknown to A, B has a weak heart. The assault causes B to suffer a stroke from which he dies. A would probably not be convicted of murder. Although A did intend to cause bodily harm, he did not know the injury was likely to cause death and, therefore, s.212(a)(ii) would not apply.

(ii) s.212(b)

This subsection merely provides that where a person's conduct would fall under s.212(a) but, by accident or mistake, the wrong person dies, he has still committed murder, even though he had no intent to harm the person who died. So, if A tries to poison B and by accident C takes the poison and dies, A's intent to harm B will be *transferred* to C.

A case which illustrates the operation of s.212(a)(ii) and s.212(b) is *Hyam v. D.P.P.* [11] This is an English case but the English law in this area is similar to Canadian law. The accused had been the mistress of a man who had become engaged to another woman, B. Early one morning the accused went to B's house and poured gasoline through the letter box, stuffed it with newspaper and lit it with a match. The house caught fire and although B and one of her children escaped through a window, B's two daughters were suffocated by the fumes. The accused's defence was that she had set fire to the house only in order to frighten B so that she would leave the neighborhood. However, the court found that the accused acted with the knowledge that setting fire to the house would probably cause bodily harm and thus the accused was liable for whatever death resulted.

(iii) s.212(c)

This subsection makes homicide murder where a person for an *unlawful object* does something which he *knows* or *ought to know* is dangerous to life and which causes the death of a human being. Because of the use of the words "ought to know", an objective test may be used to determine whether the accused is responsible for the death. Unlike s.212(a)(ii) which uses a subjective test, (i.e. did the accused actually know the harm was likely to cause death?) this section asks, would a reasonable man have known that the thing being done was dangerous to life? As one court stated the test: "If the accused had the capacity to form the intent necessary for the unlawful object and had knowledge of the relevant facts which made his conduct such as to be likely to cause death, he is guilty of murder if a reasonable man should have anticipated that such conduct was likely to cause death."[12]

It is essential that the accused acted for an unlawful object. In other words, the act which caused the death must have been done to further or to achieve an unlawful purpose. For example, if A shoots a gun at B for the purpose of robbing him and B dies, A can be charged with murder since he fired the gun for the unlawful object of robbing B.

It may be wondered why liability for murder is imposed where a person did not intend to cause death or bodily harm and may not have realized that one of these results was likely. The reasoning is that, as a matter of public policy, any person who acts for an unlawful object *should know* whether death is a likely result, and if it is likely and death does result, he should be held responsible. For example in the case of *R. v. Tennant and Naccaroto*,[13] the deceased, Johnson, had been at a party where he argued with and finally violently assaulted two men. Tennant and Naccaroto talked to one of the men later that night and agreed to talk to Johnson to try and make peace between them. They arrived at Johnson's apartment and exchanged a few words with him. Johnson, who answered his door armed with a crutch and a knife, then started swinging the weapons at the men. Naccaroto ran home to get a gun. When he came back to rescue Tennant, he, either accidentally or intentionally (the evidence on this point was contradictory), shot and killed Johnson. The court held that a jury could find Naccaroto guilty of murder under s.212(c) if the jury was satisfied beyond a reasonable doubt that the gun was obtained for the unlawful purpose of assaulting Johnson and that Naccaroto knew or ought to have known that his conduct was likely to bring about a situation in which someone might be killed. In other words, Naccaroto had unlawfully obtained the pistol (i.e. by carrying a loaded pistol for a purpose dangerous to the public, see s.83) for the unlawful object of assaulting Johnson.

B. SECTION 213 Under this section culpable homicide is murder where a person causes a person's death whether or not he knew death was likely and whether or not he intended to cause death. This section only applies to situations where the death is caused while one of the offences mentioned in s.213 is being attempted or committed. Further, the conduct and intent of the accused must fall within one of the subsections (a) – (d).

> **213. Culpable homicide is murder where a person causes the death of a human being while committing or attempting to commit high treason or treason or an offence mentioned in section 52 (sabotage), 76 (piratical acts), 76(1) (hijacking an aircraft), 132 or subsection 133(1) or sections 134 to 136 (escape or rescue from prison or lawful custody), 143 or 145 (rape or attempt to commit rape), 149 or 156 (indecent assault), subsection 246(2) (resisting lawful arrest), 247 (kidnapping and forcible confinement), 302 (robbery), 306 (breaking and entering), or 389 or 390 (arson), whether or not the person means to cause death to any human being and whether or not he knows that death is likely to be caused to any human being, if**
> > **(a) he means to cause bodily harm for the purpose of**
> > > **(i) facilitating the commission of the offence, or**
> > > **(ii) facilitating his flight after committing or attempting to commit the offence,**
> >
> > **and the death ensues from the bodily harm;**
> > **(b) he administers a stupefying or overpowering thing for a purpose mentioned in paragraph (a), and the death ensues therefrom;**
> > **(c) he wilfully stops, by any means, the breath of a human being for a purpose mentioned in paragraph (a), and the death ensues therefrom; or**
> > **(d) he uses a weapon or has it upon his person**
> > > **(i) during or at the time he commits or attempts to commit the offence, or**
> > > **(ii) during or at the time of his flight after committing or attempting to commit the offence,**
> >
> > **and the death ensues as a consequence.**

An essential element of murder under s.213 (a), (b), and (c), is that the death must be caused while the offence is being attempted or committed. It is necessary then to first show that the offence was in fact attempted or committed and second that the death occurred during the commission of the offence or its attempt. *R. v. Warner*[14] illustrates both these points. In this case the accused testified that he had been drinking heavily when a stranger, the deceased, invited him to go in his car to the country to drink a bottle of whiskey. When the car stopped near a farm house the stranger asked the accused to get in the back seat to drink the liquor. The stranger then asked the accused to perform an indecent act. At that point a struggle took place. The accused seized the stranger by the neck and choked him. The accused said when he came to his senses he tried to revive the man but was unsuccessful. After feeling his pulse he thought the man was dead. The accused then drove the car to a ditch where he dragged the body. Although the accused was unclear on this point, there was evidence that he had placed a belt around the man's neck to assist him in dragging the body. The accused then testified that he took the man's wallet to delay identification and escaped in the deceased man's car. Medical evidence was presented at the trial which indicated that the deceased died from strangulation caused by the belt.

The key issue in this case, the court held, was whether the accused formed the intent to rob the stranger before he thought he was dead or afterwards. If the intent to take the man's wallet and car had not been formed until the accused thought the man was dead, then the accused could not be held liable for robbery, and therefore was not liable for murder under s.213. The court, hearing the case on appeal, found that the trial court erred in not defining for the jury the offence of robbery and in misdirecting it regarding the necessity of finding robbery. The court set aside the murder conviction and substituted a conviction of manslaughter.

Section 213(d) provides the widest circumstances in which a culpable homicide may be murder. Notice that under this paragraph, a person may be charged with murder if he has a gun on his person, even if he isn't using it, if the death occurs while the offence is being attempted or committed or while he is in flight after attempting to commit or committing the offence. This means, for example, if the gun is fired accidentally the accused can be charged with murder if the other elements of the offence under s.213 are present. A case which involved an alleged accidental firing and considered the meaning of "in flight" is *R. v. Rowe*,[15] a 1951 decision of the Supreme Court of Canada.

In *Rowe* the accused and another man committed an armed robbery in Windsor. The men then hired a taxi driver to drive them to London. The taxicab driver became suspicious when he overheard their conversation. He stopped at a gas station to attempt to call the police. The accused followed him into the station, however, and when the taxicab driver asked the operator to call the police, the accused pulled a gun and ordered everyone to the rear of the station. The taxicab driver then ran through a doorway and slammed a wooden door behind him. The gun fired and a bullet passed through the door killing another man whose presence was unknown to the accused. There was conflicting evidence as to whether the gun was fired intentionally or accidentally. The question was left with the jury as to whether Rowe was "in flight" from the Windsor robbery and thus liable for murder under s.213(d)(ii). Rowe argued that this question should not have been left with the jury. Since he was not being pursued, it could not be said that he was "in flight." The court held that whether or not Rowe was "in flight" was a subjective matter as far as Rowe was concerned (i.e. did he believe he was being pursued?) and the fact that the police had not been informed of the Windsor robbery at the time of the shooting was not relevant. There was sufficient evidence, the court stated, for a jury to find that Rowe was "in flight" at the time of the shooting. The evidence was summed up by one of the judges as follows:

> *[Rowe] knew he had committed a robbery at Brown's house; he was anxious to dispose of the weapons taken from the house; he spent only 15 minutes endeavouring to find a purchaser in Windsor; it was Bechard [Rowe's accomplice] who made the arrangements with the taxi driver but it was Rowe, who had not been seen by Mrs. Brown [the woman who was robbed] who identified himself to Jolly [the taxi driver] when the latter was raising a question as to being paid for the trip to London. Rowe never let Jolly out of his sight, and coupled with this are the circumstances under which he pulled out [the gun]. . . .*

In sum, it is not necessary that a person be pursued or even be near the scene of the crime to be considered "in flight." This case raises some doubt as to when flight actually ends. For example, what if the shooting had occurred the next day or the following week; or what if the shooting had occurred in Toronto or in Halifax? Would the accused still be "in flight"?

The issue of when does a person cease to be in flight is especially important since an accidental killing may be murder if the circumstances fit within s.213. In the *Rowe* case, the accused claimed that he slipped on the floor of the grease-pit room and accidentally discharged the gun. If a jury believed that the shooting was accidental and that Rowe was not in flight and not committing any of the offences listed in s.213 then Rowe would probably have been convicted of manslaughter instead of murder.

C. CLASSIFICATION OF MURDER

In 1976 legislation was enacted by Parliament to abolish capital punishment. Before this new legislation was brought into effect murder was punishable either by death or by life imprisonment. Generally, the only murder cases punishable by death were those in which a police officer, prison guard or other similar person was killed while in the course of duty.

Murder is now classified as either first degree or second degree murder. Section 214, in part, states:

> **214.(1) Murder is first degree murder or second degree murder.**
>
> **(2) Murder is first degree murder when it is planned and deliberate.**

Further subsections of s.214 provide that murder is also first degree even if not planned and deliberate where the victim is a police officer, prison guard or person working in a prison or other similar person acting in the course of duty. It is also first degree murder, whether or not planned and deliberate, to cause a person's death while committing or attempting to commit the following offences: s.76(1) (highjacking aircraft), s.247 (kidnapping and forcible confinement), s.144 (rape), s.145 (attempted rape), s.149 (indecent assault on a female), and s.156 (indecent assault on a male). A person can also be charged with first degree murder where he has been previously convicted of first or second degree murder. All murder that is not first degree is second degree.

(i) the meaning of "planned and deliberate"

The words "planned and deliberate" were used in the Code prior to 1967 to describe one type of capital murder (i.e. murder for which the punishment was the death penalty). So there is some case law on what these words mean and how they are to be applied.

In sum, the cases make the following points:

1. Before considering whether the death was planned and deliberate, the Crown must prove beyond a reasonable doubt that the accused is guilty of murder.[16]
2. The Crown must then prove that the murder was *both* planned and deliberate. It would be possible for a murder to be planned but not deliberate. For example, a man might make plans over a period of days to kill his wife but at the moment of the actual killing be acting impulsively and not deliberately.[17]
3. The term "deliberate" as used in the Code means more than intentional and is closer in meaning to, "considered, not impulsive".[18] One judge stated, " . . . deliberation proceeds from the will enlightened by an intelligence which has had time to reflect upon the nature and the quality of the incriminating act."[19]
4. In considering whether a murder has been planned and deliberate, the jury is concerned with the accused's "mental processes." It should consider the accused's actions, his conduct, his statements, and his capacity to plan and deliberate.[20]

(ii) punishment for first and second degree murder

Both first and second degree are punishable by life imprisonment. The difference between the two offences with regard to punishment concerns only eligibility for parole. A person convicted of first degree murder can not be paroled until he has served twenty-five years of his sentence. Where a person has been convicted of second degree murder, he may be eligible for parole after serving ten years of his sentence.

2. Manslaughter

While the common law defined murder as unlawful killing with malice aforethought, manslaughter was defined as unlawful killing without malice aforethought. Today manslaughter is still defined in relation to murder:

> **217. Culpable homicide that is not murder or infanticide is manslaughter.**

The effect of this section is that once a homicide is found to be culpable, the next step is determining whether it is murder or infanticide; if the culpable homicide is neither then the offence is manslaughter. It follows that it is not uncommon where a person has been charged with murder for a jury to be instructed that it may bring in a verdict of guilty of manslaughter where it finds that the killing has been unlawful but the Crown has failed to prove beyond a reasonable doubt the additional element needed for murder. Similarly, if an accused appeals his conviction for murder, the appeal court may substitute a verdict of guilty of manslaughter. For example, in the case of *Molleur v. R.,*[21] the accused was a doctor, a general practitioner, who performed an abortion on a woman who was in her third month of pregnancy. The woman died and the doctor was charged with murder under s.212(c), i.e. that he had performed for an unlawful purpose an act that he knew or ought to have known was likely to cause death. The accused was found guilty and appealed. The Quebec Court of Appeal, after considering the evidence that the doctor had no specialized knowledge of obstetrics or gynaecology and that he was unaware of the advanced state of the woman's pregnancy, held that he was not in a position where he knew or should have known the dangerous nature of the operation. The court then substituted a verdict of guilty of manslaughter.

A. BY AN UNLAWFUL ACT OR CRIMINAL NEGLIGENCE Manslaughter most often arises where the death is caused by means of an unlawful act or by criminal negligence. Where the death is a result of an unlawful act, such as assault, it is not necessary to prove that the accused intended to cause the harm. In fact, many cases of manslaughter involve accidental deaths which occur as a result of an unlawful act. For example, in *R. v. Chisholm,*[22] a boy, aged 14, without justification or excuse, rushed at his young playmate, who then fell backwards. The fall dislocated the spinal column at the base of the boy's skull causing his death. Chisholm's defence was that the homicide was accidental. The court however, found him guilty of manslaughter. In its judgment it stated:

> *Homicide by misadventure [i.e. accident], . . .only occurs where an accused is doing a lawful act and accidentally kills another person. In the case before me the blow by the accused was an unlawful act which rendered him amenable for any consequences resulting from it. It is no defence to a charge of manslaughter that the unfortunate fatality was not anticipated by the accused and would not ordinarily result from such a blow.*

It is possible that a person could be convicted of manslaughter based on either an unlawful act or criminal negligence. In *R. v. Mack,*[23] three men, including the deceased and the accused, were sitting in a mobile home. Each of the men had taken heroin that evening. While still feeling the effects of the drug the accused found a gun in the bedroom and took it to the kitchen table to examine it. Although he claimed that he did not remember pointing the gun at any person, at some point in the evening he fired three shots striking the deceased twice and the other man once. The court held that a jury could find the accused guilty of manslaughter if they believed beyond a reasonable doubt either that the accused committed the unlawful act of pointing the gun at the deceased, or that the accused was criminally negligent in the manner he handled the gun.

B. MURDER REDUCED TO MANSLAUGHTER A person also may be convicted of manslaughter where he has been charged with murder in two special situations: 1) where he successfully raises the defence of intoxication; 2) where he successfully raises the defence of provocation. Both of these situations have been discussed previously in the chapter on defences and reference to that chapter should be made for a complete discussion.

Briefly, an accused may be able to reduce his charge of murder to a conviction of manslaughter where he proves beyond a reasonable doubt that at the time of the killing he was so intoxicated that he could not form the specific intent necessary for murder.

Section 215 sets out the defence of provocation. It provides that where a culpable homicide would be murder, it may be reduced to manslaughter if the accused committed the offence in the heat of passion.

3. Infanticide and Offences Concerning Childbirth

216. A female person commits infanticide when by a wilful act or omission she causes the death of her newly-born child, if at the time of the act or omission she is not fully recovered from the effects of giving birth to the child and by reason thereof or of the effect of lactation consequent on the birth of the child her mind is then disturbed.

220. Every female person who commits infanticide is guilty of an indictable offence and is liable to imprisonment for five years.

2. "Newly-born child" means a person under the age of one year.

As mentioned previously, this offence is rarely used. It was first introduced into the law of Canada in 1948. It is based on the reasoning that a woman may be mentally disturbed from the effects of giving birth or of lactation and thus be less responsible for her actions. In this situation the law mitigates the severity of punishment for what would otherwise be murder or manslaughter.

In *R. v. Marchello*,[24] the judge listed the elements of the offence which the Crown would have to prove:

> (a) the accused must be a woman;
> (b) she must have caused the death of a child;
> (c) the child must have been 'newly born';
> (d) the child must have been the child of the accused;
> (e) the death must have been caused by a wilful act or omission of the accused;

(*f*) at the time of the wilful act or omission the accused must not
      have fully *recovered from the effect of giving birth to the child;*
      and
(*g*) *by reason of giving birth to the child the balance of her mind was*
      disturbed.

Since the *Marchello* case, s.590 has been added to the Code. It states as follows:

**590. Where a female person is charged with infanticide and
the evidence establishes that she caused the death of her child but
does not establish that, at the time of the act or omission by
which she caused the death of the child,**
  **(a) she was not fully recovered from the effects of giving birth
      to the child or from the effect of lactation consequent on
      the birth of the child, and**
  **(b) the balance of her mind was, at that time, disturbed by
      reason of the effect of giving birth to the child or of the
      effect of lactation consequent on the birth of the child,**
**she may be convicted unless the evidence establishes that the act
or omission was not wilful.**

The purpose of s.590 is to avoid the problems which arise from a situation where the
Crown is able to prove all the elements of the offence except those concerning the
woman's mental state.[25] However, it appears that the accused can still raise as her
defence that she was fully recovered or that her mind was not disturbed. The result
would be that she would be entitled to be acquitted of infanticide and could not be
charged later with murder or manslaughter since an accused can not be tried twice
for the same homicide.

Two offences somewhat related to infanticide are neglect to obtain assistance in
childbirth and concealing the body of a child. They are set out in the Code as
follows:

**226. A female person who, being pregnant and about to be
delivered, with intent that the child shall not live or with intent to
conceal the birth of the child, fails to make provision for
reasonable assistance in respect of her delivery is, if the child is
permanently injured as a result thereof or dies immediately
before, during or in a short time after birth, as a result thereof,
guilty of an indictable offence and is liable to imprisonment for
five years.**
**227. Every one who in any manner disposes of the dead body
of a child, with intent to conceal the fact that its mother has been
delivered of it, whether the child died before, during or after
birth, is guilty of an indictable offence and is liable to
imprisonment for two years.**

Neither of these offences is used very often today. They seem to be left over from a
time when there was greater stigma attached to bearing an illegitimate child.

QUESTIONS FOR STUDY AND REVIEW

1. What is the difference between culpable and non-culpable homicide?
2. When may a homicide be justified? excused?
3. List the offences of culpable homicide.
4. List the methods by which culpable homicide can be committed.
5. What types of unlawful acts are considered unlawful for the purposes of s.205(5)(a)?
   How would you classify the following unlawful acts?
   a. failure of a person to file his income tax return by the deadline.
   b. failure of a person to provide necessaries of life for his children.
   c. failure of a person to have his pet dog vaccinated for rabies.
   d. driving through a stop sign.
6. Why does the Code state that a person has not committed culpable homicide where the death has been caused by influence on the mind alone unless the deceased is a child or sick person? Do you agree with the law on this point? Why does the law make an exception in the case of children and sick persons?
   Question for research:
   Is it possible to hypnotise someone and convince him to kill himself?
7. How does the Code define "human being"?
8. Is it homicide to cause the death of a child before it becomes a human being? What if the injury is caused before the child becomes a human being but the child does not die until after it becomes a human being?
9. Under what circumstances is it an offence to cause the death of a child that is not a human being?
10. A shoots and wounds B. B's religion forbids him to have blood transfusions. B dies from the wound although he would probably have survived if he would have allowed a transfusion.
    Has A caused B's death? Which Code section is relevant?
11. Where a person inflicts an injury on another person and the injured person dies, has the person who inflicted the injury caused the death if the effect of the injury was only to accelerate the death from other causes? Which Code section is relevant?
12. Explain what is meant by the statement: "It can be presumed that a person intends the natural consequences of his acts." Give examples where this rule would apply.
13. Distinguish the offences of murder under s.212. Which subsection deals with "transferred intent" and what does this phrase mean? Which subsection sets out the simplest form of murder? Which subsection uses an "objective test" and what does this mean?
14. Discuss the basic elements of murder under s.213. What are the specific intents required? Do you agree that it should be possible for an accidental killing to be murder under s.213?
15. a. What has the Supreme Court of Canada said about the meaning of "in flight"?

b. The following statement was made by Mr. Justice Cartwright who disagreed with the majority in *R. v. Rowe* on the meaning of "in flight". "I do not think it is necessary to decide whether the existence of a pursuit is in all cases a necessary condition of the existence of a flight; but for an offender's conduct to fall within the meaning of that word as used in clause (d) after he has got well away from the scene of the crime, I think it necessary that there be in progress a pursuit continuing from such scene." Discuss the opinion of the majority of the judges and of Cartwright. With which do you agree and why?

16. List the differences between first and second degree murder.

17. How have courts interpreted the words, "planned and deliberate" as used in the Code?

18. How did the common law distinguish manslaughter from murder? How is manslaughter defined today?

19. How does manslaughter most often arise?

20. Under what circumstances may a charge of murder be reduced to manslaughter?

21. Why is infanticide a difficult offence to prove?

22. Brown had been drinking in a tavern for most of the evening with Smith. At closing time he agreed to drive Smith home. However, he first drove to an empty field for the ostensible purpose of drinking some beer. While there, Brown savagely beat Smith, inflicting many minor injuries and several facial wounds, not mortal in themselves. Smith was abandoned in the field, where he died after some extended but uncertain time. The doctor who performed the autopsy stated in his opinion the deceased died from loss of blood through the facial wounds, but that the injuries would not have caused death if they had received attention. He said that he did not think death was caused by pneumonia resulting from exposure to the cold night air, but he could not exclude that possibility.

    a. Has Brown caused Smith's death? Does it make any difference whether the death was a result of loss of blood or of pneumonia?

    b. If Brown assaulted Smith for the purpose of robbing him, with what offence or offences can he be charged and under what section(s) of the Code? What will the Crown have to prove?

    c. If the injuries to Smith were a result of a fight over money Smith owed Brown, with what offence or offences could Brown be charged? What will the Crown have to prove?

    d. Does the fact that Brown had been drinking all evening give him any special defence? Explain.

    See *R. v. Popoff* (1959), 125 C.C.C. 116 (B.C.C.A.)

23. John Silvers had lost his job and was deeply in debt. He decided that the only answer to his problems was to commit suicide. He purchased a gun and went home to shoot himself. Just as he put the gun to his head, his wife walked into the room and, realizing what John was attempting, grabbed his arm to push

the gun away from his head. The gun fired and Mrs. Silvers was fatally shot in the heart.

With what offence, if any, should John be charged? What will the Crown have to prove?

See *R. v. Hopwood* (1913) 8 Cr.App. R 143 and *Wexter v. R.* (1939) S.C.R. 350, 72 C.C.C. 1.

24. Jane Snow, aged 14, was walking home from school one day when a car pulled beside her. A man, Sam Luther, rolled down the window and asked Jane for directions to a certain street. When she stopped to answer him Luther pointed a gun at her and told her to get into the car. Jane, very frightened, obeyed him. Luther drove to a highway and started heading out of town. As the car approached an intersection and slowed down to make a turn, Jane opened the door and jumped out. She hit her head on a rock and died almost instantly. Has Luther caused Jane's death? If yes, with what offence can he be charged? Explain. See *R. v. Valade* (1915), 26 C.C.C. 233 (Que.C.A.).

25. Bernie Shiftless walked into a small corner grocery store and pulled a knife on the owner. He then demanded all the money in the cash register. As he left the store with the money he put the knife in his coat pocket and started to run. Quite accidentally, a policeman was walking down the street in front of the store and Bernie ran into him. The store owner ran out and yelled "Help, I've been robbed." Bernie tried to get away but the policeman, figuring that Bernie was the thief, tried to hold him. They struggled and somehow the knife which was in Bernie's pocket pierced the policeman's throat, cutting his jugular vein. The policeman died before the ambulance arrived.

With what offence can Bernie be charged and under what Code section? Explain.

[1] (1927), 48 C.C.C. 127 (Ont.C.A.).
[2] (1938), 70 C.C.C. 384 (Man.K.B.).
[3] (1913), 21 C.C.C. 44 (S.C.C.).
[4] (1913), 5 W.W.R. 838 (Man.).
[5] (1971), 3 C.C.C. (2d) 309, 14 C.R.N.S. 209 (Alta.C.A.).
[6] (1959) 2 Q.B. 35. (1959) 2 All E.R. 193.
[7] *R. v. MarKuss* (1864), 176 E.R. 598. Whether or not the original assailant would be liable would depend on whether or not the court found that the original injury actually contributed to the death.
[8] *R. v. Nicholson* (1926), 47 C.C.C. 113.
[9] 1961 *Criminal Law Review*, 348.
[10] *R. v. Krafchenko* (1914), 22 C.C.C. 277 (Man.Ct.K.B.).
[11] (1974) 2 W.L.R. 607 (House of Lords).
[12] *R. v. Tennant and Naccarato* (1975), 23 C.C.C. (2d) 80, 31 C.R.N.S. 1 (Ont.C.A.).
[13] *Ibid.*
[14] (1960) 127 C.C.C. 394, (Alta.C.A.), affd. 34 C.R. 246, 128 C.C.C. 366 (S.C.C.).
[15] (1951), 100 C.C.C. 97 12 C.R. 148 (S.C.C.).
[16] *R. v. Mitchell,* (1965) 1 C.C.C. 155, 43 C.R. 391 (S.C.C.).
[17] *More v. R.,* (1963) 3 C.C.C. 289, 41 C.R. 98 (S.C.C.).
[18] *Ibid.*
[19] *Pilon v. R.* (1966) 2 C.C.C. 53, 46 C.R. 272 (Que.C.A.).

[20] *R. v. Mitchell, supra.*
[21] *Molleur v. R.* (1948), 93 C.C.C. 36, 6 C.R. 375 (Que.C.A.).
[22] (1908), 14 C.C.C. 15.
[23] (1975), 29 C.R.N.S. 270 (Alta.C.A.).
[24] (1951), 100 C.C.C. 137, 12 C.R. 7, (Ont.H.Ct.).
[25] For example, see *R. v. Jacobs* (1952), 105 C.C.C. 291 (Ont.Cty.Ct.).

Chapter Ten

Criminal Negligence And Legal Duties

A. CRIMINAL NEGLIGENCE

202(1) Every one is criminally negligent who
(a) in doing anything, or
(b) in omitting to do anything that it is his duty to do, shows wanton or reckless disregard for the lives or safety of other persons.
(2) For the purpose of this section, "duty" means a duty imposed by law.

Section 202 of the Code defines criminal negligence. Notice that it does not refer to a specific type of conduct. Any act that shows wanton or reckless disregard for the lives or safety of other persons may be a criminally negligent act. Similarly, any omission, or failure to act, where there is a legal duty to act, may be criminally negligent if the omission shows wanton or reckless disregard for the lives and safety of others.

"Duty" is defined as a duty imposed by law. Duties include not only those specified in the Code or other statutes but also those imposed by the common law. For example, under the common law, a person carrying a dangerous weapon, such as a rifle, is under a duty to use it with reasonable care.[1] An example of a duty imposed by the Code is contained in s.77. This section provides that a person who possesses explosive substances is under a duty to use reasonable care to prevent bodily harm or death to persons, or damage to property. Similarly, under s.242, a person who makes an opening in ice, which is open to or frequented by the public, is under a duty to guard the opening in a manner adequate to prevent accidents. The duties in the Code under the heading "Duties Tending to Preservation of Life," such as the duty of a parent to provide the "necessaries of life" for his child, are discussed later in this chapter.

It is important to note that for a breach of a duty to be criminally negligent, the omission must show reckless and wanton disregard for the lives and safety of others. So, for example, in the case of *R. v. Baker,* [2] the Supreme Court of Canada found the accused not guilty of criminal negligence even though he had breached a very strict duty imposed for the protection of workmen. In this case, the accused was operating hoisting machinery in a mine shaft. An unusually loud noise attracted his attention for a moment, causing him to fail to stop the descent of a cage or "skip." The cage struck and killed a workman. Although the accused had breached a duty required by *The Mining Regulations* by not stopping the descending cage, the court held that the almost involuntary act of the accused in directing his attention to the loud noise was not an act of criminal negligence. That is, his failure to act did not show reckless and wanton disregard for the lives and safety of others.

1. Criminal Negligence Distinguished from Civil Negligence

It is important to distinguish criminal negligence from civil negligence. Generally speaking, the civil law imposes on all persons a duty to act in a manner that does not cause harm to other persons or their property. If a person breaches a duty to take care and causes harm to a person, he may be found to be negligent by a civil court and ordered to make compensation to the injured person. A person is civilly negligent when he fails to meet the standards of a *reasonable man*. For example: A fails to keep the stairs leading to his store in a safe condition. While climbing the stairs, B, a customer, is injured because a step collapses. To determine if A must make compensation to B, the court will ask what a reasonable man would have done if placed in A's situation. The question is not whether A actually knew that the stairs were in a dangerous condition and failed to take precautions but whether a reasonable man would have known and would have repaired them or at least posted a warning. If A has not acted as a reasonable man, he will be found civilly negligent.

To be found criminally negligent there must be a greater degree of misconduct than that required for civil negligence. All human beings occasionally fail to meet the standard of the reasonable man. When a failure results in a loss to another person usually the wrongdoer will not be punished but merely required to compensate the victim for his loss. However, when conduct becomes reckless and wanton, the failure is so great that the wrongdoer becomes guilty not only of civil negligence but also of a criminal offence and liable to punishment.

The key difference then between criminal negligence and civil negligence is that criminal negligence requires reckless or wanton conduct (i.e. conduct which shows a reckless or wanton disregard for the lives and safety of others), while civil negligence requires only a failure to meet the standard of conduct of the reasonable man.

2. Determining Whether Conduct Is Reckless and Wanton

Although the term "reckless" is commonly understood and used in everyday language, Canadian courts have not been able to agree on its precise meaning. As for the term "wanton", when it is considered at all, courts have usually said that it has a meaning similar to reckless.[3] Since courts have not agreed on the meaning of reckless, different tests have been used to decide if a person's conduct has been criminally negligent.

The courts have developed two main approaches to judging a person's conduct. The first is the approach used by some English courts. For example, in *R. v. Bateman*,[4] the court gave the following test for criminal negligence: " . . . in order to establish criminal liability, the facts must be such that in the opinion of the jury, the negligence of the accused went beyond a mere matter of compensation between subjects and showed such disregard for the life and safety of others as to amount to a crime against the State and conduct deserving punishment." This approach seems to say that criminal negligence consists of negligence that goes beyond ordinary negligence. This is sometimes called *gross* negligence. The difference between criminal and civil negligence is then one of degree, criminal negligence being a gross departure from the standard of the reasonable man. In this sense, recklessness merely means very great negligence.

The second approach is similar to the first but requires one additional element before conduct can be said to be criminally negligent. The additional element is that the person accused of criminal negligence must have actually foreseen that his conduct would probably cause harm and then must have chosen without justification to run the risk. This approach requires a *subjective* awareness on the part of the accused of the danger involved. In other words, it is not enough that a reasonable man would have realized the dangerous nature of the conduct; the accused himself must have actually realized or "adverted to" the danger. Thus, this approach says that the law does not punish those persons who are inadvertently negligent, i.e. those who did not think about the risk they were taking, but only those who adverted to or consciously were aware of the risk. The Supreme Court of Canada in the case of *O'Grady v. Sparling*[5] has clearly favoured the second approach. The court stated that criminal negligence is a fundamentally different matter than civil negligence and that Parliament intended to define criminal negligence as advertent negligence. The meaning given to recklessness in this approach is then "advertent negligence." It should be recalled that in the discussion of *mens rea* in Chapter Three this was the definition given to recklessness. It was discussed there as a type of *mens rea* or "guilty mind" which is a necessary element for most criminal offences.

Possibly because of the difficulty of determining the state of a person's mind and because of the great damage caused by the seemingly thoughtless acts of people, Canadian courts have found it difficult to follow *O'Grady v. Sparling*. Some courts have been content to merely look at the conduct of the accused. If objectively considering the surrounding circumstances, the conduct appears reckless or wanton (i.e., grossly negligent), the courts have found it criminally negligent.[6] This means the courts look at the conduct through the eyes of a reasonable man and ask whether he would know that the conduct was reckless. What about the necessity of *mens rea?* Most courts have said that the guilty or blameworthy mind is to be *inferred* or *imputed* to the accused once it is shown that his conduct was reckless.[7] Other courts have taken a more extreme view and said that only the conduct is to be considered, which is measured objectively or against the standard of a reasonable man.[8] The court in *R. v. Coyne* said: "The conduct of an accused, rather than the belief entertained by him, must be the dominant factor and criterion in assessing the applicability of the provisions of s.191 (now 202) to such conduct."[9] This case was decided before *O'Grady v. Sparling* but seems to represent the position taken by the majority of the courts which have considered the issue.

It may be wondered why the courts have not followed *O'Grady v. Sparling* and have seemed to follow English case law since the principle of *stare decisis* requires lower courts to follow the decisions of higher courts.[10] There is no clear explanation for this rather confusing situation. The *O'Grady* case concerned a constitutional rather than criminal issue. At least one court has suggested a court should be very careful before applying the terms of advertent and inadvertent negligence as used in the *O'Grady* case to a criminal case.[11]

The position taken by these courts can probably best be understood by considering the kinds of situations usually encountered in a case of criminal negligence. Automobile and hunting accidents make up a large portion of the cases. The courts are, perhaps, recognizing the fact that the misuse of guns and cars can result in great suffering and that society expects persons who cause damage through the careless, even though thoughtless, use of these instruments to be punished. For example, the man who has had one drink too many and finds himself driving on the wrong side of the road, and causing a major accident, may not have "adverted to" or thought about the dangerous nature of his conduct. However, courts have found it difficult not to condemn such actions through the use of criminal penalties.

To summarize, although the case of *O'Grady v. Sparling* indicates that an essential element of criminal negligence is that the accused "adverted to" or directed his thoughts to the danger of his conduct, other Canadian courts have frequently in practice followed English law and demanded only proof that a reasonable man would have realized that the conduct was reckless.

3. The Offences of Criminal Negligence

> **203. Every one who by criminal negligence causes death to another person is guilty of an indictable offence and is liable to imprisonment for life.**
> **204. Every one who by criminal negligence causes bodily harm to another person is guilty of an indictable offence and is liable to imprisonment for ten years.**

In addition to the offences set out in s.203 and s.204, the Code also provides in s.205(5)(b) that culpable homicide (i.e. homicide that is a criminal offence) can be caused by criminal negligence. Also, s.233(1) makes it an offence to be criminally negligent in the operation of a motor vehicle.

In brief, any person who recklessly causes death or bodily harm, or who recklessly operates a motor vehicle, has committed the offence of criminal negligence.

The following cases are examples of conduct which courts have found to be criminally negligent. The purpose of discussing them is to convey an idea of the wide variety of situations to which criminal negligence may apply:

1. *R. v. Petzoldt:*[12] The accused was an unemployed animal trainer and performer. He owned two chimpanzees which he kept in the basement of his house. While he was walking the female chimp, which was five feet tall and weighed 200 lbs., on a busy street, the chimp reached out and grabbed an eight-year-old girl. The girl was bitten on her head and shoulder by the chimp. There had been several previous instances that demonstrated the aggressive and dangerous character of the animal. The animal trainer was found guilty of criminal negligence causing bodily harm. The judge said that in knowing the dangerous nature of the animal and in taking it for a walk on a main street, the accused showed wanton and reckless disregard for the safety of others.

2. *R. v. Barek:*[13] The accused, a farmer's son, was walking home after a day of hunting. Although his gun had been unloaded, when he smelled the odour of a skunk, he reloaded it. When he reached the road, he met some school children. One boy, who was walking about three or four feet in front of the accused, without warning, turned around and faced the accused. The gun went off, killing the boy. At his trial, it was shown that the gun was in terrible condition. The hammers were so loose that the slightest jar would cause the gun to fire if the hammers were cocked. Furthermore, the accused was carrying the gun at its point of balance or about six inches in front of the hammers. The judge decided, based on the facts, that the gun was cocked. The accused was convicted of criminal negligence causing death.

3. *R. v. Moroz:*[14] The accused was charged with and found guilty of criminal negligence causing death in a case involving an automobile accident. Evidence was presented at his trial that showed the accused had been impaired by alcohol, that he had been driving on the wrong side of the road, and had a few moments before the fatal accident, forced a car off the road.

4. *R. v. Rogers:*[15] This case involved criminal negligence caused by breach of a duty imposed by s.198. This section states that where a person undertakes to provide medical or surgical treatment, he is under a duty to have and use reasonable knowledge, skill and care in doing so. Rogers was an unlicenced physician. At the time of the events leading to the charge, he was registered as a naturopathic physician. The practice of naturopathy is defined as the art of healing by natural methods or therapeutics. Rogers prescribed a low calorie, low protein diet for a young child who was suffering from a skin disease. After following the diet from April 22nd to June 11th, the child's condition became so severe that he was hospitalized. The day after he entered the hospital, he died. The testimony of medical doctors at Rogers' trial indicated that the child died from gross

malnutrition. The court of appeal upheld Rogers' conviction for criminal negligence causing death, stating that in judging whether the conduct is wanton or reckless, the court must look at the standards of reasonable people, not the standards of the accused.

5. *R. v. Gagnon:*[16] The accused with three others was riding in a car traveling at about 60 to 70 m.p.h. After the four drank a number of bottles of beer, the accused threw the empty bottles out on the roadside. One bottle smashed against a rock and its fragments hit and seriously injured a woman sitting nearby. The court considered that the road was one heavily traveled at that time of year and that it was well known that many travelers stop by the wayside to go for walks or to sit and rest. The accused, the court found, had thrown the bottles at random with no concern for the consequences of his act. The accused was found guilty of criminal negligence causing bodily harm.

B. DUTIES TENDING TO PRESERVATION OF LIFE

The following sections impose on the described persons certain duties. Unlike most criminal offences which require active misconduct, these sections make it possible for a person to be guilty of a crime by *not* doing something. As discussed previously, a breach of one of these duties may be the basis for a charge of criminal negligence if the failure to act shows wanton and reckless disregard for the lives and safety of others.

1. Duty of Persons to Provide Necessaries

A. THE DUTY

197.(1) Every one is under a legal duty
(a) as a parent, foster parent, guardian or head of a family, to provide necessaries of life for a child under the age of sixteen years.
(b) as a married person, to provide necessaries of life to his spouse; and
(c) to provide necessaries of life to a person under his charge if that person
(i) is unable, by reason of detention, age, illness, insanity or other cause, to withdraw himself from that charge, and
(ii) is unable to provide himself with necessaries of life.
(2) Every one commits an offence who, being under a legal duty within the meaning of subsection (1), fails without excuse, the proof of which lies upon him, to perform that duty, if
(a) with respect to a duty imposed by paragraph (1)(a) or (b),
(i) the person to whom the duty is owed is in destitute or necessitous circumstances, or

       (ii) the failure to perform the duty endangers the life of the person to whom the duty is owed, or causes or is likely to cause the health of that person to be endangered permanently; or

    (b) with respect to a duty imposed by paragraph (1)(c), the failure to perform the duty endangers the life of the person to whom the duty is owed or causes or is likely to cause the health of that person to be injured permanently.

    (3) Every one who commits an offence under subsection (2) is guilty of

    (a) an indictable offence and is liable to imprisonment for two years; or

    (b) an offence punishable on summary conviction.

This section places upon parents, spouses, and persons in charge of other persons, the duty to provide the necessaries of life for their children, spouses or charges. It should be noticed that for an offence to have been committed, it is not enough that there has been a failure to provide without lawful excuse. If the person to whom the duty is owed falls under paragraph (1)(a) or (b) the person must, because of the failure to provide either be in destitute or necessitous circumstances, or his health or life must be endangered. So, for example, a man who fails to support his wife cannot be convicted of this offence if his wife has sufficient means of her own. If, however, the person to whom the duty is owed falls under paragraph (1)(c), the offence is only committed if his health or life is endangered.

B. PERSONS WHO MUST PERFORM THE DUTY

    196. In this Part ...
    "child" includes an adopted child and an illegitimate child; ...
    "guardian" includes a person who has in law or in fact the custody or control of a child.

Since s.196 defines "child" as including an illegitimate or adopted child, parents of these children are included in s.197. Section 197(4)(b) further provides that evidence that a person has in any way recognized a child as being his child, is, in the absence of any evidence to the contrary, proof that the child is his child. So, for example, if a man supports an illegitimate child, this would be evidence that he has recognized the child as his own. Unless evidence is presented which provides another explanation for his actions, the child will be presumed to be his.

The definition of "guardian" is very broad. It would cover a situation where, for example, a parent has left the child in the care of a person who has then, *in fact,* the custody and control of the child.

Until recently, the Code only required husbands to provide the necessaries of life for their wives. Then, in 1975, the *Statute Law (Status of Women) Amendment Act* was passed. This act amended certain sections of several statutes, including the Criminal Code, so that men and women could be treated more equally by the law.

Because of this act, the duty to provide necessaries is now placed on both spouses.

Where a person has another person under his charge, the duty to provide is only imposed if the person under charge is unable, for a reason listed in s.197(1)(c)(i), to withdraw himself from the charge and if the person under charge is unable to provide for himself. An example of a case where the court found the accused had failed to provide for a person under his charge is *R. v. Instan.*[17] Although this is an English case, which based its decision on English law, it is a good illustration of the type of situation in which a duty under the Code could arise. In *Instan,* the accused was living with her elderly aunt. The aunt became ill with gangrene and was confined to bed. Only the accused was aware of the aunt's condition. The accused did not give or attempt to obtain any medical assistance for her aunt. She also neglected to provide food for her, although the accused accepted food which was brought to the house by tradesmen. Although the aunt died from the gangrene, the court found that the aunt's death was substantially accelerated by neglect, want of food and of nursing and medical attention. The accused was found guilty of manslaughter.

C. NECESSARIES OF LIFE Necessaries in this section of the Code are those things necessary for the preservation of life. Ordinarily, this includes food, shelter, clothing and medical treatment. However, this is probably not a complete list, especially since what is considered a necessary will depend on the particular circumstances of the case.[18]

D. LAWFUL EXCUSES The failure to provide necessaries must be without "lawful excuse." The Code has not clearly defined what may be considered a lawful excuse. However, courts have stated that inability to provide because of lack of money where, for example, the parents are unable to find employment, is a lawful excuse.[19] Also, the person must be aware that the necessaries are required before he can be found guilty of the offence.[20] If the spouse or child has adequate means of his own, an accused would also have a lawful excuse since the spouse or child would not be in destitute or necessitous circumstances.

There have been a number of reported cases involving members of religious sects who do not believe in the use of medical treatment. These cases clearly indicate that the parents' religious beliefs will not be accepted as a lawful excuse for failing to provide necessary medical treatment.[21]

Notice that s.197(2) places the burden on the person who has failed to provide necessaries to show that he acted with lawful excuse. Section 197(4)(c) also provides that where a person has left his spouse and has failed for one month subsequent to the time of leaving to maintain his spouse or child, this is, in the absence of any evidence to the contrary, proof that he has failed to provide.

E. DESTITUTE AND NECESSITOUS CIRCUMSTANCES The fact that a spouse or child is on welfare or receiving charity from friends or relatives does not mean that they are not in destitute or necessitous circumstances. As one judge aptly pointed out, families receive relief because they are in destitute or necessitous circumstances.

They do not cease to be in such circumstances because they have received relief to keep them from famishing or suffering.[22]

Furthermore, s.197(4)(d) states that the fact that a spouse or child is receiving or has received necessaries from a person who is not under a legal duty to provide them cannot be used as a defence by an accused. So, for example: A wife has been deserted by her husband. She is forced to live with her parents because she has no means of her own. Even if the parents support her at a very high standard of living, the husband cannot defend himself on the grounds that she is not destitute or in necessitous circumstances.

F. DANGER TO HEALTH OR LIFE The offence may be committed where the failure to provide necessaries endangers the life of the person to whom the duty is owed, or causes, or is likely to cause, the health of that person to be permanently endangered. Whether a person's life has been endangered or health permanently endangered, depends on the particular facts of each case. It has been said that the words have no special technical meaning.[23] An example of a case where the court found that the wife's health was permanently endangered is *R. v. Wood,* a 1911 decision of the Ontario Court of Appeal. In this case, the accused deserted his wife and child. The wife was forced to work at very hard menial labour, which was breaking her health, to support herself and child. Although she needed a serious operation, she was unable to undergo it because she had no money to pay for the operation and had to continue working so that she could maintain herself and child.

2. Duties of Persons Undertaking Dangerous Acts

A. WHERE MEDICAL OR SURGICAL TREATMENT IS ADMINISTERED

> **198. Every one who undertakes to administer surgical or medical treatment to another person or to do any other lawful acts that may endanger the life of another person is, except in cases of necessity, under a legal duty to have and to use reasonable knowledge, skill and care in doing so.**

This section does not create an offence but merely defines the duty persons who administer medical or surgical treatment are under. Section 198 would most often be used in conjunction with the offence of criminal negligence. This means if a person breaches a duty under s.198, he has not committed an offence unless the breach of the duty is criminally negligent. Notice there is an exception "in cases of necessity" where no duty is imposed. Presumably this would apply in an emergency situation to protect a person who attempted to give aid but failed to have or use reasonable knowledge, skill, or care.

B. WHERE OMISSION IS DANGEROUS TO LIFE

> **199. Every one who undertakes to do an act is under a legal duty to do it if an omission to do the act is or may be dangerous to life.**

This section provides that where a person begins to do an act, he is under a legal duty to complete it if the omission of the act is or may be dangerous to life. So, for example: A sees B drowning. A is under no legal obligation to save B. But if A throws B a rope and before B can grab it, pulls it back in, A has breached a legal duty to act. He undertook to act and B's life has been endangered by the omission. Like s.198, this section does not create an offence but could be used as the grounds for a charge of criminal negligence.

3. Child Abandonment

> **200. Every one who unlawfully abandons or exposes a child who is under the age of ten years, so that its life is or is likely to be endangered or its health is or is likely to be permanently injured, is guilty of an indictable offence and is liable to imprisonment for two years.**
> **196. In this Part**
> **"abandon" or "expose" includes**
> **(a) a wilful omission to take charge of a child by a person who is under a legal duty to do so, and,**
> **(b) dealing with a child in a manner that is likely to leave that child exposed to risk without protection; ....**

This section makes it an indictable offence to abandon a child under the age of ten. Notice that the offence can be committed by either a failure to act (i.e. a "wilful omission") or by positive misconduct (i.e. dealing with the child in a manner that exposes the child to risk). "Abandon" has also been defined by the courts as "leaving children to their fate."[24]

An example of a case of child abandonment is *R. v. Motuz*.[25] In this case, parents left their two children aged four and five, alone and locked in a farmhouse while they went out drinking. The farmhouse was 3/4 of a mile from the nearest neighbour. After the parents had been gone for three hours, the house caught fire, burned down and killed both children. In finding the parents guilty, the judge described the parents' conduct as a total abandonment of parental responsibility.

QUESTIONS FOR REVIEW AND DISCUSSION

1. To what type of conduct does criminal negligence refer?
2. What essential elements must be present before an omission to act can be criminally negligent?
3. What are the main differences between civil negligence and criminal negligence?
4. Discuss the two main approaches used by the courts to determine if a person's conduct has been reckless (i.e. criminally negligent). Which approach do you prefer? Why? Which approach have most courts seemed to use?
5. List the offences of criminal negligence.

6. The following cases have been discussed in this chapter as furnishing examples of types of conduct courts have found to be criminally negligent. For each case, describe the criminally negligent conduct and discuss the approach used by the court to determine if the conduct was reckless. If there is not enough information given for any particular case to answer these questions, state what information is needed and why.
   a. *R. v. Petzoldt*
   b. *R. v. Barek*
   c. *R. v. Moroz*
   d. *R. v. Rodgers*
   e. *R. v. Gagnon*
7. Describe the following:
   a. The persons who are under a duty to provide necessaries,
   b. The persons to whom the duty is owed,
   c. Under what circumstances is a breach of the duty an offence?
8. What are "necessaries of life"?
9. Under what circumstances may a person who is under a duty to provide necessaries of life have a lawful excuse for not providing them?
10. Why does the law in "cases of necessity" where medical or surgical treatment is administered, not impose a duty to have and use reasonable knowledge, skill and care?
11. Does the law always impose a duty to act if the failure to act will endanger a person's life? If not, under what circumstances does a person have a duty to act? Do you agree with the present law? Explain.
12. Do you think the offence of child abandonment should only apply to children under ten years of age?
13. Mr. & Mrs. Simon and their seven children lived in a two-room house on a farm in Saskatchewan. For the past two months, Mrs. Simon's 20-year-old brother, Rodney, had been living with them. Because of the limited space, Mrs. Simon did not want her brother staying in the house. She had complained about this to Mr. Simon on several occasions. One night after Mr. Simon and Rodney had returned from work, Mr. and Mrs. Simon argued about whether Rodney should continue living with them. Mrs. Simon finally said there wasn't room for everyone and that she was leaving. She then put on a jacket and hat. She had, however, nothing on her feet except house slippers and stockings and was otherwise thinly clad. Before she left, she told her 10-year-old son, Jimmy, to put on his coat and to come with her. A few minutes after Mrs. Simon and Jimmy left, Rodney asked Mr. Simon if they should go after them. The temperature that night was −40°F. Mr Simon said no, that they had probably gone to a neighbour's for the night. The neighbour lived one and a half miles to the south. The next day, Rodney went to the neighbour's to see if Mrs. Simon and Jimmy were there. On the way, he found their bodies frozen stiff. Apparently they had taken a wrong turn and lost their way.

With what offence or offences, if any, could Mr. Simon or Rodney be charged? What would the Crown have to show? What other information would be relevant? See *R. v. Sidney* (1912) 20 C.C.C. 376 (Sask. C.A.).

[1] *R. v. Coyne* (1958), 31 C.R. 335, 124 C.C.C. 176 (N.B.C.A.).

[2] (1929), 51 C.C.C. 352 (S.C.C.).

[3] See e.g. *R. v. Walker* (1974), 18 C.C.C. (2d) 179, 26 C.R.N.S. 268 (N.S.C.A.) where the court said "wantonness is perhaps a subclass of recklessness. It is a wild, mad or arrogant kind of recklessness . . . . "

[4] *R. v. Bateman* (1925), 19 Cr.App.R.8. See also *Andrews v. D.P.P.,* (1937) 2 All E.R. 552, 26 Cr. App.R. 34 for a similar statement on the meaning of "reckless."

[5] (1960), 33 C.R. 293, 128 C.C.C. 1 (S.C.C.)

[6] See e.g. *R. v. Rogers,* (1968) 4 C.C.C. 278 (B.C.C.A.), 4 C.R.N.S. 303; *R. v. Torrie* (1967) 3 C.C.C. 303 (Ont.C.A.), *R. v. Belbeck,* (1966) 2 C.C.C. 331, 3 C.R.N.S. 173 (N.S.C.A.)

[7] See e.g. *R. v. Fortin* (1957), 121 C.C.C. 345, 29 C.R. 28 (N.B.C.A.), *R. v. Torrie supra.*

[8] See e.g. *R. v. Rogers, supra.*

[8] *R. v. Coyne, supra.*

[10] See discussion of this principle of law in Chapter One.

[11] *R. v. Belbeck, supra.*

[12] (1973), 11 C.C.C. (2d) 320 (Ont.Co.Ct.).

[13] (1947), 90 C.C.C. 189 (Ont.C.A.).

[14] (1972), 5 C.C.C. (2d) 277 (Alta.C.A.)

[15] *R. v. Rogers, supra.*

[16] (1956), 115 C.C.C. 82 (Que.Ct. of Sessions of the Peace).

[17] (1893), 17 Cox's C.C. 602.

[18] See e.g. *R. v. Sidney* (1912), 20 C.C.C. 376 (Sask.C.A.)

[19] See e.g. *R. v. Bunting* (1926), 45 C.C.C. 135 (Ont.C.A.).

[20] *R. v. Steele* (1952), 102 C.C.C. 273, 14 C.R. 285(Ont.)

[21] See e.g. *R. v. Lewis* (1903), 7 C.C.C. 261 (Ont.C.A.), *R. v. Brooks* (1902), 5 C.C.C. 379 (B.C.C.A.), *R. v. Elder* (1925), 44 C.C.C. 75 (Man.C.A.).

[22] *R. v. Wilson* (1933), 60 C.C.C. 309 (Alta.C.A.).

[23] *R. v. Bowman* (1893), 3 C.C.C. 410 (N.S.C.A.).

[24] *Re Drummond Infants Adoption* (1968), (D.L.R.) (3d) 309 (B.C. Sup. Ct. Chambers).

[25] *R. v. Motuz and Motuz,* (1965) 2 C.C.C. 162 (Man.C.A.).

Chapter Eleven

Offences Involving Motor Vehicles

The Criminal Code contains a number of offences that involve the operation of a motor vehicle. Driving that is criminally negligent [s.233(1)] or dangerous [s.233(4)], and impaired driving [s.234] are examples of driving offences included in the Code. Certain of the driving offences included in the Code are very similar to provincial highway traffic offences, that is, offences which are contained in provincial highway traffic statutes such as the Highway Traffic Act of Ontario. For instance, the Criminal Code contains an offence dealing with drivers who fail to stop at the scene of an accident [s.233(2)], and most of the provincial statutes concerned with highway traffic regulations create an offence, "failing to remain at the scene of an accident," which is very much like s.233(2). When there is a Code offence and a provincial offence that appear similar in nature, it is helpful to remember that the Code offence is a more serious offence (violation of the driving conduct being prohibited). In other words the driving behaviour of the accused must be such that it warrants a criminal charge, and not a less serious quasi-criminal charge under a provincial highway traffic act. Only Criminal Code driving offences will be discussed in this chapter. If a Code offence is similar in nature to a provincial highway traffic offence this fact will be mentioned to avoid confusing the two offences.

A "motor vehicle" is defined in s.2 of the Code as a "vehicle that is drawn propelled or driven by any means other than by muscular force." This definition does not include a train or anything that operates on train tracks. Nor does it include a boat or a ship. Section 240 of the Code creates specific offences for the operation of a boat or ship. The definition of motor vehicle *does* include such means of transportation as cars, farm tractors, snowmobiles and motorcycles.

A. CRIMINALLY NEGLIGENT OR DANGEROUS DRIVING

1. Criminal Negligence in Operation of a Motor Vehicle

The general meaning of the term "criminal negligence" was defined in Chapter Ten (see page 171). Briefly, criminal negligence is an act, or omission, which "shows wanton or reckless disregard for the lives or safety of others" (s.202).

Section 233(1) provides for an offence which involves criminal negligence in the operation of a motor vehicle. Section 233(1) states:

> **233.(1) Everyone who is criminally negligent in the operation of a motor vehicle is guilty of**
> **(a) an indictable offence and is liable to imprisonment for five years, or**
> **(b) an offence punishable on summary conviction.**

In applying Section 233(1) the courts appear, in their decision-making process, to favour what is best described as an objective approach. That is to say they treat the phrase, "wanton or reckless disregard for the lives or safety of others," as an adjective. If a person's driving behaviour is so negligent, in other words, *the driving is such a marked departure from the standard of care expected of a reasonable driver,* that it can be described, by an onlooker, as showing wanton or reckless disregard for the lives or safety of others, then the driving amounts to criminal negligence.

However, another way the courts have sometimes interpreted the phrase, "wanton or reckless disregard for the lives or safety of others," hinges, essentially, on the word "reckless" as it is used in that phrase. Was a person's driving behaviour so reckless, that is, so thoughtless, that it is deserving of criminal punishment? Recklessness in this context dictates that the driver *advert to,* or foresee, the possible consequences of his manner of driving. Consider an example. A is driving his car, and is in a hurry to get home. It is raining and the highway is very slippery. He comes to an intersection marked by a yield sign but he does not slow down and approach the sign with caution. He is in such a hurry that he decides to ignore the sign and "take his chances," hoping that there is no traffic on the other road. As he enters the intersection he collides with a motorcycle. In such a set of circumstances it would be fair to say that A's manner of driving was reckless, because he adverted to, or foresaw, the consequences of his ignoring the yield sign, i.e., that he might be involved in an accident if he didn't yield, yet he deliberately chose to take the risk.

If the objective approach was applied to the set of facts described in this example, the following question would be asked. Can "running" a yield sign, on a slippery road, be described as "showing a wanton or reckless disregard for the lives or safety of others"? The element of "advertence," or "foreseeability," does not, directly, enter the analysis. This approach determines the driver's intentions by making the assumption that the driver *intended the natural consequences of his acts.* And, as was noted earlier, it is this approach which the courts appear to favour. In other words, if a jury, or judge, can describe the accused's driving behaviour as being such a marked departure from the standard of care expected of a reasonable man, that it amounts to a wanton or reckless disregard for the safety of others, the offence of criminal negligence, (in the operation of a motor vehicle), is made out. The two cases which follow are examples of driving behaviour which resulted in charges of driving in a criminally negligent manner.

In *R. v. Torrie*,[1] the accused was driving north when he collided with a motor vehicle which was proceeding south. The driver and four passengers in the southbound car were killed. The accused was the only occupant of the northbound car.

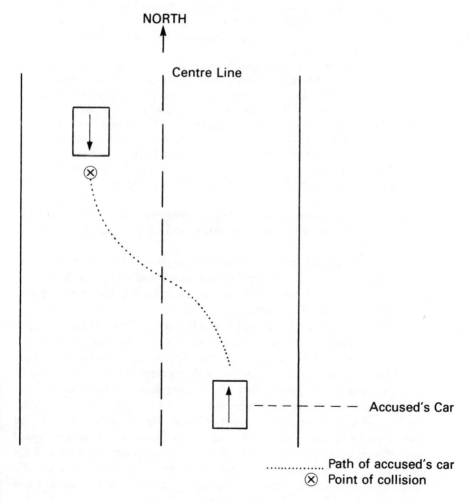

Figure 11-1

The highway was a regular surface, 22 ft. wide with 8 ft. shoulders bordered by guard rails. The highway was marked in the centre with a clearly visible broken white line. Visibility was unobstructed for a considerable distance on either side of the accident scene. It was a cool, dark night. The highway was wet, but no rain was falling and it was not freezing.

The collision occurred at the approximate centre of the south-bound lane. (See figure 11-1) The accused was, therefore, on the wrong side of the road. He had consumed a very substantial amount of alcohol shortly before the collision. There was no evidence of tire marks attributed to either vehicle.

The court concluded in its reasons for judgment:

> *The words of s.191(1), now s.202, and s.221(1), now s.233(1), in their plain meaning indicate an intention to prohibit a type of conduct in driving a motor vehicle which demonstrates, on the part of the motorist, a recklessness of consequences or an indifference to the lives or safety of others.*
>
> *In the present case, the conduct of the accused in driving on a main highway while his faculties were impaired by alcohol; his failure to appreciate the significance of the center line of the highway, or to recognize the imminent danger of collision with the oncoming vehicle; his unexplained position on the 'wrong' side of the highway; his failure to keep a proper look-out — all of which acts and omissions are undisputed in the evidence — indicate conduct on the part of the accused which falls within the description of wanton or reckless disregard for the lives or safety of others.*

R. v. Ciesielski[2] is a case which provides another example of driving conduct which the courts described as showing "wanton or reckless disregard for the lives or safety of others."

The accused collided with another car, seriously injuring the driver of the second car. The road at the scene of the accident was paved and straight with concrete curbs. At the time of the collision it had a visible, painted center line. The pavement was free of ice and snow. The weather was clear.

At the time of the collision the accused's vehicle had its left wheels 2 ft. to the left of the center line. There was evidence that the accused's vehicle was travelling at a greatly excessive speed at the moment of impact. One witness estimated his speed to be 70 m.p.h. The same witness stated that at the moment of impact the accused's vehicle leaped into the air with its four wheels completely off the road. Another witness said that his car was overtaken and passed by the accused's car about three-quarters of a block from the point of collision. He stated that after passing him, the accused's car drove over the center line and continued to pick up speed until the collision occurred. At the moment of impact he placed the accused's car half the width of a car across the center line. He further testified that the accused's car was going at a tremendous rate of speed immediately prior to the collision and that at no time before the accident were the brakes applied.

On the above facts the accused was convicted of criminal negligence in the operation of a motor vehicle.

2. Dangerous Driving

Section 233(4) defines the offence of dangerous driving:

> **233.(4) Everyone who drives a motor vehicle on a street, road, highway or other public place in a manner that is dangerous to the public, having regard to all the circumstances including the nature, condition and use of such place and the amount of traffic that at the time is or might reasonably be expected to be on such place, is guilty of**
> **(a) an indictable offence and is liable to imprisonment for two years, or**
> **(b) an offence punishable on summary conviction.**

A "public place" as it is used in s.233(4) generally means any place to which the public has a degree of access. A privately owned driveway used for customer parking was held to be a "public place" in *R. v. English*.[3] Other cases have described shopping center parking lots, churchyards, and school grounds as public places.

"The public" does include *passengers* in the car which is the subject of a dangerous driving charge. It is important to note that for a conviction to be registered under s.233(4) an injury, or death, *need not* have been caused as a result of the accused's driving.

As with the offence of criminally negligent driving, the offence of dangerous driving is considered with reference to what is best described as an objective standard. That is, the driver's conduct is usually viewed without direct reference to the issue of whether he foresaw the dangerous consequences of his driving. Once again, as for criminally negligent driving, the driver's intention is presumed from the idea that he intended the natural consequences of his acts. This objective approach was demonstrated by an Ontario case, *R. v. Beaudoin*.[4] In *Beaudoin* the court said that the essence of the offence of dangerous driving is the *manner or character of the accused's driving*. It is not necessary that the jury find a given state of mind to convict, but from evidence of the observable conduct of the vehicle driven and the attendant circumstances, it is the task of the jury to determine the actual behaviour of the driver. In other words the jury must decide whether, in the light of the relevant conditions prevailing at the time of the alleged offence, *of which a reasonably prudent man should have been aware or anticipated,* the driving amounted to dangerous driving.

The court went on to state:

> ... *to support a conviction of dangerous driving the prosecution must prove beyond a reasonable doubt:*

1. that the lives or safety of others were endangered by the accused's driving; and
2. that such jeopardizing resulted from the driver's departure from the standard of care that a prudent driver would have exercised having regard to what actually were or might reasonably have been expected to be the condition, nature or use of the place where he was driving (including the amount of traffic thereon).

R. v. Peda[5] is another case in which the accused was charged with dangerous driving. He was driving his taxi-cab (in Toronto), easterly on the exit lane from the Gardiner Expressway, which runs into Lakeshore Boulevard. Between the exit lane and the southerly lane of Lakeshore Boulevard is a narrow strip separating the two lanes. This dividing strip is several inches higher than the level of the exit lane and Lakeshore Boulevard. The two eastbound lanes are separated from the westbound lanes by a median the level of which is higher than the highway. (See figure 11-2).

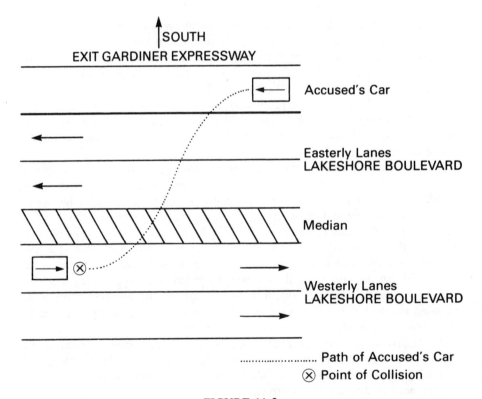

FIGURE 11-2

The prosecutor contended that the accused's dangerous driving occurred when he drove his car from the exit lane, across the dividing strip, then across the two eastbound lanes of Lakeshore Boulevard and over the median, striking a car being driven westerly on the north side of Lakeshore Boulevard. There was no evidence as to the speed at which the accused was driving. The accused stated that he was driving down the exit lane when the driver of the car in front of him suddenly applied his brakes and that after that he remembers nothing until after the accident.

The trial judge in his address to the jury used the following words: "So, briefly, dangerous driving is driving a car on a street, road, or highway, or other place in a manner that is dangerous to the public, and again, gentlemen, there is really no ambiguity in that language [of s.233(4)], it is a matter which you will have to decide: was the manner in which the accused drove the car, under the circumstances which have been related to you, was it dangerous to the public having regard to all the circumstances."

The jury concluded that the circumstance of the accused's driving, as described to the court, did amount to driving that was dangerous to the public; and he was therefore found guilty as charged.

3. Summary

A comparison of the cases would indicate that the practical difference between the offence of dangerous driving, and driving that is criminally negligent is one of degree, as opposed to a difference in the character of the driving. Criminally negligent driving, when compared to dangerous driving, involves a *greater departure* from the standard of driving expected of a reasonable man. That is, it is a more serious offence. This point is reinforced by the fact that under s.233(1), criminally negligent driving, the maximum penalty is five years and under s.233(4), dangerous driving, it is only two years.

At this point you may be wondering where the common provincial offence of "careless driving" enters the picture. Careless driving is the least serious of the three offences. A test for this offence was stated as follows, in *R. v. Beauchamp*[6] (an Ontario case): "The test . . .is whether it is proved beyond a reasonable doubt that this accused in the light of existing circumstances of which he was aware or of which a driver exercising ordinary care would have been aware, failed to use the care and attention or to give to other persons using the highway the consideration that a driver of ordinary care would have given in the circumstances."

In other words careless driving uses an objective test, and involves conduct which is not dangerous, or wanton or reckless, but which is sufficient enough a departure from the standard of care of a reasonable man that it is deserving of some form of punishment.

In *R. v. Furlong*[7] the accused was on his way home from work. He was driving within the city speed limit. He looked down for a second to switch on his car radio. At that moment a man stepped off the sidewalk and was struck by the accused's car. The accused was charged with dangerous driving. The court held that at most the accused was only guilty of a *momentary lack of care,* and that to be convicted of dangerous driving he would have had to have been far more negligent. The court went on to say, however, that the accused's driving would probably support a conviction of "careless" driving.

B. FAILING TO STOP WHEN INVOLVED IN AN ACCIDENT

Section 233(2) provides that:

> **233.(2) Everyone who, having the care, charge or control of a vehicle that is involved in an accident with a person, vehicle or cattle in the charge of a person, with intent to escape civil or criminal liability fails to stop his vehicle, give his name and address and, where any person has been injured, offer assistance, is guilty of**
> **(a) an indictable offence and is liable to imprisonment for two years, or**
> **(b) an offence punishable on summary conviction.**

This subsection actually contains three separate and distinct offences:
1. failure to stop altogether;
2. failure to give name and address after having stopped; and
3. failure to render assistance, to a person who has been injured, once stopped.

In 3. above this does not mean applying first aid. It means taking the necessary steps to ensure that medical assistance or first aid help reaches the scene of the accident as quickly as possible.

The common constituent elements for each of the above three offences are:
(1) Having the *care, charge* or *control* of a vehicle;
(2) *Involvement* in an *accident* with a person, another vehicle or cattle; and
(3) The *intent to escape civil or criminal liability*.

Section 233(3) provides:

> **233.(3) In proceedings under ss.(2), evidence that an accused failed to stop his vehicle, offer assistance where any person has been injured and give his name and address is, in the absence of any evidence to the contrary, proof of an intent to escape civil and criminal liability.**

In other words, an accused is required to give an explanation as to why he didn't stop, once it has been demonstrated he was involved in an accident.

As a general rule, an ''accident'' occurs the instant two vehicles, a vehicle and a person, or a vehicle and an ''object'' come into contact. It is immaterial whether or not damage actually occurs as a result of the contact. For instance, if A, driving his car, sees B suddenly step out onto the road, and applies his brakes so that he is able to stop without hurting B, but his bumper still made contact with B's body then an accident would have occurred. In certain circumstances, to be involved in an accident does not require the accused's car to have actually collided with another car, or another person or another object. If the accused, for instance, *caused* an accident, or helped to cause it, and *witnessed* the accident occurring, then he would be ''involved'' in the accident. For example: if a person changed lanes abruptly and caused a car travelling behind him to brake suddenly, go out of control, hit the curb, and roll off the highway, he would have been involved in the accident. However, if he could prove that *he did not see the accident and was unaware that it had occurred* even though he in fact caused it, he would not be guilty of "failing to stop" in contradiction of s.233(2).

C. IMPAIRED DRIVING

1. General

Section 234 provides:

> **234. Everyone who, while his ability to drive a motor vehicle is impaired by alcohol or a drug, drives a motor vehicle or has the care or control of a motor vehicle, whether it is in motion or not, is guilty of an indictable offence or an offence punishable on summary conviction and is liable:**
> **(a) for a first offence, to a fine of not more than two thousand dollars and not less than fifty dollars or to imprisonment for six months or to both;**
> **(b) for a second offence, to imprisonment for not more than one year and not less than fourteen days; and**
> **(c) for each subsequent offence, to imprisonment for not more than two years and not less than three months.**

Section 234 creates two separate offences: 1. *Driving* a motor vehicle *while impaired;* and 2. Having the *care or control* of a motor vehicle *while impaired.* "Motor vehicle" is defined in section 2 of the Code (see page 183). Whether or not a motor vehicle can move under its own power at the time of the offence is not material. It is the *type or nature* of the vehicle and *not* its actual state of operability that is the determining factor. In *Saunders v. R.,*[8] even though the motor vehicle in question was wedged into a ditch so that it could not move under its own power (it was eventually moved by a tow truck) the accused, who was in the car and impaired at the time, was found guilty of impaired driving under section 234.

Offences under section 234 do not require that the vehicle be on a highway or road or other "public place." In *R. v. Murray,*[9] a case from Prince Edward Island, the accused was convicted of impaired driving (having "care or control" of his car) while the car was parked in the private driveway beside his house.

A. IMPAIRED In general an accused is impaired within the meaning of section 234 if he has been so affected by the consumption of alcohol, or drugs, he is no longer in *complete* control of his motor vehicle. The proof that he is impaired can come from a number of evidentiary sources: eg. his actual driving behaviour, a breathalyzer test, or his appearance and behaviour (i.e. slurred speech, smell of alcohol on his breath, etc.), when he is examined by the police.

In *R. v. McKenzie*[10] the court made the following statement about proof of impairment: "There appears to be no single test or observation of impairment of control of faculties, standing alone, which is sufficiently conclusive. There should be consideration of a combination of several tests and observations such as general conduct, smell of the breath, character of the speech, manner of walking, turning sharply, sitting down and rising, picking up objects, reaction of the pupils of the eyes, character of the breathing."

An accused is under *no legal obligation* to perform any physical tests, (excluding the breathalyzer test), calculated to prove or disprove his degree of impairment.

As a general rule the result of a breathalyzer test, alone, will be *insufficient* to sustain a conviction of impaired driving. On the other hand erratic driving by the accused is relevant but not essential to a conviction. In certain situations a high breathalyzer test reading alone, without evidence of erratic driving, can result in a conviction for impaired driving. In *R. v. Brissette*[11] the court stated that the question is not whether the accused drove erratically, but rather, was his *ability to drive* impaired.

B. "CARE OR CONTROL" Usually a person has "care or control" of a vehicle when he is sitting in the driver's seat. However, it is not essential for the accused to be in the driver's seat in order for him to have "care or control" of the vehicle. In *R. v. Kemsley*[12] the court was prepared to hold that an impaired accused, who was found with his hand on the car door handle (the keys were in the ignition), was in "care or control" of his car.

In *R. v. Rupolo*[13] the investigating officer found the accused (who was impaired), two to five feet away from his car which was stuck in mud on the median of a four-lane highway. The motor was not running, the lights were off, the doors were locked and the keys were in the possession of the accused. The court concluded that in such circumstances the accused had "care or control" of his car, for the purpose of a charge under s.234.

If a person is found in the driver's seat, s.237(1)(a) creates the following rebuttable presumption:

> **Where it is proved that the accused occupied the seat ordinarily occupied by the driver of a motor vehicle, he shall be deemed to have had the care or control of the vehicle unless he establishes that he did not enter or mount the vehicle for the purpose of setting it in motion.**

In other words, a person who is impaired and is found "behind the wheel" of his vehicle, may not be "in care or control" if he can establish that he *did not get in the vehicle with the idea of driving it.*

In *R. v. McPhee*[14] the accused attempted to call his supervisor to request someone to come and take his car (a taxi) off the road, but the line was busy. He therefore went to his taxi-cab and turned on the ignition in order to use the car radio to call his dispatcher to relay a request to his supervisor to come and take his car off the road. He then fell asleep while waiting for the supervisor. In response to his call the dispatcher sent out the supervisor, to pick up the cab. Fifteen to twenty minutes later, but before the supervisor had arrived, the police found the accused asleep in the car with his head on the passenger side and his feet on the driver's side, with the keys in the ignition and the motor running. At this time he was impaired by alcohol.

The judge concluded that in a prosecution under section 234, if the *only proof* offered by the prosecutor of "care or control" of a motor vehicle is that the accused occupied the seat ordinarily occupied by the driver, and the accused establishes, as the taxi cab driver did, that he did not enter the vehicle for the purpose of setting it in motion, he must be acquitted.

In *R. v. Mullen,* [15] M and a friend, G, set out in M's car from Sudbury, with the intention of going to Ottawa. Shortly after their departure G said he had some MDA (a drug) which M asked to try. M asked G to drive. When the MDA did not at first affect M, he took two or three more capsules which produced a considerable effect. As they were approaching North Bay, M asked G to turn back and G turned the car around. M then asked G to stop the car so that he could get out and walk around. After both men got out of the car, there was an altercation in which G was struck by M, and G then left, apparently hitch-hiking into North Bay. According to M he was hallucinating at this time and was uncertain of what was happening. M returned to his car and sat in the driver's seat. He testified that he did not intend to drive because he was still suffering the effects of the drug and was waiting to "come down." Constable C observed M sitting in the driver's seat of the car stopped on the shoulder of the highway. M explained his physical condition to the officer by stating he had taken four MDA capsules.

M was charged with having the care or control of his car while impaired by the drug MDA. He was found not guilty because the court believed that he had not entered his car with any intention of driving it.

2. The Question of Voluntariness

An accused may avoid a conviction of impaired driving, (having "care or control" or "driving" while impaired), if he became impaired *non-voluntarily and was neither aware nor should reasonably have been aware,* that he would become impaired. In other words if an accused's impairment was caused by prescribed medication and he was unaware, *before* taking the medication, of its "impairing" qualities, *and after* taking it, he did not become aware as the medication took effect, of his impairment, his impairment would not be voluntarily induced.

Whether or not an accused's impairment was voluntary or involuntary was discussed in *McLeod v. A.G. Sask.* [16] The accused was charged with impaired driving. He testified that he had two drinks of whisky and then, intending to take two "222" pills, he mistakenly took two pills prescribed for his diabetes. A doctor testified that the diabetes medication could cause symptoms of impairment, and that the accused would be *unaware* of such symptoms. The court held that through no act of his own will, the accused became incapable of appreciating that he was, or might become impaired. In such circumstances the accused could not be convicted of impaired driving.

In *R. v. Saxon*[17] the accused after taking two tranquillizers at approximately 3:00 p.m. drove to a local beer parlour and consumed four beers between 4:00 p.m. and 5:00 p.m. (There was some conflict in his evidence as to whether it was four glasses or four bottles of beer.) At 5:00 p.m. he left, entered his car, drove it, and was involved in an accident.

The accused, at his trial, testified that in 1973 he consulted a doctor who prescribed some tranquillizers for him, and told him not to drink alcohol for a period of six weeks. He took the tranquillizers for about three days. The accused stated that the pills made him very drowsy and that because of their effect he was unable to work (he was employed as a research mathematician) and, therefore, he stopped taking them. However, some months later, on the day of the accident, the accused stated that he was feeling nervous so he decided to start taking the tranquillizers again. He took a single pill at 8:00 a.m., and another at 11:00 a.m., and at 3:00 p.m. he took two more. He was supposed to take only one pill every 6 hours. The accused then went to the beer parlour and the last thing he said he remembered before the accident, was pushing the door open to leave. The accused was charged with impaired driving.

The accused's doctor gave the following evidence about the effect of the tranquillizers and the alcohol:

> *Q. A person who has had four tranquillizers, two of them at the same time in the day, what would be the effect of one bottle of beer on such a person?*
> *Would he begin to feel upset after the first bottle of beer?*
> *A. I think he would begin to notice it, yes.*
> *Q. He would begin to notice and the second beer would make the condition worse?*
> *A. Likely, yes.*
> *Q. Four would make it very bad?*
> *A. By four I think he would notice it absolutely.*

The accused tried to argue that his impairment was not voluntarily induced in that he had taken tranquillizers prescribed by his doctor, and that he did not know, and had not been told by his doctor, what their effect would be when the tranquillizers were combined with alcohol. The court did not accept the accused's defence and found him guilty of impaired driving under section 234. The court stated that if an accused *knew*, or had any *reasonable grounds for believing,* that the consumption of drugs and alcohol *might cause him to be impaired,* then if he consumes these substances and becomes impaired, he has *voluntarily* become impaired. The accused in this case should have known from his own prior use of the drugs that they would impair his judgment and make him drowsy and less alert. Yet after taking four pills over seven hours, instead of the prescribed one pill every six, he proceeded to a beer parlour and consumed alcohol. He should have known the beer would increase the impairment caused by the tranquillizers alone. Furthermore, the accused's doctor testified that two beers, let alone the four he had actually consumed, when taken in conjunction with the tranquillizers, should have alerted him to the fact that he was impaired.

D. THE BREATHALYZER

There are two sections in the Code which authorize a police officer to make a breathalyzer test demand to a driver.

Section 234.1 states:

> **234.1(1) Where a peace officer reasonably suspects that a person who is driving a motor vehicle or who has the care or control of a motor vehicle, whether it is in motion or not, has alcohol in his body, he may, by demand made to that person, require him to provide forthwith ...a sample of his breath ...to enable a proper analysis of his breath to be made by means of an approved roadside screening device. ...**

An "approved roadside screening device" is an instrument which can evaluate a person's blood alcohol level immediately. Such an instrument, or device, is the Alcohol Level Evaluation Roadside Tester (ALERT), an electronic instrument that flashes red or green when a driver breathes into it. If it flashes red, it indicates that the driver's blood alcohol level is probably over the 80 milligram limit. If the device signals red, the driver will then be taken to the police station for the regular breathalyzer test.

Section 235 provides:

> **235.(1) Where a peace officer on reasonable and probable grounds believes that a person is committing, or at any time within the preceding two hours has committed, an offence under s.234 or 236, he may, by demand made to that person forthwith or as soon as is practicable, require him to provide then or as soon thereafter as is practicable ...samples of his breath ...and to accompany the peace officer for the purpose of enabling such samples to be taken.**

Section 234.1 was enacted to assist police officers in preventing and controlling the problem of "the drinking driver." At one time s.235(1) was the only authority a police officer could use to make a demand for a breathalyzer test. Section 235(1) dictates that *reasonable and probable grounds* have to be evident before a demand can be made. In other words prior to s.234.1 a driver had to be obviously drunk, or openly careless and erratic in the handling of his vehicle, before he could be required to take a breathalyzer test. And of course, under s.235(1) a driver had to be taken to the police station to perform the breathalyzer test. (Section 234.1 provides that the breathalyzer test is to be conducted at the "roadside".)

Such strict grounds proved to be inadequate when it came to preventing and controlling, as opposed to only "catching", impaired drivers. Section 234.1 lowered the test so that the police only need *reasonably suspect* that a person has alcohol in his body. If they have a reasonable suspicion a driver can be stopped and required to provide a sample of his breath.

More specifically, the difference between a test that is based on a "reasonable suspicion" (s.234.1), and one that is based on "reasonable and probable" grounds (s.235), is that the latter test ("reasonable and probable") *sets a much higher standard*. The police officer must believe that the accused *probably* has committed the act. That is to say, it is more likely than not, that the accused has "done the thing" said of him. A "reasonable suspicion" test is generally satisfied if the officer believes it is *possible* that the accused committed the act. That is to say, the accused might have done the thing said of him.

Under s.234.1 a police officer must actually observe the accused either driving, or having care or control of his vehicle, before he can make a demand. If an officer suspects a motorist had alcohol in his body while driving, but did not observe him driving, (or having "care or control"), a demand could *not* be made pursuant to s.234.1. The officer would have to satisfy the reasonable and probable grounds test that the motorist was impaired, while driving within the two hours preceding the demand, as provided for in s.235.

This is perhaps best illustrated by an example:

B, a witness, reports to a police officer that he observed a car being driven erratically, and is able to positively identify the driver as A. The police officer proceeds to A's home and discovers a car parked in the driveway. The car is registered in A's name. A answers the door, and the police officer observes he smells of alcohol, is glassy-eyed and has slurred speech. He asks A if he has been driving in the last hour or so. A says yes. In such circumstances the police officer would be entitled to demand that A take a breathalyzer test under authority of section 235, because he has reasonable and probable grounds for believing A did drive, (within the last two hours), while he was impaired. The police officer, however, could not use section 234.1 because he did not observe A while he was driving.

Suppose in the above example A, when he was questioned by the officer, appeared to be completely sober. Then the only evidence that A might have been driving while impaired, would be the evidence of the witness. In such circumstances the officer would *not* have reasonable and probable grounds to believe that A had been guilty of impaired driving, and he would not be entitled to make a demand under s.235. And once again even if the officer suspected A had alcohol in his body, he could not make a demand under s.234.1 because he did not observe A driving.

Consider a second example. A police officer observed B coming out of a tavern. B is walking in a perfectly normal manner, he is completely in control of himself. B gets into his car and drives away. His driving is not erratic. Under s.235 the officer could not make a demand that B take a breathalyzer because he would not have reasonable and probable grounds for believing B was driving while impaired. However, the officer could make a demand under section 234.1, because it is *reasonable to suspect* that B, exiting from a tavern, has alcohol in his body while he is driving. In this example the officer could have made a demand for a breathalyzer as soon as B entered his car because, at that time, B would have "care or control" of his car.

The following briefly summarises when, under the authority of s.234.1 and 235, a police officer may make a demand for a breathalyzer test:

1. The officer observes the accused driving, or in care or control of a motor vehicle, and he *reasonably suspects* he has alcohol in his body (s.234.1).

2. The officer, not relying on section 234.1, has *reasonable and probable* grounds to believe the accused is driving, or has care or control while impaired (s.235).

3. The officer believes, on reasonable and probable grounds, that the accused, within the two hours preceding the demand, was driving, or had care or control of his vehicle, while impaired (s.235).

1. Refusal to Take a Breathalyzer Test

Both s.234.1(2) and 235(2) make it an offence, unless the accused has a reasonable excuse, to refuse to take a breathalyzer test, once the demand is made. Section 234.1(2) and s.235 both state:

> **(2) Every one who, without reasonable excuse, fails or refuses to comply with a demand made to him by a peace officer under subsection (1) is guilty of an indictable offence or an offence punishable on summary conviction and is liable**
> **(a) for a first offence, to a fine of not more than two thousand dollars and not less than fifty dollars or to imprisonment for six months or to both;**
> **(b) for a second offence, to imprisonment for not more than one year and not less than fourteen days; and**
> **(c) for each subsequent offence, to imprisonment for not more than two years and not less than three months.**

A refusal, by the police, to allow the suspected motorist a private conversation with his lawyer is an excuse for the accused's refusal to provide a breath sample. However the police do not have to wait for the accused's lawyer to actually visit with his client and attend the test. Once the accused has made his phone call he then must take the test. If an accused is unable to contact his lawyer he *may not* delay taking the test.

Establishment that an accused's state of mind was so affected by alcohol, or a drug, that he could not understand the demand at all, is a reasonable excuse for not providing a sample. In a New Brunswick case, *R. v. Nadeau,*[18] the judge concluded that a "reasonable excuse" must entail some circumstance which renders compliance with the demand either extremely difficult, or likely to involve a substantial risk to the health of the person on whom the demand has been made.

2. Excessive Blood Alcohol Level

Section 236 makes it an offence to drive, or have care or control of a motor vehicle, while having a blood alcohol reading in excess of ''.08.''
Section 236(1) states:

> **236.(1) Every one who drives a motor vehicle or has the care or control of a motor vehicle, whether it is in motion or not, having consumed alcohol in such a quantity that the proportion thereof in his blood exceeds 80 milligrams of alcohol in 100 millilitres of blood, is guilty of an indictable offence or an offence punishable on summary conviction and is liable**
> > **(a) for a first offence, to a fine of not more than two thousand dollars and not less than fifty dollars or to imprisonment for six months or to both;**
> > **(b) for a second offence, to imprisonment for not more than one year and not less than fourteen days; and**
> > **(c) for each subsequent offence, to imprisonment for not more than two years and not less than three months.**

Offences under s.234 and 236 are separate and distinct. Therefore, a person may be charged under both s.234, (impaired driving), and s.236, even though the charges arose out of the same set of facts.

E. DRIVING WHILE PROHIBITED

It is an offence for a person to drive while his licence or driving permit is suspended.
Section 238(3) states:

> **238.(3) Every one who drives a motor vehicle in Canada while he is disqualified or prohibited from driving a motor vehicle by reason of the legal suspension or cancellation, in any province, of his permit or licence ...to drive a motor vehicle in that province is guilty of**
> > **(a) an indictable offence and is liable to imprisonment for two years; or**
> > **(b) an offence punishable on summary conviction.**

If an accused is genuinely ignorant of the fact that his licence has been suspended, or cancelled, he cannot be convicted of an offence under s.238(3).

QUESTIONS

1. B has been driving all night. He knows that he is very drowsy but decides to keep driving. A short time later he falls asleep, loses control of his car and runs off the road. No other cars are involved in the accident. Should B be charged with:
   (i) driving that is criminally negligent, [section 233(1)].
   (ii) dangerous driving, [section 233(4)].
   (iii) the provincial offence of "careless driving."
2. Would your answer to the above question change if B did collide with another car after he fell asleep?
3. What is the difference between driving that is criminally negligent [section 233(1)], and driving that is dangerous [section 233(4)]?
4. Define the offence of impaired driving [section 234].
5. Can a person be convicted of impaired driving without the evidence of a breathalyzer test?
6. In what circumstances can a police officer make a demand that a motorist submit to a breathalyzer test?
7. What does "reasonable excuse" mean, in sections 234.1 and 235?

[1] (1967) 50 C.R. 300 (Ont.C.A.).
[2] (1958) 122 C.C.C. 247, 29 C.R. 312 (Alta.C.A.)
[3] (1970) 1 C.C.C. 338 (Ont.C.A.)
[4] (1973) 12 C.C.C. (2d) 81 (Ont.C.A.)
[5] (1969) 4 C.C.C. 245; 7 C.R.N.S. 243 (S.C.C.)
[6] (1971) 1 C.C.C. 101 (Ont. H.C.J.)
[7] (1947) 90 C.C.C. 197 (Ont.Co.Ct.)
[8] (1967) 3 C.C.C. 278; 1 C.R.N.S. 249 (S.C.C.)
[9] (1973) 11 C.C.C. (2d) 296 (P.E.I. S.C.)
[10] (1955) 111 C.C.C. 317; 20 C.R. 412 (Alta.S.C.).
[11] (1966) 57 W.W.R. (B.C. S.C.)
[12] (1971) 1 C.C.C. (2d) 272 (Ont.S.C.)
[13] (1963) 40 C.R. 245 (Alta.S.C.)
[14] (1976) 25 C.C.C. (2d) 412 (Ont.C.A.).
[15] (1975) 30 C.R.N.S. 4 (Ont.C.A.).
[16] (1972) 6 C.C.C. (2d) 81 (Sask.D.C.)
[17] (1975) 22 C.C.C. (2d) 370 (Alta.C.A.).
[18] (1974) 19 C.C.C. (2d) 199 (N.B.C.A.).

Chapter Twelve

Assaults and Related Offences Against the Person

A. ASSAULT DEFINED

> 244. A person commits an assault when,
> (a) without the consent of another person or with consent, where it is obtained by fraud, he applies force intentionally to the person of the other, directly or indirectly;
> (b) he attempts or threatens, by an act or gesture, to apply force to the person of the other, if he has or causes the other to believe upon reasonable grounds that he has present ability to effect his purpose;
> or
> (c) while openly wearing or carrying a weapon or an imitation thereof, he accosts or impedes another person and begs.

Section 244 sets out the definition of assault. Notice that the section defines three different sets of circumstances in which an assault may occur. Under ss.(a), force must be actually used and lack of valid consent is an essential element. Where the use of force is only threatened or attempted, ss.(b) requires that the person accused of assault must have either had the ability to carry out the assault, or must have caused the victim to believe upon reasonable grounds that he had the ability to carry out the assault. Subsection (c) is a relatively new addition to the Code, being added by the *Criminal Law Amendment Act, 1975*. This subsection defines a specific situation in which it may be implied that the use of force is being threatened. At the time of this writing, there have been no reported cases applying or interpreting this section. The following discussion will, therefore, relate to assault as defined in ss.(a) and ss.(b). However, the general principles derived from the application of ss.(a) and ss.(b) should also apply to ss.(c).

1. Assault: Section 244(a)

The main issue involving assault under s.244(a) (i.e. where physical force is actually applied), is whether or not the victim gave valid consent. This issue is important since lack of valid consent must be established before it can be said that an assault has occurred. It might be wondered why any person would consent to force being applied to himself. The reason becomes obvious when one considers the fact that any touching of a person may be an assault if done without that person's consent. Thus, what in one situation might be a gesture of love and affection, in another situation might be grounds for a charge of criminal assault.

·It is essential then that the prosecutor show that there was no valid consent. Before a person can give his consent to an act, he must understand the nature of the act. The law draws a distinction between mere submission and positive consent. As one court stated: " ...consent means an active will in the mind of the [victim] to permit the doing of the act complained of; and that knowledge of what is to be done, or of the nature of the act that is being done, is essential to a consent to the act."[1] In this case, the accused had performed indecent acts upon two eight-year-old boys. He argued that the boys had consented to the acts being performed. The boys, however, testified that the accused had not told them what he was going to do to them and that they did not understand what he had done. In this situation, the court ruled that because of their ignorance of the acts, they could not give valid consent.

Similarly, there have been cases where a person has impersonated a doctor and with the consent of the patient, who is usually a woman, given a physical examination. In these cases, where the charge is often indecent assault, it has been decided that the patient's consent was obtained by fraud and was, therefore, invalid.[2] Some persons are incapable of giving consent, for example, insane persons or very young children. So, before a child receives medical treatment, unless emergency conditions exist, a doctor will obtain the consent of the child's parents or guardian.

It is important to point out that an assault may result where the amount of force exceeds that to which consent has been given. This situation could arise during a sports event, such as a hockey game, where a fight breaks out on the ice. It is generally agreed that players of sports which involve physical contact consent to a certain amount of force being applied to them by other players. But as one judge has said: " ...there is a question of degree involved, and no athlete should be presumed to accept malicious unprovoked or overly violent attack."[3]

Although the Code seems to clearly require lack of consent for assault under s.244(a), some courts have said that a person cannot give valid consent where the physical force is used in anger or where it is likely to or does cause bodily harm. For example, in the case of *R. v. Squire*[4] two men argued in a tavern and went outside to fight. One of the men, an off-duty police officer, pulled a gun during the fight and shot and killed the other man. He was charged with murder. Whether or not the fight was lawful was one factor in determining whether or not the accused could rely on the defence of provocation. The court ruled that consent itself would not make the fight lawful. The court said: "Where two persons engage in a fight in anger by mutual consent, the blows struck by each constitute an assault on the other unless justifiable in self defence...."

There have been, however, cases which have said that there must be proof of actual lack of consent before the accused can be convicted of assault. In *R. v. Dix,*[5] the facts were similar to those in the *Squire* case. Two men who had been drinking in a tavern argued and agreed to go outside to fight. The fight was over in about one minute leaving one man unharmed and the other badly beaten. The victor in the fight was charged with assault causing bodily harm. The accused was found not guilty by the court because the Crown failed to prove that the physical force was applied without the victim's consent.

Although there were factual differences in the cases and the charge in *Squire* was more serious, these differences do not provide an explanation for the contrary decisions regarding the effect of consent.

It appears that while the court in the *Dix* case relied basically on a straightforward reading of s.244 of the Code, the court in the *Squire* case was strongly influenced by English law, particularly a 1934 court decision. This case, *R. v. Donovan,*[6] stated that although exceptions exist, generally it is an unlawful act to beat a person with such violence that bodily harm is a probable consequence. Consent in such circumstances, the court said, is immaterial since the act itself is unlawful. Clearly some acts are unlawful even if the victim consents. A good example is the offence of murder which can be committed even with a willing victim. The Code in s.14 specifically denies the defence of consent to those accused of murder:

> **14. No person is entitled to consent to have death inflicted upon him, and such consent does not affect the criminal responsibility of any person by whom death may be inflicted upon the person by whom consent is given.**

However, with regard to the offence of assault under s.244(a), Parliament seems to have plainly made lack of consent an essential ingredient of the offence.

In summary, it is unclear whether the English common law which states it is an unlawful act, even if the victim consents, to inflict bodily harm, should be read into s.244(a) of the Code; or whether lack of consent is always necessary for the commission of this kind of assault, even where bodily harm is caused. It is likely that until more cases are decided by the courts of Canada, the law will remain in doubt.

Until that time, at least where an act causes serious injury to a person, the courts may avoid confronting the issue of the effect of consent by ruling that the injurious act was not within the scope of the victim's consent. This was the method used by the court in the case of *R. v. MacTavish.*[7] In this case, two high school boys agreed to meet outside the school at noon to fight. Shortly after the fight began, the accused knocked the other boy to the ground, pulled the fallen boy's sweater over his head and kicked him several times. The court of appeal upheld the accused's conviction by finding that there was no consent given by either of the boys to kicking. The court stated: "Kicking involves bodily injury as a probable consequence and is a kind of act which cannot reasonably have been in the contemplation of either when they agreed to engage in a school boy's fight."

By finding that there was no consent, the court found it unnecessary to state what its decision would have been if consent had been given to the acts.

2. Assault: Section 244(b)

Under this subsection of s.244 an attempted or threatened use of force is defined as an assault. This means actual physical contact is not necessary for the offence to have been committed. An example of this type of assault is the case of *R. v. Judge*.[8] In this case a court of appeal upheld the conviction of an accused who, accompanied by other men, approached the victim, who was inside a locked car, and while using words and gestures which indicated he had a weapon, threatened to "burn" the victim. Similarly, pointing a gun at a person without a lawful excuse such as self-defence would be an assault.[9] Even where the accused does not intend to carry out the threat, if the victim reasonably believes that the accused has the ability to carry out the threat, the offence will have been committed. This point is illustrated by a New Brunswick case where an argument between a husband and wife led to the husband taking up a gun and threatening to shoot his wife. It was argued that the husband was not guilty of assault because the accused did not intend to actually shoot his wife. The Court of Appeal disagreed however and entered a verdict of guilty of common assault. The court ruled that the making of the threat itself, coupled with the ability to carry it out, constituted the offence of assault.[10]

Interestingly, the courts have held that words *alone,* no matter how threatening, do not constitute an assault. In the case of *R. v. Byrne,*[11] the accused was charged with robbery under s.288(c) (now s.302(c)) which states:

> **Everyone commits robbery who . . . . (c) assaults any person with intent to steal from him. . . .**

The accused had walked up to the box office of a movie theatre and said to the cashier, "I've got a gun, give me all your money or I'll shoot." Although he had a coat draped over his arm, no gun was visible. Then, while the cashier was gathering the money, the accused fled. The court held that the accused had not committed an assault since there were no acts or gestures accompanying his verbal threats and he could not, therefore, be found guilty of robbery as charged.

3. The Permissible Use of Force

Under certain circumstances, the law allows persons to apply physical force to other persons. In Chapter Five under the discussion of arrests, it was mentioned that a police officer, or a person assisting a police officer, can use as much force as reasonably necessary to make an arrest. Similarly, in Chapter Four on Defences, it was pointed out that a person can use a reasonable amount of force to defend himself, his family, or property. Likewise, parents or a person standing in their place (e.g. a teacher) can use a reasonable amount of force for the correction of a child. In all these situations, however, once the amount of force exceeds that which is reasonable and necessary under the circumstances, an assault is committed.

B. THE OFFENCES OF ASSAULT

Once it is established that an assault as defined in one of the subsections of s.244 has taken place, the person who has committed the assault will be charged under one of the other Code sections which define the several different offences of assault. The reason that there is more than one offence of assault is because the nature and the seriousness of the assault will depend on other circumstances surrounding the actual use of, or attempted or threatened use of, force. For example, it is usually a more serious offence to assault an on-duty police officer than a private individual. Also, if serious bodily injury is caused, a more serious offence will be charged.

1. Assault Offences Under s.245

245.(1) Every one who commits a common assault is guilty of an offence punishable on summary conviction.

(2) Every one who unlawfully causes bodily harm to any person or commits an assault that causes bodily harm to any person

    (a) is guilty of an indictable offence and is liable to imprisonment for five years; or

    (b) is guilty of an offence punishable on summary conviction.

The section creates two different offences:
1. s.245(1), common assault;
2. s.245(2), committing an assault that causes bodily harm.
Common assault is the least serious type of assault. It may be used when the assault consists only of threats or attempts, or when the victim has not suffered any bodily harm. Where bodily harm does occur, the accused may be charged under s.245(2).

While an exact definition of "bodily harm" has never been given, it appears that the "least bodily harm" would be sufficient for a s.245(2) charge.[12] One English case even considered an injury of the victim's "state of mind for the time being" as within the definition of "actual bodily harm." In this case, *R. v. Miller*,[13] a husband had forced his wife from whom he was separated to have intercourse with him. He could not be charged with rape since, generally speaking, a man can not be guilty of raping his wife. His conviction for assault causing actual bodily harm was proper, however, since the husband was not justified in using force and the attack had left the woman in a hysterical and nervous condition. Another English case defined bodily harm as including:" . . . . any hurt or injury calculated to interfere with the health and comfort of the [victim]. Such hurt or injury need not be permanent, but must, no doubt, be more than merely transient and trifling.''[14]

Courts have held that *unlawfully causing bodily harm,* which is mentioned in the first part of s.245(2), is an offence distinct from *assault causing bodily harm.*[15] This means that a person could be charged either with the offence of assault causing bodily harm or with the offence of unlawfully causing bodily harm. There have been no court decisions which discuss what the actual differences between the two offences are. Presumably unlawfully causing bodily harm could apply to a situation where injury was caused by means other than by assault.

2. Assault Offences Under Section 246

> **246.(1)** Every one who assaults a person with intent to commit an indictable offence is guilty of an indictable offence and is liable to imprisonment for five years.
>
> **(2)** Every one who
>
> **(a)** assaults a public officer or peace officer engaged in the execution of his duty, or a person acting in aid of such an officer;
>
> **(b)** assaults a person with intent to resist or prevent the lawful arrest or detention of himself or another person; or
>
> **(c)** assaults a person
>
>   **(i)** who is engaged in the lawful execution of a process against lands or goods or in making a lawful distress or seizure,
>
>   or
>
>   **(ii)** with intent to rescue anything taken under a lawful process, distress or seizure
>
> is guilty of
>
> **(d)** an indictable offence and is liable to imprisonment for five years, or
>
> **(e)** an offence punishable on summary conviction.

An essential element of assault under s.246(1) is that the assault must be committed with intent to commit an indictable offence. So, for example, if A points a gun at B for the purpose of kidnapping B (an indictable offence), A could be charged with "assault with intent" under s.246(1) rather than with the less serious offence of common assault.

The offences listed under s.246(2) have the common element of an assault of a person who is engaged in an act of law enforcement such as a police officer making an arrest or a person seizing property under lawful process (e.g. a court order). A frequent question which arises under this section is whether the person assaulted was acting within the scope of his authority at the time of the assault. If, for example, a police officer is assaulted while making an illegal arrest, the accused cannot be charged under s.246(2), although another type of assault may be charged. An interesting case which illustrates this point is *Carrier v. R.*,[16] a 1972 decision of the New Brunswick Court of Appeal. In this case, the police were investigating the theft of two wheels from a car. After searching the accused's trunk and finding nothing, the accused was told his car was being seized "to check it out." Apparently, the police wanted to take the car to the station to examine the wheels on the car. Upon being told that his car was being seized, the accused rolled up the car window, catching the police officer's arm between the glass and car frame, and drove off. The officer was able to free his arm but the accused then attempted to run him over. The court found that the police officer, by attempting to seize the car over the owner's objection and without arresting him had exceeded the powers given to him. The accused, therefore, could not be convicted under s.246(2). However, the court substituted a conviction of common assault since the accused had used more force than necessary to resist the seizure of his car.

The extent of the police officer's authority is not always easy to determine. The Supreme Court of Canada recently considered this issue in *R. v. Stenning.*[17] The case involved police constables who, while investigating a disturbance outside a building and seeing a suspicious movement inside, entered the building through an open window. The police found two men in the building who refused to identify themselves. One of the men struck one of the constables in the face. It turned out that this man was the son of the owner of the building and was not involved in the outside disturbance. The court found that the accused was guilty of assault under s.246(a). The court stated: "Assuming that Wilkinson (the constable) did technically trespass on the premises, the fact remains that he was there to investigate an occurrence which had happened earlier in the evening, which involved the firing of a rifle. He was charged under s.47 of the *Police Act,* R.S.O. 1960, c.298, with the duty of preserving the peace, preventing robberies and other crimes, and apprehending offenders. He was in the course of making an investigation, in carrying out that duty, when he was assaulted by the respondent."

Both the *Stenning* case and the following case, *R. v. Tunbridge,*[18] which had the opposite result, demonstrate the difficulty in deciding when police are engaged in the execution of their duty. In *Tunbridge,* the police were called to investigate a domestic quarrel. The husband appeared to be intoxicated and the wife said she wished to take the children and leave the home. While the wife was dressing one child, the other child was taken by the father onto his lap. When the wife was ready to leave, the man refused to let the child go. The police then scuffled with the accused in an attempt to take the child from him. The man was charged with assault under s.246(2). The court directed that the accused be acquitted and stated: "In the absence of reasonable apprehension of injury to the child or of some breach of the peace I think the constables exceeded their duty when they purported to decide that the child should be taken from the father and then proceeded with their attempt physically to take it."

C. OFFENCES OF CAUSING BODILY HARM

1. Causing Bodily Harm With Intent

> **228.** **Every one who, with intent**
> **(a) to wound, maim or disfigure any person,**
> **(b) to endanger the life of any person, or**
> **(c) to prevent the arrest or detention of any person,**
> **discharges a firearm, air gun or air pistol at or causes bodily harm in any way to any person, whether or not that person is the one mentioned in paragraph (a), (b), or (c), is guilty of an indictable offence and is liable to imprisonment for fourteen years.**

The offence of "causing bodily harm with intent" always requires a specific intent to bring about one of the consequences listed in subsections (a) – (c) of s.228. Of course, the necessary intent may be presumed if it is a natural consequence of a person's act. So, if A fires a gun at close distance at B, it may be presumed that A intended to wound B or to endanger his life. However, if, for example, A shows that the firing was accidental, he will have rebutted the presumption.

Maiming means disabling a person in such a way that he is less able to fight or to defend himself.[19] Such injuries as broken limbs, or lost eyesight, are maims. Wounding involves breaking the skin,[20] while to disfigure seems to refer to harming a person so that he is less physically attractive. So, to cut off a man's nose would not be a maiming but it would be a wounding and disfiguring.

One question that was settled in a 1962 case decided by the Alberta Court of Appeal was whether the injury had to be caused by some type of weapon. The court decided that the section does not require a weapon and that the accused was guilty of the offence. He had, using his hands, tried to wrap the victim's leg around a telephone pole, breaking the leg badly.[21]

2. Other Offences of Causing Bodily Harm

There are several other offences in the Code which prohibit the causing of bodily harm by specific means. Some of these are the following: Sections 77–79 create offences concerning the causing of bodily harm through the use of explosive or dangerous substances. Section 229 makes it an offence to cause a person to take a poisonous or noxious substance. Section 230 sets out the offence of choking, suffocating or strangling a person to enable, or assist in, the commission of an indictable offence. Section 231 makes it an offence to set a trap with intent to cause death or bodily harm. Section 232 defines the offence of interfering with transportation facilities with intent to endanger others. Section 242 places upon everyone who makes an opening in the ice or an excavation on land a duty to guard the opening to prevent accidents.

D. OTHER OFFENCES AGAINST THE PERSON

1. Threatening

> **331.(1) Every one commits an offence who by letter, tele-gram, telephone, cable, radio, or otherwise, knowingly utters, conveys or causes any person to receive a threat,**
> **(a) to cause death or injury to any person, or**
> **(b) to burn, destroy or damage real or personal property, or,**
> **(c) to kill, maim, wound, poison or injure an animal or bird that is the property of any person.**

The Supreme Court of Canada in the recent case of *R. v. Nabis*[22] fully discussed the main elements of the offence of threatening. The issue which the court had to decide was whether an oral threat made face-to-face was an offence under s.331. Notice that the section lists several ways that the threat may be conveyed, e.g. by letter, telegram, telephone, etc. The list then ends with the words "or otherwise." The specific question for the court was whether oral face-to-face threats are included in these words, "or otherwise." The decision of the court was that the making of purely oral threats is not a criminal offence. The intent of Parliament, the court stated, was to only prohibit threats conveyed either by those means listed or by means similar to, or of the same category, as those listed. The court went on to suggest several possible reasons for only prohibiting certain types of threats:

> *Some have reasoned that a person who goes to the trouble of writing a threatening letter, for example, has already proceeded from words to deeds and, therefore, manifested his resolve. Also, the use of certain means may conceal the identity of the person making the threat or prevent the prospective victim from judging what steps he can take to ensure his safety. Lastly, it is possible that resort to any means other than the one which human beings most usually employ to communicate with each other is likely to amplify the threat . . . .*

Likewise, the court stated that making the simple expression of a threat a serious crime would be likely to lead to many difficulties since "countless are those who do not weigh their words."

The court also made the following points about the offence of threatening.

> *To be convicted of the offence, it does not matter if the accused intended to carry out the threat, what his specific purpose was for making the threat, what his motive was, whether the threat raised the possibility of imminent or remote danger to the victim, or what effect the threat had on the victim.*

There are several other offences in the Code which may be committed through the use of threats. Examples are: assault (s.244), which may be committed by the use of threatening acts or gestures; rape (s.143), which may be committed where consent to intercourse is obtained by the use of threats of bodily harm; and the offence of extortion by libel (s.266), which may be committed by threatening to publish a defamatory libel. It is also an offence to threaten a clergyman or minister to prevent or obstruct him from performing a service or other function (s.172). Extortion with intent to unlawfully gain anything (s.305) can be committed through the use of threats to induce a person to do or cause anything to be done.

2. Intimidation

381.(1) Every one who, wrongfully and without lawful authority, for the purpose of compelling another person to abstain from doing anything that he has a lawful right to do, or to do anything that he has a lawful right to abstain from doing,
   (a) uses violence or threats of violence to that person or to his wife or children, or injures his property,
   (b) intimidates or attempts to intimidate that person or a relative of that person by threats that, in Canada or elsewhere, violence or other injury will be done to or punishment inflicted upon him or a relative of his, or that property of any of them will be damaged,
   (c) persistently follows that person about from place to place,
   (d) hides any tools, clothes or other property owned by or used by that person, or deprives him of them or hinders him in the use of them,
   (e) with one or more other persons follows that person, in a disorderly manner, on a highway,
   (f) besets or watches the dwelling-house or place where that person resides, works, carries on business or happens to be, or
   (g) blocks or obstructs a highway,
is guilty of an offence punishable on summary conviction.

(2) A person who attends at or near or approaches a dwelling-house or place, for the purpose only of obtaining or communicating information, does not watch or beset within the meaning of this section.

Section 381, as well as s.380 (Criminal Breach of Contract) and s.382 (Offences by Employers) are contained in the Code under the heading, "Breach of Contract, Intimidation and Discrimination Against Trade Unionists." As the heading suggests, these sections have most often been employed during trade disputes. Besetting and watching is often called the "legislative equivalent" to picketing.[23] Similarly, one purpose of s.381(2) is to clarify the conditions under which picketing is unlawful.[24] However, it has also been pointed out that s.381 does not apply only to trade and labour disputes but prohibits general types of conduct. So, for example, in *R. v. LeBlanc*,[25] a priest was convicted of an offence under s.381 where he made threats of violence against two Jehovah's Witnesses who were making house calls in his parish. After telling them to leave his parish, he said to them that the four men standing nearby might give them a "licking" and he would be glad to pay their fines. He and the four men then, in their cars, followed the couple's car for a few miles. The court held that the threats were made for the purpose of compelling the Jehovah's Witnesses to leave the area and to abstain from calling on people. Since the couple had a lawful right to propagate their religion in such a manner, the priest was guilty of the offence.

Before a person can be convicted of an offence under s.381 for doing one of the acts listed in (a) – (g), it must be proved by the prosecution that the purpose of the conduct was that set out in s.381(1). So, for example, in the case of *R. v. Brancombe*,[26] although it was proved that the accused had "besetted or watched" the dwelling place of the complainant, there was no evidence of what his purpose was. Since it was not shown that the accused's purpose was to compel the complainant to do something she had a lawful right to abstain from doing, or not to do something she had a lawful right to do, the Crown failed in making out its case against the accused, who was then found not guilty of the offence.

3. Kidnapping

247.(1) Every one who kidnaps a person with intent
(a) to cause him to be confined or imprisoned against his will,
(b) to cause him to be unlawfully sent or transported out of Canada against his will, or
(c) to hold him for ransom or to service against his will, is guilty of an indictable offence and is liable to imprisonment for life.

(2) Every one who, without lawful authority, confines, imprisons or forcibly seizes another person is guilty of an indictable offence and is liable to imprisonment for five years.

(3) In proceedings under this section, the fact that the person in relation to whom the offence is alleged to have been committed did not resist is not a defence unless the accused proves that the failure to resist was not caused by threats, duress, force or exhibition of force.

This section creates the offences of kidnapping, forcible seizure, confinement and imprisonment. Kidnapping is the most serious offence and requires specific intent to carry out one of the purposes in ss.(1)(a) – (c).

The term "kidnapping" is not defined in the Code and Canadian courts have not been called upon to give a definition. It has, however, long been an offence at common law, being considered a form of aggravated false imprisonment. Many of the older English cases of kidnapping involved sending the victim out of the country.[27] However, an early Canadian case established that kidnapping does not necessarily mean that the stolen person must be taken out of the country.[28] This broader definition is reflected in the present wording of the section. Some help in defining the term is given by the English case of *R. v. Reid.*[29] In this case, a husband had been charged with kidnapping his wife. In finding that a man can be convicted of the offence even though the victim is his wife, the court accepted a definition of kidnapping that referred to the stealing, carrying away or secreting of a person against that person's will. The offence, the court stated, is complete when the victim is seized and carried away.

Since the kidnapping must be done "against the person's will," it is important to examine the meaning of this phrase. Section 247(3) clearly states that the non-resistance of the victim can not be used by the accused as a defence unless he proves that the failure to resist was not caused by "threats, duress, force or exhibition of force." In other words, a person who does not resist being taken by an armed gunman has still been taken "against his will." What if a person willingly goes with another person because of the false statements made by that person, would this constitute a taking against his will? This was one of the questions considered recently by the Ontario Court of Appeal in the case of *R. v. Brown.*[30] In this case, the accused picked up a 10-year-old girl by falsely telling her that her father had asked him to drive her to school. Instead, the accused drove the girl out of the city to an isolated spot. When he approached her, she attempted to get out of the car. The accused then choked her until she was unconscious. Believing her to be dead, he put her body in the car trunk and drove 25 miles to a garbage dump where he threw the body and covered it with garbage. After the accused drove away, the girl escaped to a farm house. For the accused's defence, it was argued that since the child went with the accused willingly, the accused could not be convicted of kidnapping.

The court, however, found the accused guilty of the offence since his actions of choking her, placing her in the trunk and driving her 25 miles to a garbage dump were, the court said, "clearly within the kidnapping section." However, the court also indicated that the kidnapping occurred as soon as the accused's false statements induced the victim to enter the car. This case is then support for the proposition that a person does not act willingly when his actions are induced by false statements and, therefore, can be considered "unwilling" for the purposes of the offence of kidnapping.

4. Abduction

> **248. Every one who takes away or detains a female person, against her will, with intent**
> **(a) to marry her or to have illicit sexual intercourse with her, or**
> **(b) to cause her to marry or to have illicit sexual intercourse with a male person,**
> **is guilty of an indictable offence and is liable to imprisonment for ten years.**
> **249.(1) Every one who, without lawful authority, takes or causes to be taken an unmarried female person under the age of sixteen years out of the possession of and against the will of her parent or guardian or of any other person who has lawful care or**

charge of her is guilty of an indictable offence and is liable to
imprisonment for five years.

(2) For the purpose of proceedings under this section, it is not
material whether

   (a) the female person is taken with her own consent or at her
        own suggestion, or
   (b) the accused believes that the female person is sixteen years
        of age or more.

250.(1) Every one who, with intent to deprive a parent or
guardian or any other person who has lawful care or charge of a
child under the age of fourteen years of the possession of that
child, or with intent to steal anything on or about the person of
such a child, unlawfully,

   (a) takes or entices away or detains the child, or
   (b) receives or harbours the child

is guilty of an indictable offence and is liable to imprisonment for
ten years.

(2) This section does not apply to a person who, claiming in
good faith a right to possession of a child, obtains possession of
the child.

An offence similar to kidnapping is abduction. Sections 248 – 250 create three
distinct offences which are mainly distinguishable from one another by the age and
sex of the victim. Notice that the chief differences between kidnapping and the
offences of abduction are first, the intents or purposes for the taking of the person
differ; and second, except where the offence is one under s.248, abduction can be
committed even though the victim is willing. Thus, the fact that the victim
consented to the abduction is not usually a defence.

Section 249(2)(a) specifically provides that where a person takes an unmarried
female under the age of sixteen out of the possession of her parents or guardians, it
is not a defence that the female consented to or even suggested the taking. A 1963
Ontario Court of Appeal case, *R. v. Langevin,* found the accused guilty of
abducting two fourteen-year-old girls even though the court said that the girls had
taken a very active if not leading part in the occurrence.[31] Although there has been
some disagreement on the point among judges, the court in *Langevin* held that it is
not necessary that there be any persuasion on the part of the abductor which has
encouraged the girl to consent to the taking for the offence to be committed.

An essential element of the offence is that the female be taken out of the
possession of her parents by the accused. So, if a girl, on her own, leaves home and
later goes with a person, he cannot be found guilty of abduction. Of course, if he
aided the girl in leaving home by giving her money for transportation or other
encouragement, the fact that he did not physically "take" her will not save him.
The case of *R. v. Blythe* demonstrates the necessity of parental possession before the
offence can be committed.[32] In the *Blythe* case, the girl resided in the United States
in the state of Washington. She received letters and money for tickets which
persuaded her to leave her home and meet the accused in Victoria. The accused was

charged with abduction but was found not guilty. The court held that when the girl arrived in Victoria, she had abandoned her father's possession by traveling to a foreign country. So, when the accused met her and took her to a boarding house where they spent the night, it could not be said that he had taken her out of her parent's possession. Although the letters and money from the accused encouraged her to leave, since they were received outside of Canada, the court had no jurisdiction over those events. In other words, the essential element of the offence, i.e. being taken out of the possession of her parents, had occurred in another country and, thus, the accused could not be found guilty of the offence in a Canadian court.

The case of *R. v. Cox*[33] considered the issue of whether a female is taken against the will of her parents when the parent allows the girl to be taken based on the accused's fraudulent statements. In this case, the accused told the girl's mother that he needed a baby sitter for his three children. The mother allowed her fifteen-year-old daughter to go with the accused in his car. When the accused did not turn at the street where he said his house was located, the girl became alarmed and escaped from the car. At his trial, it was found that the accused had used a false name and address and had lied about his employment situation. The Court of Appeal held that a consent obtained from fraud or trick is not consent and before a person can be said to do an act willingly, he must be consciously consenting to the act.

Section 250 refers to the abduction of a child under fourteen. It should be noticed that the offence is committed even if the accused only "harbours" or "receives" the child. For example, if a twelve-year-old runs away from home and is allowed to stay in the home of a person, if the necessary intent is proven, that person may be convicted of the offence. It will not matter that he did not entice or encourage the child to leave home. The cases reported under this section often involve separated parents, who, in fighting over the custody of their children, engage in child-stealing. Courts have ruled that where one parent is given legal custody of a child by a court with authority to do so, the parent who does not have legal custody may be convicted of abduction under s.250.[34]

An interesting case which involved the operation of s.250(2) is *R. v. Austin.*[35] In this case, the parents separated and the mother was given custody of the child by an Ontario Family Court judge. The mother and child then moved to British Columbia. The father met them in B.C. and a brief reconciliation was tried. Both parents believed that the order of the Ontario judge had no legal effect in B.C. and were unaware of a British Columbia statute that, under the circumstances, gave the mother the right to custody. Furthermore, the father's belief regarding the effect of the court order was based on information given to him by a magistrate at the Ontario Family Court at the time when his wife and child moved to B.C. When the couple again separated, the father took the child with him and returned to Ontario. The father was then charged in B.C. with abduction under s.250. The Court of Appeal found the accused not guilty because of the effect of s.250(2) since the father believed in good faith he had a right to possession of the child. The court did not however, rule on the question of whether or not the Ontario Family Court order was effective in British Columbia. The court noted that this was an unusual case since ignorance of the law is not usually a defence. But because of s.250(2), if the accused mistakenly but in good faith claims a right to possess the child, he cannot be guilty of abduction.

5. Abortion

> **251.(1)** Every one who, with intent to procure the miscarriage of a female person, whether or not she is pregnant, uses any means for the purpose of carrying out his intention is guilty of an indictable offence and is liable to imprisonment for life.
>
> **(2)** Every female person who, being pregnant, with intent to procure her own miscarriage, uses any means or permits any means to be used for the purpose of carrying out her intentions is guilty of an indictable offence and is liable to imprisonment for two years.
>
> . . . .
>
> **(4)** Subsections (1) and (2) do not apply to
>
> (a) a qualified medical practitioner, other than a member of a therapeutic abortion committee for any hospital, who in good faith uses in an accredited or approved hospital any means for the purpose of carrying out his intention to procure the miscarriage of the female person, or
>
> (b) a female person who, being pregnant, permits a qualified medical practitioner to use in an accredited or approved hospital any means described in paragraph (a) for the purpose of carrying out her intention to procure her own miscarriage, if, before the use of those means, the therapeutic abortion committee for that accredited or approved hospital, by a majority of the members of the committee and at a meeting of the committee at which the case of such female person has been reviewed,
>
> (c) has by certificate in writing stated that in its opinion the continuation of the pregnancy of such female person would or would be likely to endanger her life or health, and
>
> (d) has caused a copy of such certificate to be given to the qualified medical practitioner.

Unless an abortion is obtained by following the procedure set out in s.251, it is a criminal act for both the pregnant woman and the person performing the abortion. To summarize, before a doctor can perform an abortion he must obtain a certificate of approval from the therapeutic abortion committee of the hospital where the abortion will be performed. The committee will review the case and by majority vote decide whether the continuation of the pregnancy would or would be likely to endanger the woman's life or health. If a majority agree that the abortion is necessary, a certificate will be issued.

Notice that the only hospitals in which abortions may be performed are those which are "accredited" or "approved." Hospitals are accredited by the Canadian Council on Hospital Accreditation as ones in which diagnostic services and medical, surgical and obstetrical treatment are provided. Approved hospitals are those approved by the provincial Minister of Health for performing abortions. Another requirement is that the therapeutic abortion committee must be appointed by the board of the hospital. Also the doctor who performs the operation must be qualified to practice medicine in the province in which the hospital where the abortion will be performed is located.

It is also an offence under s.252 to unlawfully supply or procure a drug or other noxious thing or instrument knowing it is intended to be used to procure an abortion.

A person may be convicted of attempting to procure an abortion even though he was not the person who performed the operation. In *R. v. Tass*,[36] a doctor arranged for a person to abort a woman who had asked him to perform the operation. The doctor drove the abortionist to the woman's house and waited outside while the operation was being performed. When the woman collapsed and died the doctor was called into the house. After confirming that the woman had died, he drove the abortionist to the police station. The doctor was found guilty of an attempt to procure a miscarriage.

It is immaterial whether or not the method used to procure the miscarriage is one which can be used successfully. In *R. v. Smith*[37] the accused attempted to use "slippery elm" to cause the miscarriage. The court held that whether or not "slippery elm" could be used successfully was not an issue in the case. The only question, the court said, was: did the accused have the *intent* to bring about a miscarriage and did he attempt to do so by the use of *any means?* The case *R. v. A*[38] used similar reasoning in finding the accused not guilty because he had only pretended to perform an abortion. In this case the accused only intended to encourage the woman who wanted an abortion and had thought about committing suicide. The court found that the accused had no intent to cause a miscarriage.

It should be noticed that the procedure set out in s.251 is detailed and lengthy. Generally, abortions should be performed as early in the pregnancy as possible. It could happen that by attempting to follow s.251 a pregnant woman might find that she had delayed too long in obtaining the abortion. Are there any exceptions to s.251? To take an extreme example suppose A lives in an isolated region of northern Canada. She has been told another pregnancy will endanger her life. She becomes pregnant during the winter season when it is impossible to travel to the nearest "accredited or approved" hospital. If she waits until spring it will be too late to safely have the abortion. If a doctor performed an abortion on A would he have any defence for violating the law? The case of *R. v. Morgentaler*,[39] a 1975 decision of the Supreme Court of Canada, has raised the possibility that a doctor in such a case could rely on the defence of *necessity*.

Dr. Morgentaler was a Montreal physician who was charged with the offence of performing an abortion on a twenty-six year old unmarried university student. The woman did not suffer any complications from the operation and there was no question of the doctor's competency. Furthermore, there was substantial evidence presented which indicated that if the woman had gone to an accredited hospital, she would have received committee approval to have an abortion. The main issues, therefore, involved the validity and scope of s.251.

The doctor's defence was based on several arguments including that the law is unconstitutional and violates the Canadian *Bill of Rights*. These arguments were rejected however by a majority of the judges hearing the case. Although the defence of necessity was also unacceptable, the judges indicated that in the proper situation necessity *might* be a successful defence.

In brief, necessity is a common law defence which is preserved by s.7(3) of the Code. This defence is said to arise where a person performs an illegal act to avoid the happening of a great evil or harm. In other words, in a very unusual and urgent situation, a person may be excused from violating the law. However, as one judge in *Morgentaler* pointed out, the defence of necessity has never been used successfully in Canada and has only been used possibly once in England. Six of the judges (all nine Supreme Court judges heard the case) also expressed some doubt as to whether the defence does exist since as one judge said it is "ill-defined" and "elusive." However, the judges stated that assuming it does exist, the defence could only be used where "(1) the accused in good faith considered the situation so emergent that failure to terminate the pregnancy immediately could endanger life or health, and (2) that upon any reasonable view of the facts compliance with the law was impossible." In this case the woman had no medical insurance, was ineligible as a foreign student for employment and had no close friends or relatives in Canada. The costs of obtaining a legal abortion were beyond her means. Since discovering her pregnancy, she was anxious, depressed, not sleeping or eating properly and was prone to vomiting. Her studies had been adversely affected. A majority of the judges felt that these facts did not justify the doctor's violation of the law.

E. RECOGNIZANCES TO KEEP THE PEACE

745.(1) Any person who fears that another person will cause personal injury to him or his wife or child or will damage his property may lay an information before a justice.

(2) A justice who receives an information under subsection (1) shall cause the parties to appear before him on or before a summary conviction court having jurisdiction in the same territorial division.

(3) The justice or the summary conviction court before which the parties appear may, if satisfied by the evidence adduced that the informant has reasonable grounds for his fears,

    (a) order that the defendant enter into a recognizance, with or without sureties, to keep the peace and be of good behaviour for any period that does not exceed twelve months, and comply with such other reasonable conditions

>prescribed in the recognizance as the court considers
>desirable for securing the good conduct of the defendant,
>or
>
>(b) commit the defendant to prison for a term not exceeding
>twelve months if he fails or refuses to enter in the
>recognizance.

This is a very useful section which gives magistrates the authority to exercise what is sometimes called "preventative justice." By entering a recognizance the defendant agrees to an obligation to keep the peace and to comply with any other conditions prescribed by the court. A *surety* is a person who is willing to be answerable if the defendant fails to keep the peace. Sometimes a sum of money must be given to the court by the defendant or the surety as additional encouragement for the defendant to keep the peace. The money is forfeited if the defendant does not honour his obligation. This section is frequently used by wives who, because they have been previously threatened or assaulted by their husbands, fear future attack. Although it is not necessary that an assault or any other offence be committed before a justice uses the powers given to him by this section, the powers can only be exercised upon "reasonable and probable grounds" that a breach of the peace will occur in the future.[40]

In addition to the authority given to a justice under this section, he has a general authority derived from the common law of England to maintain order and preserve the peace by ordering persons whom he thinks may breach the peace, to enter a recognizance.[41] The difference between the common law authority and that given under s.747 was explained by a judge of a British Columbia Supreme Court in *R. v. White* as follows: "Under s.717 (now s.745) of the Code a defendant cannot be bound over unless the magistrate is satisfied that the informant has reasonable grounds for his fears whereas the prerequisite to the exercise of the common law jurisdiction is that the magistrate (on facts established to his satisfaction) has probable grounds to suspect or be apprehensive that there may be a breach of the peace."[42]

In other words, under s.745, it is the informant who must have reasonable grounds for the fears of future injury, while under the common law, it is the justice who must have reasonable grounds for the fears. So, for example, a justice could require a person to enter a recognizance even though no other person had complained. This was, in fact, what the magistrate in the case of *R. v. Cholan* had attempted to do. He could not decide whether the informant or the defendant was telling the truth so ordered them both to enter recognizances. The British Columbia Supreme Court, however, found that the magistrate did not have reasonable grounds to exercise his common law authority since being unable to determine which person was telling the truth, his decision was based on speculation and conjecture as to what the actual facts of the case were.

QUESTIONS FOR REVIEW AND DISCUSSION

1. Briefly describe the three sets of circumstances under which an assault may occur.
2. Explain the various positions taken by the courts when considering the effect of the victim's consent on an alleged assault.
3. Why does the law make an attempted or threatened use of force an offence?
4. Has the offence of assault been committed where the alleged assailant threatened a person but did not actually intend to apply force to his victim?
5. Can threatening words alone constitute the offence of assault?
6. Discuss the circumstances under which the use of force may be lawful.
7. Why is there more than one offence of assault? What are they?
8. How have the courts defined "bodily harm"?
9. Distinguish the following terms: wounding, maiming, disfiguring.
10. What is the main difference between the offence of assault causing bodily harm and the offence of causing bodily harm with intent?
11. Discuss the decision of the court in *R. v. Nabis,* which considered the offence of threatening. Do you agree with the court's reasoning?
12. What is the main difference between kidnapping and the offences of forcible seizure, confinement and imprisonment?
13. Can a parent ever be found guilty of abducting his own child? Explain.
14. Discuss whether necessity should be a defence to performing an illegal abortion and if so, under what circumstances. See *R. v. Bourne,* (1938) 3 All E.R. 615, 108 L.J.K.B. 471 (1939) 1 K.B. 687.
15. What is a recognizance? a surety?
16. What is the main difference between the court's common law authority to order persons to enter recognizances and the authority given by the Code?
17. Is it necessary that an offence be committed before a judge can order a person to enter a recognizance?
18. Bob and Tony are two high school students. One afternoon they were playing basketball in the gym when Bob ran into Tony knocking him to the floor. Tony got up angrily and punched Bob in the mouth. At that point they began fighting violently until some other students were able to separate them. What charges if any could be laid and against whom? Explain.
19. The town of Marlboro closed off a downtown street one summer to create a mall. The area became a hangout for teenagers who sometimes became quite rowdy. One evening Constable Jones observed two young persons, a man and woman, kissing and wrestling in the middle of the sidewalk. Constable Jones told them to get up and stop acting like idiots. At that point another young woman, Molly Brown, yelled an obscenity at him. Jones then arrested Molly and attempted to take her to his police cruiser. By this time a crowd had developed and were making it difficult for Jones to escort Molly to his cruiser. While this was happening, Sandra stepped forward and slapped Jones in the face and was promptly arrested.

Sandra was charged with assaulting a peace officer while engaged in the execution of his duty. Constable Jones gave evidence at her trial that he had not arrested Molly for yelling at him but said "his authority had been flaunted" and that he wanted to have her arrested "to prevent further trouble." Should the court find Sandra guilty of the charge? Explain. If not, what other offence could she be charged with?

See *R. v. Allen* (1971), 4 C.C.C. (2d) 194 (Ont.C.A.).

20. Sam Smith, age 19, had been dating Barbara Bright, age 15. Barbara's parents did not like Sam and thought he was a bad influence on their daughter. Last Wednesday they forbade Barbara to see him any longer. Friday night Barbara packed a suitcase and slipped out of the house. She went to Sam's apartment and told him that she had run away from home. He let her in and she spent Friday and Saturday night at his apartment. Sunday night her parents found out where Sam lived. They went to Sam's place and forced her to go home with them.

Can Sam be charged with abduction? What difference would it make if Sam had picked her up Friday night and driven her to his apartment? What if Sam had called her and encouraged her to leave home and live with him? What would the results be if Barbara were 13 instead of 15?

[1] *R. v. Lock* (1872) 12 Cox C.C. 244.
[2] For further discussion see Chapter Seven on sex offences.
[3] *R. v. Maki* (1970), 1 C.C.C. (2d) 333, (Ont.)
[4] (1975), 31 C.R.N.S. 314 (Ont.C.A.).
[5] (1972), 10 C.C.C. (2d) 324 (Ont.C.A.).
[6] (1934) 2 K.B. 498, 25 CR App. R 1, 30 Cox C.C. 187.
[7] (1972), 8 C.C.C. (2d) 206, 20 C.R.N.S. 235 (N.B.C.A.)
[8] (1957), 118 C.C.C. 410 (Ont.C.A.)
[9] *Kwaku Mensah v. R.* 2 CR 113, (1946) A.C. 83.
[10] *R. v. Horncastle* (1972), 8 C.C.C. (2d) 253 (N.B.C.A.)
[11] (1968) 3 C.C.C. 179, 3 C.R.N.S. 190 (B.C.C.A.).
[12] *R. v. Hosteller* (1902), 7 C.C.C. 221 (S.Ct. of the N.W.T.)
[13] (1954) 2 All E.R. 529, (1954) 2QB 282
[14] *R. v. Donovan, supra*
[15] See for example: *R. v. Prpich* (1971) 4 C.C.C. (2d) 325 (Sask.C.A.); *R. v. Dix* (1972), 10 C.C.C. (2d) 324 (Ont.C.A.).
[16] (1972), 19 C.R.N.S. 308 (N.B.C.A.)
[17] (1970) 3 C.C.C. 145 (S.C.C.).
[18] (1971), 3 C.C.C. (2d) 303, (B.C.C.A.).
[19] *R. v. Schultz* (1962), 30 W.W.R. 23 (Alta.C.A.)
[20] *R. v. Hostetter, supra*
[21] *R. v. Schultz, supra*
[22] *R. v. Nabis* (1974), 18 C.C.C. (2d) 144 (S.C.C.)
[23] *Allied Amusements Ltd. v. Reaney*, (1937) 4 D.L.R. 162 (Man.C.A.)
[24] *Canadian Dairies Ltd. v. Seggie* (1940), 74 C.C.C. 210.
[25] (1964) 3 C.C.C. 40 (N.S.Cty.Ct.)
[26] *R. v. Branscombe*, (1956) O.W.N. 897, 25 C.R. 88 (Ont.C.A.).
[27] See for example: *Attorney General v. Edge* 1943 I.R. 115 and *R. v. Hale* (1974) 1 All E.R. 1107 where the historical sources of the offence are discussed.

[28] *Cornwall v. The Queen*, (1872-3) 33 Upper Can. Q.B. 106.

[29] *R. v. Reid*, (1972) 2 All E.R. 1350 (C.A.).

[30] (1972), 8 C.C.C. (2d) 13 (Ont.C.A.).

[31] (1962) 38 CR 421 (Ont.C.A.).

[32] (1895) 1 C.C.C. 263 (S.C.B.C.).

[33] (1969) 4 C.C.C. 321 5 C.R.N.S. 395 (1960).

[34] For a case which found the father not guilty of abduction because custody had not been given to the mother by a "competent" court see *R. v. Anagnotis*, (1970) 1 C.C.C. 234.

[35] (1957), 120 C.C.C. 118 (B.C.C.A.).

[36] 1 CR 378, 86 C.C.C. 97 (Man.C.A.) and (1947) S.C.R. 103, 2 C.R. 503, 87 C.C.C. 97.

[37] (1960), 128 C.C.C. 140 (B.C.C.A.).

[38] (1944), 83 C.C.C. 94 (Que.Mag.Ct.).

[39] (1975), 20 C.C.C. (2d) 449 (S.C.C.).

[40] See, for example, *R. v. White*, 5 C.R.N.S. 30, 64 W.W.R. 708 (1969) 1 C.C.C. 19 (Sub-nom. *R. v. White; exparte Cholan*) (B.C.S.C.).

[41] See for example *Mackenzie v. Martin* (1954) S.C.R. 361, 180 C.C.C. 305 (S.C.C.) where it was established that power exists in Ontario.

[42] *R. v. White, supra.*

Chapter Thirteen

Offences Against Property Rights

The offences to be discussed in this chapter are those which involve violations of a person's *property rights*. A property right includes a right of possession, or ownership, of a place or a "thing." Owning a car, or a home, or renting an apartment are examples of property rights. Common offences against property rights include theft and "breaking and entering." Excluding the offences of robbery and extortion, crimes of this nature do not involve violence or the threat of violence to the person.

A. THEFT

1. Elements Of The Offence

Generally, theft is the act of a person who dishonestly *takes* property belonging to another with *intention of depriving* the owner of it either permanently, or temporarily.

Section 283(1) of the Code defines the offence of theft:

> **283.(1) Every one commits theft who fraudulently and without colour of right takes, or fraudulently and without colour of right converts to his use or to the use of another person, anything whether animate or inanimate, with intent,**
>> **(a) to deprive, temporarily or absolutely, the owner of it or a person who has a special property or interest in it, of the thing or of his property or interest in it,**

(b) **to pledge it or deposit it as security,**

(c) **to part with it under a condition with respect to its return that the person who parts with it may be unable to perform or,**

(d) **to deal with it in such a manner that it cannot be restored in the condition in which it was at the time it was taken or converted.**

(2) A person commits theft when, with intent to steal anything, he moves it or causes it to move or to be moved, or begins to cause it to become movable.

Section 294 provides:

294. Except where otherwise provided by law, every one who commits theft:

(a) **is guilty of an indictable offence and is liable to imprisonment for ten years, where the property stolen is a testamentary instrument or where the value of what is stolen exceeds two hundred dollars; or**

(b) **is guilty**

(i) **of an indictable offence and is liable to imprisonment for two years, or**

(ii) **of an offence punishable on summary conviction, where the value of what is stolen does not exceed two hundred dollars.**

To constitute an offence of theft under section 283(1), several elements must be proved:

(1) a "thing" must be *taken or converted* (generally a conversion occurs when a person keeps, for his own use, a "thing" which he was loaned on a temporary basis only). To establish this ingredient the prosecutor must prove that the thing is owned by someone other than the accused;

(2) the thing must be taken *fraudulently and without colour of right;* and

(3) the person taking must *intend* to:

a. *deprive,* temporarily or permanently, the owner of the thing taken, (Note: the term "special property" as it is used in s.283(1)(a) includes rented or loaned property), *or*

b. *pledge* the thing, or *deposit it as a security* (for example, using "borrowed" stocks or bonds as collateral in order to raise cash), *or*

c. *part* with the thing *under a condition* which he may be *unable to perform, or*

d. *deal* with the thing taken in *such a manner* that it *cannot be returned in the same condition* as when it was taken.

In general, the theft is committed when the offender moves the thing, or causes it to move, with the intent to steal it.

A. "FRAUDULENTLY AND WITHOUT COLOUR OF RIGHT"

(i) fraudulently

For a "thing" to be taken *fraudulently,* it must be taken without mistake, and with a dishonest or criminal intent.

In *Cooper v. R.,* [1] the accused was charged with the theft of an aircraft. The accused went to the grounds of the flying school where he had begun taking flying lessons. Using a canoe he went out to the aircraft which was moored at a buoy. Without permission he got in and started the plane, intending to bring it alongside a dock. He missed the dock once and was making a second attempt when he was stopped. The evidence indicated that the accused intended only to show the plane to some friends. The court found the accused innocent of the charge of theft. It was held that he had not taken the aircraft fraudulently. Even though the accused had taken the plane within the meaning of s.283, (he deprived the owner of it temporarily), he did so only to show it to his friends and thus, he *did not take it with a criminal,* or dishonest, intent.

In *Handfield v. R.,* [2] the accused was charged with the theft of an election poster. His defence was lack of criminal intent. He and two of his brothers spent the evening together. On their way home they passed the residence of someone on which was standing an election poster, inviting the electorate to vote Progressive Conservative. The accused removed the poster and placed it on the lawn of a person he knew to be a Liberal party supporter. The accused said that he took the poster to "play a trick" and that he never meant to steal it.

The court held that the accused did not take the election poster fraudulently. The judgment concluded: "What was done may, to some people, seem reprehensible and might possibly subject the accused to some punitive measures, but not in my opinion subject them to conviction as common thieves and to a criminal record for the future."

In *R. v. Kerr,* [3] the accused was celebrating with considerable conviviality a victory in a retriever dog championship competition. For some reason, the accused and two companions went to the International Airport where they were seen by a cleaner at the airport. All three were staggering and acting in a foolish manner. The accused was carrying one of the ashtrays belonging to the airport. The cleaner saw the ashtray being carried out by the accused. The ashtray was of a floor type and several feet in height. The behaviour of the men made the cleaner think that the ashtray was being carried away as a prank, and he thought it would be left outside the airport door. Later two police officers visited the accused's home and saw the ashtray resting on the lawn in front of the house. The accused said he did not mean to take the ashtray, and that he had intended to return it but the police arrived before he was able to do so. The court decided that the accused did not commit the offence of theft: "The circumstances in connection with the accused's stupid and foolish actions clearly showed the absence of any criminal intent."

(ii) "Colour of Right"

The term *colour of right* generally refers to a situation where there is an assertion of a possessory right, that is, a claim of ownership or lawful possession, to the thing which is alleged to have been stolen. In other words, if someone asserts what he believes to be an *honest* claim of ownership, even though he may, in fact, be mistaken, he will have a colour of right to the "thing" and cannot be found guilty of the offence of theft.

In *R. v. Wudrick,*[4] the accused, who was a railway employee, believing certain watermelons in a car on the railroad tracks had been abandoned, took two. In fact, the melons had not been abandoned and the accused was charged with theft. The accused's defence was that he had a "colour of right," in other words a possessory claim to the watermelons. The court concluded the accused's belief, that the melons were waste, and that there was nothing wrong in taking them, was an honest belief. The accused was, in such circumstance, acquitted of the charge.

In *R. v. Howson,*[5] the accused was charged with the theft of a car. The complainant parked his car on a private parking lot without the permission of the owner. The accused, at the request of the superintendent of the lot, towed the complainant's car to his premises where it remained until the complainant located it there. The complainant demanded the return of his car but the accused refused to deliver it until he was paid a towing and storage charge. The complainant eventually paid the amount demanded, under protest, recovered his car and laid an information charging the accused with stealing his car.

The accused, in actual fact, *could not legally keep the complainant's car.* The accused stated he took the car believing, honestly, that he had a possessory claim to it until such time as he was paid a towing and storage charge. In other words, the accused claimed he honestly believed he had a "colour of right" to the car. The court accepted this argument and he was acquitted on the charge of theft.

2. Summary

A summary of the above cases indicates that certain conduct is not fraudulent merely because it is unauthorized. The conduct must be committed with a criminal, or dishonest, intent. Thus behaviour that can be described as a "joke" or a "prank" is not fraudulent. As well, if a person honestly believes he has a claim of ownership to the thing allegedly stolen, he has a defence to a charge of theft for taking the thing. In other words, not only must the taking of the thing be with the intent to deprive temporarily or absolutely, or one of the other situations listed in s.283(1), [that is, s.283(1)(b), (c) and (d)], but also the taking must be "fraudulent and without colour of right," for the offence of theft to be committed.

3. Specific Theft Offences

The Criminal Code contains a number of sections which create specific theft offences. Some of these are described in the following paragraphs.

A. THEFT OF GAS, ELECTRICITY, OR TELECOMMUNICATIONS Section 287 provides:

> **287.(1) Every one commits theft who fraudulently, maliciously, or without colour of right,**
> **(a) abstracts, consumes or uses electricity or gas or causes it to be wasted or diverted, or**
> **(b) uses any telecommunication facility or obtains any telecommunication service,**
> **(2) In this section and in section 287.1, "telecommunication" means any transmission, emission or reception of signs, signals, writing, images, sounds or intelligence of any nature by radio, visual, electronic or other electromagnetic system.**

Section 287(1)(a) deals with situations in which gas or electricity is stolen. For example, if an accused diverts electricity from a public utility commission so that it does not pass through the commission's meter, he is guilty of the theft of electricity.

In *R. v. Brais,* [6] the accused was charged with theft, contrary to s.287(1)(b), in that she fraudulently obtained long distance telephone services. An operator of the telephone company took a call from the accused who said she wanted to make a credit card call to Toronto. The accused gave the Toronto number and the credit card number. The call lasted 64 minutes and the charge for it was $41.60. After 30 minutes certain checking was done and it was found that the card number was not a genuine number, and that the telephone company could not charge the call to anyone.

The accused was convicted under s.287(1). The court held that the accused placed the telephone call *intentionally, without mistake,* and with *knowledge* that she was obtaining the call by using a credit card number which did not exist.

Section 287.1(1) (not reproduced) creates the offence of *making, owning,* or *selling,* any instrument or device which is designed to obtain a *telecommunication service* (telephone, telegram, etc.) without paying for the "service."

B. THEFT BY A PERSON REQUIRED TO ACCOUNT Section 290(1) provides:

> **290.(1) Every one commits theft who, having received anything from any person on terms that require him to account for or pay it or the proceeds of it or a part of the proceeds to that person or another person, fraudulently fails to account for or pay it or the proceeds of it or the part of the proceeds of it accordingly.**

Section 290(1) covers situations in which an accused has received money, or a "thing", from one person and must turn it over to another person. In *R. v. Mckenzie,* [7] a taxi driver was convicted of theft under s.290, because he failed to turn over to the taxi's owner all of the fare money he owed to the owner.

C. THEFT BY HUSBAND OR WIFE Section 289 provides:

> **289.(1) Subject to subsection (2), no husband or wife, during cohabitation, commits theft of anything that is by law the property of the other.**
>
> **(2) A husband or wife commits theft who, intending to desert or on deserting the other or while living apart from the other, fraudulently takes or converts anything that is by law the property of the other in a manner that, if it were done by another person, would be theft.**

If a husband and wife are still *living together,* neither spouse can be convicted of theft if he or she takes property belonging to the other. However, if one of the spouses *deserts, intends to desert,* or is *living apart,* and takes property belonging to the other, he is guilty of theft.

The property taken must belong, *in law,* to the other spouse. For example, if a car is the object taken, the car, in most situations, would have to be registered in the name of the "wronged" spouse. Property that a spouse *brings into a marriage* is property which belongs to him, or her, by law, and therefore, if this property is stolen, the offence of theft is committed. Also, if one spouse is *given a gift* by the other, and there is no question that the person giving the gift relinquished all control over it, the gift is "by law" the property of the other.

Generally, if there is any doubt as to whether the property stolen belongs, in law, to a spouse, the person taking the property will not be charged with theft. This general rule usually applies to property that is owned "jointly" by both the husband and the wife. In such situations, the wronged spouse must start an action in a civil court to *sue* the person for return of the stolen property. In such an action, the court will make up its mind as to who the rightful owner of the property is. If the court finds the property belongs to both spouses, it may order the property to be sold and the proceeds be split evenly among the spouses.

Section 289(3) states:

> **289.(3) Every one commits theft who, during cohabitation of a husband and wife, knowingly,**
>
> **(a) assists either of them in dealing with anything that is by law the property of the other in a manner that would be theft if they were not married, or**
>
> **(b) receives from either of them anything that is by law the property of the other and has been obtained from the other by dealing with it in a manner that would be theft if they were not married.**

If a third party assists one of the spouses in taking property belonging, in law, to the other, he or she will be guilty of theft. Also, if the third party receives property from one of the spouses and the property was stolen by the spouse, the third party will also be committing theft. In such situations the third party must know the spouse is removing property which belongs to the other before the offence of theft can be made out. For example, if a husband removed from the matrimonial home his wife's silver collection, the silver having belonged to the wife before the marriage, and he gave the silver to another woman, and she *knew to whom the silver belonged,* and was *aware the husband had taken it,* she would also be guilty of theft.

4. Offences Resembling Theft

A. MOTOR VEHICLES It is possible to "take" a motor vehicle without the consent of its owner, and *not* be committing the offence of theft.

Section 295 provides:

> **295. Every one who, without the consent of the owner, takes a motor vehicle . . .with intent to drive [or] use it or cause it to be driven [or] used . . .is guilty of an offence punishable on summary conviction.**

The difference between the taking of a car that amounts to theft under s.283, and the taking of a car that amounts to the lesser offence of "taking a vehicle without consent" (an offence often described as "joy-riding") under s.295, is decided by the factor of *fraudulent* intent. To be found guilty of theft under s.283, the accused must be shown to have "fraudulently" taken the thing stolen (see page 223). He must have taken the thing dishonestly or with a criminal intent. In other words, if a person takes a car without consent of the owner, intending only to go for a drive, and intending to return it thereafter to its owner, he *may* be guilty of "taking a vehicle without consent," rather than theft.

In *Hirshman v. Beal,*[8] the issue was whether a person had stolen a car within the definition of "theft." The car was left by the owner for repair at a garage. The mechanic, having repaired the car, took it for a test drive. However, having completed the road test, the mechanic, instead of returning the car to the garage, used it to go home for lunch. On his way back to the garage after lunch he drove his wife around town so that she could complete various shopping errands. The mechanic was stopped by the police before he could return the car to the garage.

The court concluded that the mechanic had not committed the offence of theft, because he did not fraudulently take the car. The court did, however, mention that the act of the mechanic in temporarily converting the car to his own use came perilously close to the crime of theft and that such a "taking," in slightly different circumstances, would be theft.

In *Marsh v. Kulchar,*[9] the question of whether a car was stolen or "wrongfully taken" was considered by the Supreme Court of Canada. M, a farm hand, was told to look after his employer's car. M, who did not have a driver's licence, decided to drive the car to a coffee shop a short distance away. Before he could return the car to the farm from the coffee shop, he had an accident. The court said that M "took" the car but did *not steal* it. He lacked the element of fraudulent intent necessary for a conviction of theft.

In *R. v. Wilkins*, [10] the accused took a policeman's motorcycle, while the latter was standing on the sidewalk making out a ticket, intending to drive it a short distance for the purpose of playing a joke on the policeman. He was charged with theft of the motorcycle under section 283. The court held that the accused should have been charged under s.295 and that he was not guilty of theft under s.283. In its judgement, the court stated: "In the instant case, the facts could not possibly justify a conviction of theft. The accused did not intend to steal the vehicle, that is, to convert the property to his own use, but only to drive it as contemplated by s.295. His intention was merely to play a joke on the policeman — the intention to perpetrate this joke, stupid though it was, is incompatible with the evil intent which is inherent in the crime of theft."

B. TAKING FROM MAIL Section 314 creates a special offence for the theft of mail:

> **314.(1) Every one who**
> **(a) steals**
>   **(i)   anything sent by post, after it is deposited at a post office, and before it is delivered,**
>   **(ii)   a bag, sack or other container or covering in which mail is conveyed, whether it does or does not contain mail, or**
>   **(iii) a key suited to a lock adopted for use by the Canada Post Office, or**
> **(b) has in his possession anything in respect of which he knows that an offence has been committed under paragraph (a),**
> **is guilty of an indictable offence and is liable to imprisonment for ten years.**

C. TAKING OF A CREDIT CARD Section 301.1(1) deals with the theft or falsification of a credit card.

> **301.1(1) Everyone who,**
> **(a) steals a credit card,**
> **(b) forges or falsifies a credit card,**
> **(c) has in his possession, uses or deals in any other way with a credit card that he knows was obtained**
>   **(i)   by the commission in Canada of an offence, or**
>   **(ii) by an act or omission anywhere that, if it had occurred in Canada, would have constituted an offence, or**
> **(d) uses a credit card that he knows has expired or been revoked or cancelled**
> **is guilty of an indictable offence and is liable to imprisonment for ten years.**

Section 301.1(3) provides:

> **301.1(3) For the purposes of this section, "credit card" means any card, plate, coupon book or other device issued or otherwise**

distributed for the purpose of being used upon presentation to obtain on credit, money, goods, services or any other thing of value.

D. FRAUDULENT CONCEALMENT Section 301 creates the offence of *fraudulent concealment.*

301. Every one who, for a fraudulent purpose, takes, obtains, removes or conceals anything is guilty of an indictable offence and is liable to imprisonment for two years.

Section 301 is designed to cover situations in which the thing taken is *hidden* in the hope that the owner will not be able to find it. For instance, if a deceased had made two wills, and neglected to destroy the first, an accused who concealed the second, because it "cut out" an inheritance which the first will granted, would be guilty of fraudulent concealment under s.301.

B. ROBBERY

1. Elements of the Offence

Section 302 of the Code defines the offence of *robbery:*

302. Every one commits robbery who
(a) steals, and for the purpose of extorting whatever is stolen or to prevent or overcome resistance to the stealing, uses violence or threats of violence to a person or property;
(b) steals from any person and, at the time he steals or immediately before or immediately thereafter, wounds, beats, strikes or uses any personal violence to that person;
(c) assaults any person with intent to steal from him; or
(d) steals from any person while armed with an offensive weapon or imitation thereof.

The difference between theft and robbery is that robbery involves *violence* or the *possibility of violence* to the victim.
Section 303 states:

303. Every one who commits robbery is guilty of an indictable offence and is liable to imprisonment for life.

The violence used to commit the robbery need not be severe, nor need it cause an injury to the victim. Generally, any form of physical interference, from a push to a punch, will amount to "violence" for the purposes of s.302. Suddenly snatching a purse will usually be theft rather than robbery. However, if, in order to get the purse, the accused had to "lock" his hand around the wrist of the purse-holder, or even "shake" the purse in order to force her to let it go, the offence of robbery would be committed, because violence was used.

Similarly, a *threat* of any form of violence will generally suffice to bring the accused's action within the offence of robbery.

Section 2 of the Criminal Code provides that "to steal" means "to commit theft."

Robbery is, therefore, made up of two basic elements:

(1) *theft,* or the intention to commit theft, *and*

(2) *violence,* or the threat of violence.

2. Specific Robbery Situations

Section 302(a) sets out the basic definition of the offence of robbery, that is, theft accompanied by actual violence, or by threats of violence. To "extort" means to *compel,* or to *force.* The violence or threat of violence need not be directed at the person being robbed. If the accused struck an innocent by-stander at the scene of the theft, he would be guilty of robbery.

Section 302(b) extends the definition of robbery. If violence is used by the thief at any time *immediately before* or *after* the actual theft, he is guilty of robbery. If, for example, the accused entered a store, opened the cash register while the store owner was in a back room, ran out of the store and pushed someone to the ground who was blocking the path to his "escape" car, he would be guilty of robbery.

Section 302(c) provides that, *whether or not a theft takes place,* if the victim was *assaulted with the intent to steal,* the offence of robbery is still committed. If an accused knocked someone to the ground with the intent to grab his wallet, and was interrupted by a witness' screams which caused him to flee before he could get the wallet, he would still have committed the offence of robbery.

Section 302(d) provides that robbery is committed if a person steals while he is armed with an *offensive weapon* or with an *imitation of an offensive weapon.* Section 2 of the Code defines what is meant by the word "offensive weapon":

> **"offensive weapon" or "weapon" means**
> **(a) anything that is designed to be used as a weapon, or**
> **(b) anything that a person uses or intends to use as a weapon.**

A. OFFENSIVE WEAPON Almost any object can be categorized as an offensive weapon.

In *R. v. Sloan,*[11] the accused was charged with attempted robbery under s.302(d). The accused, whose head and upper body were partially covered with a bed sheet, had come to a hotel in the middle of the night and ordered the night desk man to open the office where the money was kept. The desk man refused. He was prodded backwards in the chest by something protruding from under the sheet. He said to the accused, "Don't push me, I've got a couple of cracked ribs." The accused then said, "If you don't open that door, you'll be in worse shape." The desk man turned and, in so doing, hit the protruding object and discovered it was a finger, not a gun barrel. At that point, the accused fled.

The court held that the accused did not have an "offensive weapon or an imitation thereof." Part of the judgment states: "In this case, all that is shown is that the accused . . .simulated the conduct of a man armed with a weapon. He acted a part or played out a pantomime to give the impression that he had a weapon. *While the conduct might have justified a conviction under ss.(a) (theft with threat of violence) or (c) (theft with assault) of s.302 of the Code, ...it does not meet the requirements of s.302(d).* To arm oneself with a weapon means to equip oneself, to acquire, to become possessed of some instrument which is either a weapon or an imitation of a weapon. I am not of the opinion that in these circumstances a man can be armed with his own finger and I am satisfied that the word 'imitation' as used in s.302(d) refers to an imitation of the weapon and cannot be stretched to include a simulation of conduct or actions."

3. Robbery of Mail

Section 304 defines a special offence for robbing anything that is used to *convey or transport mail*. Section 304 states:

> **304. Every one who stops a mail conveyance with intent to rob or search it is guilty of an indictable offence and liable to imprisonment for life.**

C. EXTORTION

1. Elements of the Offence

Section 305 defines the offence of *extortion:*

> **305.(1) Every one who, without reasonable justification or excuse and with intent to extort or gain anything, by threats, accusations, menaces or violence induces or attempts to induce any person, whether or not he is the person threatened, accused or menaced or to whom violence is shown, to do anything or cause anything to be done, is guilty of an indictable offence and is liable to imprisonment for fourteen years.**
>
> **(2) A threat to institute civil proceedings is not a threat for the purposes of this section.**

Extortion is essentially equivalent to the word "blackmail." An extortion occurs when one person *threatens* another with some consequence, such that the person is *forced* to commit an act, or to omit doing something which he otherwise would have done, if he had not been threatened. In *R. v. Natarelli and Volpe,*[12] the accused were convicted of extortion in that they threatened the life of the victim if he did not deliver to them a large sum of money.

In the *Volpe* case, the court stated that there were three ingredients to the offence of extortion:

(1) that the accused has used *threats,*
(2) that he has done so with the *intention of obtaining something* by the use of threats, and
(3) that either the use of the threats or the making of the demand for the thing sought to be obtained was without *reasonable* excuse *or justification.*

With respect to requirement (3), above, the court in *Volpe* said that once it is proved that the accused made threats to cause *death,* or *bodily harm,* with intent to obtain the money sought, then they are guilty of extortion regardless of whether they honestly believed that they had a right to the money. In other words, a person cannot threaten another with death, or harm, in an attempt to force him to do something, even if he honestly believes he has reasonable justification for making the threat. An example of a threat which *is justified* is the threat of a creditor to turn over an account to a collection agency, in an attempt to get payment from a person who owes him money. However, if the creditor threatened the person with violence if he didn't pay on time, even though he is owed the money, he would have no reasonable justification for making such a threat.

A. THREAT OR MENACE The threat, or menace, involved need not amount to a threat to harm, or murder the victim. A threat, for example, by someone that he will damage the victim's property is sufficient for the purposes of s.305. For example, a threat to break a person's windows, or let the air out of his car tires, could probably qualify as extorting threats.

B. THREAT TO SUE Section 305(2) provides that a threat to take someone to court in an attempt to force him to do something is *not* a threat for the purpose of committing the offence of extortion. Therefore, if A threatened to sue B in an attempt to get him to pay for damages he caused to A's property, A would not be committing the offence of extortion.

D. BREAKING AND ENTERING

1. Elements of the Offence

Section 306 defines the offence of *breaking and entering:*

> **306.(1) Every one who**
> **(a) breaks and enters a place with intent to commit an indictable offence therein,**
> **(b) breaks and enters a place and commits an indictable offence therein, or**
> **(c) breaks out of a place after**
> > **(i) committing an indictable offence therein, or**
> > **(ii) entering the place with intent to commit an indictable offence therein,**
> **is guilty of an indictable offence and is liable**
> **(d) to imprisonment for life, if the offence is committed in relation to a dwelling-house, or**

(e) to imprisonment for fourteen years, if the offence is committed in relation to a place other than a dwelling-house.

There are three different break and enter situations outlined in s.306:
(a) breaking and entering with the *intent to commit* an indictable offence;
(b) breaking and entering and *committing* an indictable offence; and
(c) breaking *out* after *having committed* an indictable offence, or after having entered a place with the *intent to commit* an indictable offence.
A "breaking out" as the term is used in (c) above would cover a situation in which a person concealed himself in a department store until it closed, and then, having stolen some merchandise, broke a window in order to leave the store.

Before an accused can be found guilty of the offence of breaking and entering it must be proved that he (1) *broke* and (2) *entered* (3) *a place* (4) and committed, or intended to commit, an *indictable offence*. Each one of these separate elements must be established. If an accused entered a place but did not "break" and enter, he cannot be found guilty of breaking and entering. Or, if an accused broke and entered a place but not with the intent to commit an indictable offence, he has not committed an offence under s.306. Each of these different and distinct elements will be discussed separately.

A. BREAKING *Breaking* is defined in s.282:

> **282. "Break" means**
> **(a) to break any part, internal or external, or**
> **(b) to open any thing that is used or intended to be used to close or to cover an internal or external opening.**

"Breaking" usually involves "jimmying" a door or window, "picking" a lock or breaking a window. However, "breaking" also includes a number of ways of entering a place that one would not normally associate with the word breaking. Opening a door with a stolen or "found" key, lifting a latch, raising an already open window or simply opening an unlocked door, all are examples of breaking for the purposes of the offence of breaking and entering.

In *R. v. Jewell,*[13] the accused was charged with "breaking and entering" under s.306. An excerpt from the court's decision summarizes the facts: "The building which is the subject of the charge is a house which had been unoccupied for a considerable period of time. It was in a somewhat dilapidated condition and not habitable at the date of the alleged offence. The accused entered the house through a screen door and an inner door, both of which were open wide enough to permit the accused to enter without further opening the doors."

The accused's evidence, which was the only evidence on this point, was as follows:

> A. *And do you remember entering the house in question?*
> A. *Yes, I do.*
> Q. *Yes?*

> *A. I entered through, well, it's the westerly door, and I didn't have to force it open. It was open. When we walked up, the screen door was open, the door was open wide enough to walk through, without having to push it any further.*
> *Q. You didn't even budge the door? Is that what you are saying?*
> *A. I didn't budge it at all.*

The accused admitted that he entered the house for the purpose of stealing something from the house.

The court concluded that because the accused entered through an already open door it could not be said that he "broke into" the building. However, in *R. v. Bargiamis,*[14] it was held that *further opening* an already ajar door did constitute "breaking." In the *Bargiamis* case, the door was open about one half inch and the accused pushed it open to allow himself space to enter.

It would appear that if an accused is to be said to have "broken into" (or out of) a place, he must have gained entrance, (or exit), by having used some force to "assist" his entry. If he is able to enter through an already open door or window, he will not have broken into the place.

B. ENTERING *Entering* is defined by s.308:

> **308.(a) a person enters as soon as any part of his body or any part of an instrument that he uses is within any thing that is being entered; and**
> **(b) a person shall be deemed to have broken and entered if**
> **(i) he obtained entrance by a threat or artifice or by collusion with a person within, or**
> **(ii) he entered without lawful justification or excuse, the proof of which lies upon him, by a permanent or temporary opening.**

An entrance is made as soon as *any part of the body* of the accused, or any part of the instrument used by him, is within *any part of the place* being entered. If an accused is caught by police with a hand inside a window which he opened, he has entered the place for the purpose of s.306.

In *R. v. Marshall,*[15] the accused was charged with "breaking and entering." A police officer on patrol noticed a window pane in the premises pushed in about one foot. The window pane consisted of six glass panels, five of which were broken. One police officer searching in the vicinity of the broken window found the accused lying on his back on the ground concealed in a trench some five feet from the building. His hand was cut and his left cowboy boot was off. He was arrested.

At the trial, the accused gave this testimony:

> *A. I was standing there and I went across the street to take a leak and I was standing in an empty yard there and I seen all these cars going by so I went a little further in over by the building there and I went like this, leaning against the building there and the window*

broke and then this here. So I was mad and I went like this, I just swung. I may have swung twice, I don't remember but I swung once and I hit the bottom and then I don't know. I think I had a piece of glass or something in my boot cause when I moved it hurt so I took my boot off and I was trying to empty it out and I heard the police coming so I laid down in the grass because I was scared. I thought I was going to be charged with wilful damage or something. I had no intention of entering the building whatsoever, I know the man that owns the building very well and there was nothing I wanted of his.

It was acknowledged by all parties, including the accused, that there had been a "breaking." But it was further held that there had been an "entering" as well. Even though the accused had only put his hand through the window in the process of breaking it, that was enough to constitute an entering. It was, therefore, established that the accused had broken and entered the building. However, it was not proved that he had done so *with the intent to commit an indictable offence* and he was acquitted.

Section 308(b) states that a person can be said to have broken and entered a building if he entered through a "permanent or temporary opening." *Open doors and open windows are not permanent or temporary openings. In R. v. Sutherland,*[16] the accused entered through a garage "enclosed on three sides and open on one end for the entrance of a car." He entered for the purpose of stealing gasoline and was charged with "breaking and entering." The court held that the "opening" in the garage was really not an opening but was, in fact, "an entrance." An opening in s.308 refers to a hole in a wall, or door, or an opening where a door or window has not yet been placed. Areas where people usually enter buildings are not "openings."

Section 308(b) also provides that if a person gains entry by threats or with "inside help" he will still have "broken and entered."

C. PLACE Section 306 also provides that:

306.(8) For the purposes of this section, "place" means
(a) a dwelling-house;
(b) a building or structure or any part thereof, other than a dwelling-house;
(c) a railway vehicle, vessel, aircraft or trailer; or
(d) a pen or enclosure in which fur-bearing animals are kept in captivity for breeding or commercial purposes.

"Breaking and entering" a *dwelling-house* is often described as "burglary," although there is no separate Code offence defining burglary.

D. INTENT TO COMMIT AN INDICTABLE OFFENCE If it can be established that the accused "broke" and "entered" a "place," it must still be shown that (1) he *committed an indictable offence,* or (2) he entered with *the intent to commit an indictable offence.*

The most common indictable offence that is the object of a break-in is theft. However, the offence is not restricted to break-ins of that nature. Rape and assault, or any other indictable offence, can be the object of a break-in, under a "breaking and entering" charge.

In *Macleod v. R.,*[17] the accused after being ordered out of his host's home, where he had been drinking, returned and broke into the home to retrieve a bottle of liquor which he had brought to the home earlier. The accused was acquitted on a charge of "breaking and entering" because he did not break and enter with an intent to commit an indictable offence. See also the *Marshall* case on page 234.

For the same reason, if someone breaks into a cottage only to seek shelter, he will not have committed an offence under s.306, because, in such a situation, there is no intent to commit an indictable offence.

2. Presumption of Intent

Section 306(2) provides:

> **306.(2) For the purposes of proceedings under this section, evidence that an accused**
> **(a) broke and entered a place is, in the absence of any evidence to the contrary, proof that he broke and entered with intent to commit an indictable offence therein; or**
> **(b) broke out of a place is, in the absence of any evidence to the contrary, proof that he broke out after**
> **(i) committing an indictable offence therein, or**
> **(ii) entering with intent to commit an indictable offence therein.**

This subsection requires only that the accused give an *explanation* as to why he broke and entered a place. Once this explanation is before the court, the prosecutor must still prove, beyond a reasonable doubt, that the accused broke and entered, and committed an indictable offence, or intended to commit such an offence. In other words, the accused is not required to prove he did not commit, or intend to commit an indictable offence. He need only offer an explanation for his otherwise unexplainable presence. Returning to the example of a person who breaks into a cottage seeking shelter, under Section 306(2) he would be *presumed* to have broken and entered the cottage with the intent to commit an indictable offence. However, as soon as he gave an explanation for entering the cottage then the prosecution would have *to prove,* beyond a reasonable doubt, that in fact he broke and entered for the purpose of committing an indictable offence and not merely to seek shelter.

E. BEING UNLAWFULLY IN A DWELLING-HOUSE

1. Elements of the Offence

Section 307 provides:

> **307.(1) Every one who without lawful excuse, the proof of which lies upon him, enters or is in a dwelling-house with intent to commit an indictable offence therein is guilty of an indictable offence and is liable to imprisonment for ten years.**
>
> **(2) For the purpose of proceedings under this section, evidence that an accused, without lawful excuse, entered or was in a dwelling-house, is, in the absence of any evidence to the contrary, proof that he entered or was in the dwelling-house with intent to commit an indictable offence therein.**

The place entered must be a *dwelling-house*. A dwelling-house is a place in which people are intended to live. An apartment and motel, or hotel, rooms qualify as "dwelling-houses."

For the purpose of s.307, "enters" has the same meaning as it does under s.306. (see page 234). Subsection (2) requires the accused to provide the court with an explanation to the effect that he had a lawful excuse for being found in the dwelling-house in what were otherwise suspicious circumstances.

To commit an offence under s.307, a person does not have to "break" in. In other words, if a person walked through an open door into a dwelling-house, although he could not be found guilty of the offence of "breaking and entering" (s.306), he could be found guilty of unlawfully being in a dwelling-house.

To establish an offence under s.307, it must be shown that a person entered the dwelling-house with the intent to commit an indictable offence. In *R. v. Hachey,*[18] the accused were seventeen teenagers who entered an unoccupied farm house so that they could have a party there. They were acquitted on a charge under s.307, because they did not enter with the intent to commit an indictable offence.

F. POSSESSION OF HOUSE-BREAKING, VAULT-BREAKING AND SAFE-BREAKING TOOLS

1. Elements of the Offence

Section 309 makes it an offence for a person to have in his possession, *without reasonable explanation,* any instrument suitable for crimes such as theft or "breaking and entering."

Section 309(1) states:

309.(1) Every one who, without lawful excuse, the proof of which lies upon him, has in his possession any instrument suitable for house-breaking, vault-breaking or safe-breaking, under circumstances that give rise to a reasonable inference that the instrument has been used or is or was intended to be used for house-breaking, vault-breaking or safe-breaking, is guilty of an indictable offence.

In *R. v. Singleton,*[19] the question was raised as to the definition of "house" in *house-breaking*. The court said that house included not only dwelling-houses, but almost *any other building or structure or place*.

The constituent elements of an offence under s.309(1) are:

(1) *possession of instruments;*

(2) that are *suitable for house-breaking, and vault-breaking or safe-breaking;* and

(3) are found in *circumstances that indicate they were or are intended to be used for the purpose of house-breaking, vault-breaking or safe-breaking*.

The accused is under an onus to establish that he possessed such instruments for a lawful purpose.

A. POSSESSION Possession is defined by s.3(4) of the Code. Section 3(4) provides:

3.(4)(a) a person has anything in possession when he has it in his personal possession or knowingly

> **(i) has it in the actual possession or custody of another person, or**
>
> **(ii) has it in any place, whether or not that place belongs to or is occupied by him, for the use or benefit of himself or of another person; and**

(b) where one of two or more persons, with the knowledge and consent of the rest, has anything in his custody or possession, it shall be deemed to be in the custody and possession of each and all of them.

Possession under both (a) and (b) of s.3(4) consists of (1) a measure or right of *control* over the thing *and* (2) the *knowledge* of what the "thing" is. Control over the "thing" does not necessarily mean actual "physical" or manual control. A person may still have a measure of control over a thing when he knows it is being kept, and consents to it being kept, by another person.

In other words, if a person knowingly owns a house-breaking instrument and a friend (not knowing it is a house-breaking instrument) is keeping it at his house, the owner still has possession of the instrument. If the friend did know about the unlawful character of the instrument and concealed it within his home, he, too, would be said to be in possession of the instrument. This is because, in both of the above examples, *the person has knowledge of the instrument and a measure or right of control over it*.

In *Mongeau v. R.,*[20] the accused was arrested along with L. The accused was driving L's car when he was stopped by a police officer and asked for his driving licence and the car registration.

The arresting officer testified that he had no particular suspicion of either of the parties, and that he was merely making a routine "spot" check. He asked the accused to open the trunk of the car, which the latter proceeded to do. Observing a pack-sack therein, the constable asked what it contained. The accused said that he thought the pack-sack contained tools and gave as his reason for so thinking, the fact he could see a wooden handle sticking out of the top of the bag.

As the two of them were examining the trunk, another policeman, who had remained in the police car, noticed L, who had stayed in his automobile, open the door and deposit another bag underneath the car. When this was examined, it was found to contain dynamite, caps and fuse. Both men were thereupon arrested and charged under s.309.

The accused argued that he did not have possession of the tools and dynamite, and only guessed that the bag in the trunk contained "ordinary tools." He further explained he was driving the car, which was L's, because L had an injured foot.

The court held:

1. While the accused was in control of the automobile in which the articles were found, his control was merely due to the fact that he was sitting in the driver's seat at the time the police stopped the automobile to check it. The checking of the car was merely routine and the police officer testified that he had no suspicion of either of the parties.

2. The mere fact that the accused was driving the car at the time on behalf of the owner, who was also present in the car, *did not* establish that he had *control* over, or even *knowledge,* of the tools or dynamite.

3. The explanation of the accused was a reasonable one under the particular circumstances of the case and he was entitled to the benefit of any doubt that might arise in respect thereof.

The accused was acquitted on the charge of possession contrary to s.309. L, on the other hand, was convicted as charged.

B. INSTRUMENT SUITABLE FOR HOUSE-BREAKING, VAULT-BREAKING OR SAFE-BREAKING In *R. v. Hayes,*[21] the accused was found in posssssion of certain documents. These documents consisted of elaborate plans or sketches of two villages in Ontario showing the exact location of two banks, and containing a minute and detailed description of the interior of one of them. The documents also contained recipes for making explosives, information about bullet-proof vests, and descriptions of other instruments. The sole question for determination in the case was whether or not the documents, or plans, found in the possession of the accused, came within the category of "instruments for house-breaking, vault-breaking or safe-breaking."

The court concluded a *"breaking" instrument* necessarily implies an object, or article, or tool, which may be used to break something in the sense of the meaning of "break" as it is defined by s.282 (see page 233). Objects such as crowbars, jacks, screwdrivers, or even bent coat-hangers, are all capable of being described as "breaking" instruments. Having thus defined instrument, the court decided that the documents in the possession of the accused could not be classified as "house, vault or safe-breaking" instruments.

R. v. Benischek[22] is a case in which the issue was whether articles, found in possession of the accused, were instruments for safe-breaking.

In the trunk of a motor vehicle, owned by the accused, the police seized a brief case in which was found bottles containing nitric and sulphuric acid, bicarbonate of soda, a measuring bottle and a cup, rubber gloves and a plastic spatula. The evidence established the chemicals and implements were all necessary for making nitro-glycerine, a powerful explosive used constantly for safe-breaking. Glycerine, an essential ingredient for making the explosive, was not found in the possession of the accused. However, glycerine has several legitimate uses and is readily procurable at any drug store.

The court concluded:"Having in mind that the only purpose that could be served by using all the objects found was to make nitro-glycerine they are in my opinion substantial things having physical characteristics enabling them to be used to facilitate a breaking and constitute therefore an instrument for safe-breaking."

C. SUSPICIOUS CIRCUMSTANCES If it can be shown that a person (1) *possessed* (2) *instruments* that could be used for "house, vault or safe-breaking," it must further be demonstrated that (3) there is a *link* between the instruments and an actual or intended "house, vault or safe-break."

In *R. v. Kozak and Moore,*[23] the accused were found with screwdrivers, a pair of pliers, a metal expandable tool, a wrench, two pallet knives, and two pairs of gloves. The question was whether these "otherwise innocent instruments" were to be used for an intended "house, vault or safe-break." The accused were observed to be studying the rear door of an apartment building with the assistance of binoculars. Also found in the possession of the accused was a card, on which was written the licence plate number of the car owned by the occupant of the apartment. The court held that such circumstances could be capable of giving rise to a *reasonable inference* that the instruments in possession of the accused were to be used to "break in" to the apartment they were studying.

2. Presumption of Intent

If the accused is found in circumstances that otherwise satisfy all of the elements under s.309, he is required to demonstrate that he had a lawful excuse, or reasonable explanation, for having possession of the instruments in question.

In *R. v. Sullivan and Godbolt,*[24] the accused was found in possession of possible safe-breaking instruments, (a set of pole-climbers, a three-pound hammer, two pieces of soap, steel punches, pieces of wire, a pair of pliers and a quantity of rubber tape). He was able, however, to convince the court that all of the above material and instruments could be, and were intended to be, used for a legitimate contracting business purpose.

3. Instruments for Breaking Into Coin-Operated Machines

Section 310 creates a separate offence for the possession of instruments that can be, and are intended to be used, for breaking into *coin-operated machines.* Section 310 reads:

> **310. Every one who, without lawful excuse, the proof of which lies upon him, has in his possession any instrument suitable for breaking into a coin-operated device or a currency exchange device, under circumstances that give rise to a reasonable inference that the instrument has been used or is or was intended to be used for breaking into a coin-operated device or a currency exchange device, is guilty of an indictable offence and is liable to imprisonment for two years.**

4. Automobile Master Key

Section 311 creates the offence of unlawful selling, buying or having possession of an *automobile master key:*

> **311.(1) Every one who**
> **(a) sells, offers for sale or advertises in a province an automobile master key otherwise than under the authority of a licence issued by the Attorney General of that province, or**
> **(b) purchases or has in his possession in a province an automobile master key otherwise than under the authority of a licence issued by the Attorney General of that province, is guilty of an indictable offence and is liable to imprisonment for two years.**

A key of this nature is *defined* in s.311(5):

> **311.(5) For the purposes of this section, "automobile master key" includes a key, pick, rocker key or other instrument designed or adapted to operate the ignition or other switches or locks of a series of motor vehicles.**

G. POSSESSION OF PROPERTY OBTAINED BY CRIME

1. Elements of the Offence

Section 312 provides that it is an offence for a person, *knowingly,* to have in his *possession* any "thing" (either in whole or in part) which was obtained directly, or indirectly, by the *commission of an indictable offence.* Also, if a person has in his possession *proceeds* of a transaction involving a thing obtained by a crime, he is guilty of an offence under section 312.

If the thing was obtained by an act outside of Canada and the act was such that if it had occurred *within* Canada, it would have constituted an indictable offence, then having possession of the thing would still be contrary to s.312.

Section 312(1) states:

312.(1) Every one commits an offence who has in his possession any property or thing or any proceeds of any property or thing knowing that all or part of the property or thing or of the proceeds was obtained ...directly or indirectly from

(a) the commission in Canada of an offence punishable by indictment, or

(b) an act or omission anywhere that, if it had occurred in Canada, would have constituted an offence punishable by indictment.

Section 312(2) deals with situations in which a *motor vehicle* is the thing in possession. If a person has in his possession a motor vehicle with a *tampered* identification number, the vehicle is presumed to have been stolen, or obtained by another crime.

Section 312(2) states:

312.(2) In proceedings in respect of an offence under subsection (1), evidence that a person has in his possession a motor vehicle the vehicle identification number of which has been wholly or partially removed or obliterated or a part of a motor vehicle being a part bearing a vehicle identification number that has been wholly or partially removed or obliterated is, in the absence of any evidence to the contrary, proof that the motor vehicle or part, as the case may be, was obtained, and that such person had the motor vehicle or part, as the case may be, in his possession knowing that it was obtained,

(a) by the commission in Canada of an offence punishable by indictment, or

(b) by an act or omission anywhere that, if it had occurred in Canada, would have constituted an offence punishable by indictment.

(3) For the purposes of subsection (2), "vehicle identification number" means any number or other mark placed upon a motor vehicle for the purpose of distinguishing the motor vehicle from other similar motor vehicles.

Section 313 states:

313. Every one who commits an offence under section 312

(a) is guilty of an indictable offence and is liable to imprisonment for ten years, where the subject-matter of the offence is a testamentary instrument or the value exceeds two hundred dollars; or

(b) is guilty
(i) of an indictable offence and is liable to imprisonment for two years, or
(ii) of an offence punishable on summary conviction,
where the value of what is in his possession does not exceed two hundred dollars.

The general elements of an offence under s.312 are that the accused has a thing in (1) his *possession* (2) *knowing it was obtained by commission of an indictable offence* in Canada or by an act committed outside of Canada which would have been an indictable crime within Canada.

Section 316 (not reproduced) provides that for the purposes of s.312, the offence of "having in possession" is *complete* when a person has, alone, or together with another, possession or control over the "thing." In other words, to be convicted of an offence under s.312 the accused does not have to have the thing in his physical possession at the time he is arrested. He may, himself, have disposed of the "hot property" which he received yet still have committed an offence under s.312.

Specifically, to establish an offence under s.312 the prosecutor must prove:
1. The thing or "goods" have been *obtained by an indictable offence* (theft or robbery for example);
2. the goods are the *property of a person other than the accused;*
3. the accused *received* the goods (took them into his possession); and
4. at the time of receipt or while in his possession he became *aware* the goods were obtained by an indictable crime.

A. POSSESSION The definition of possession [3(4)] was discussed on page 238. Possession applied to s.312 dictates that the accused must have knowledge that the "thing" was obtained by an indictable offence, and have a measure or right of control over it. If a person knowingly buys a stolen T.V. set and asks the seller to deliver the set to a certain address, he will be said to have possession of the set for the purposes of s.312, even though it is not actually in his immediate or physical possession. This is because:
(1) he has knowledge of the T.V. set, and
(2) he has a measure or right of control over the set.

Or if, three people together knowingly purchased the stolen T.V. set, and one of them temporarily placed it in his garage, all three people would be in possession of the set. By s.316 if, in both of the above examples, a person had helped conceal the T.V. set even though he is not an "owner" of it, he could still be said to have possession of it for the purposes of s.312.

In *R. v. Kinna*,[25] one of the issues considered was whether or not the accused had possession of a stolen typewriter. According to the evidence, the accused and W were in the accused's room in downtown Vancouver. After some time, W went across to his own room and brought back a typewriter into the accused's room. W then said it would have to be sold as they needed money. He spoke of the typewriter in terms indicating it had been stolen. W went into a store to sell the typewriter while the accused remained outside. A police officer saw him there and questioned him. The accused told the officer a false story. W was arrested in the store. The accused was not arrested until the next day.

The court held that the accused did not have possession of the typewriter. Mere knowledge of a stolen thing is insufficient, and a person (the accused), cannot be said to consent to possession by another (and thereby be in possession himself), unless he, the accused, has some control over the thing. The court concluded that the accused did not have a measure of control over the typewriter.

B. KNOWLEDGE For a successful conviction of a charge under s.312, it must be proved that the accused knew the "goods" which are the subject of the charge were obtained by an indictable crime. If a person has his suspicions aroused but then *deliberately or recklessly omits to make further inquiries,* he will be *deemed,* as a matter of law, to have "guilty knowledge." That is, it will be assumed he was aware that the goods in question were obtained by an indictable offence.

In *R. v. Mottola and Vallee,*[26] M and V were charged with having in their possession stolen money. M (male) and V (female) were in bed when the house they were staying in was raided by the police. The police did not enter the bedroom occupied by the two accused because of the latter's state of undress, but Detective Sergeant H remained near the open bedroom door, and from that vantage point saw M reach into his trousers' pocket and remove a bundle of money which he handed to V, who was in bed. V put the money under the pillow, then got up, crossed the room and put something in a cardboard box. H then entered the room and began his search. He found nothing under the pillow but upon opening the cardboard box, he found the stolen money. It was acknowledged that M knew the money was stolen. The question was whether V, in such circumstances, could be said to have the same knowledge. The court decided that she could not. At most her possession of the money was a *momentary physical handling* from which it would be unfair, in all the circumstances, to infer guilty knowledge on her part. V was therefore found not guilty of the charge. M, on the other hand, was found guilty of having possession of the stolen money.

In *R. v. Marabella,*[27] the accused, a scrap or salvage dealer, was charged with having possession of stolen copper. The police seized, in a salvage yard, over a ton of new copper which was proved to have been stolen a few nights earlier from a manufacturing company. The accused had delivered the copper to the salvage yard owner after having purchased it from B. The main issue in the case was whether the accused *should have known* the goods (the copper) were stolen, considering the circumstances in which B sold it to him.

B was not connected with a business which sold copper. The copper was purchased at a private residence, and copper is not normally found at a private residence. It was not a purchase of a quantity of scrap material. The copper was bulky, heavy, and from its size, shape and appearance, the accused must have known it was new and unused. The accused did not deal in new copper. There was also the matter of the price paid. The price paid by the accused, according to his statement, was 25 cents a pound. This was little more than one half of the amount normally paid even for scrap copper. Even in view of all of the unusual and suspicious circumstances described above, the accused never questioned B as to the source of the copper.

The court concluded that in such circumstances, the accused was guilty of having possession of stolen property. He *deliberately* refrained from asking for further information to avoid obtaining knowledge which would have been dangerous to him, namely that the copper was stolen. If a person *consciously omits* to ask questions because he wishes to remain in ignorance, he is deemed to have "guilty knowledge."

2. "Doctrine of Recent Possession"

There is a presumption present in cases which involve possession of *recently* stolen goods. In brief, once possession of recently stolen goods is established, it is presumed they were obtained with the knowledge that they were stolen. In other words, if a person has in his possession a car that was recently stolen, he is presumed to know that the car was stolen. In such a situation, the accused must offer an explanation to rebut, or overcome, this presumption. If he offers an explanation that might be reasonably true, that is an explanation which indicates he did not know the goods were stolen, he is entitled to be acquitted of a charge of possession of stolen property.

QUESTIONS

1. How can the word "fraudulent" used in Section 283 be defined?
2. What does "colour of right" mean?
3. If a person "takes" a transistor radio on Friday, without the owner's consent, and returns it undamaged on the following Monday, has he committed the offence of theft?
4. What is the difference between the *theft* (s.283) and the *taking* (s.295) of a motor vehicle?
5. A and B are husband and wife. Before the marriage, A collected valuable coins. After his marriage to B, A stopped collecting but he did keep all of the coins he had collected before the marriage. B took the coins one day, without letting her husband know, and sold them for $500.00. She spent the money on herself. A did not discover the coins were missing until a month later. His wife pretended she didn't know what had happened to them. Could B, the wife, be convicted of theft if it is found out it was she who took the coins?
6. What factors must be proved to complete the offence of robbery (s.302)?
7. A grabs at B's purse. She holds tight. Without actually touching her, A "wrenches" the purse out of B's hands. B stumbles but does not fall. Is A guilty of robbery?
8. What are the elements of the offence of extortion (s.305)?
9. What constitutes a threat for the purposes of extortion?

10. Define for the purposes of "breaking and entering" (s.306) the following words:
    a. "break"
    b. "enter"
    c. "place"
11. If it is proven an accused "broke and entered" a place, what must the accused do if he hopes to escape a conviction under s.306?
12. What is the difference between the offence of "breaking and entering" and being unlawfully in a dwelling-house (s.307)?
13. Define "house-breaking, vault-breaking and safe-breaking tools" as these words are meant to be used in s.309.
14. What are the elements of the offence of possession of property obtained by crime (s.312)?
15. Define the meaning of "possession."
16. Does a person have to know for certain that an object is stolen before he can be convicted under s.312?
17. What does the "doctrine of recent possession" mean?

[1] (1946) 2 C.R. 408 (N.S. C.A.)
[2] (1953) 17 C.R. 343 (Que.C.A.)
[3] (1965) 4 C.C.C. 37 (Man.C.A.)
[4] (1959) 123 C.C.C. 109 (Sask.C.A.)
[5] (1966) 3 C.C.C. 348 (Ont.C.A.)
[6] (1972) 7 C.C.C. (2d) 301; 20 C.R.N.S. 190 (B.C. C.A.)
[7] (1971) 4 C.C.C. (2d) 296 (S.C.C.)
[8] (1916) 28 C.C.C. 319 (Ont.C.A.)
[9] (1952) 1 S.C.R. 330 (S.C.C.)
[10] (1964) 44 C.R. 375 (Ont.C.A.)
[11] (1974) 19 C.C.C. (2d) 190 (B.C. C.A.)
[12] (1967) 1 C.R.N.S. 302 (S.C.C.)
[13] (1975) 22 C.C.C. (2d) 252; 28 C.R.N.S. 331 (Ont.C.A.)
[14] (1970) 4 C.C.C. 258; 10 C.R.N.S. 129 (Ont.C.A.)
[15] (1970) 1 C.C.C. (2d) 505 (B.C.C.A.)
[16] (1967) 50 C.R. 197 (B.C.C.A.)
[17] (1968) 2 C.R.N.S. 342 (P.E.I.S.C.)
[18] (1970) 1 C.C.C. (2d) 242; 11 C.R.N.S. 376 (N.B. C.A.)
[19] (1956) 115 C.C.C. 391 (Ont.C.A.)
[20] (1957) 25 C.R. 195 (Que.C.A.)
[21] (1958) O.W.N. 449 (Ont.C.A.)
[22] (1963) 3 C.C.C. 286; 39 C.R. 285 (Ont.C.A.)
[23] (1975) 30 C.R.N.S. 7 (Ont.C.A.)
[24] (1946) 1 C.R. 164 (B.C. C.A.)
[24] (1951) 11 C.R. 292 (B.C. C.A.)
[26] (1959) O.R. 520 (Ont.C.A.)
[27] (1957) 177 C.C.C. 78 (Ont.C.A.)

Chapter Fourteen

Offences Resembling False Pretences

Offences to be discussed in this chapter are those which might most aptly be described as "crimes of deceit." *False pretences, fraud,* and *forgery* are examples of such crimes. These offences do not involve any violence, or a threat of violence.

A. FALSE PRETENCES

1. Elements of the Offence

Section 319 defines what a *false pretence* is:

> **319(1) A false pretence is a representation of a matter of fact either present or past, made by words or otherwise, that is known by the person who makes it to be false and that is made with a fradulent intent to induce the person to whom it is made to act upon it.**
> **(2) Exaggerated commendation or depreciation of the quality of anything is not a false pretence unless it is carried to such an extent that it amounts to a fraudulent misrepresentation of fact.**

A false pretence is therefore made up of (1) a *representation* (statement) about (2) *facts,* past or present, made (3) by *words,* or other means (acts) that are *known* by the accused to be (4) *untrue* and made (5) with the *dishonest* intent to *make* someone *do* or give up something. For example, A falsely tells B that he has $500.00 in his bank account so that B will accept a cheque as payment for a motorcycle which A wants to buy. If B accepts the cheque and gives the bike to A, A will have obtained the bike by false pretences. It is important to remember that the false statement must be about an *existing* (or past) fact. In the above example, if A had told B that he would pay for the motorcycle in a week and B delivered the motorcycle to him upon such a promise, assuming A did not pay B at the end of the week, A would not be guilty of false pretences. This is because A could not be said to have made a representation about a fact, past or present. His representation was about a future event. A would be guilty of theft or fraud.

Section 312(2) provides that if a person exaggerates about the quality of an article, for example, states that his car is in excellent condition when, in fact, he knows it to be in poor shape, this exaggeration will not amount to a false pretence. The exaggeration must be such that it comes close to being an outright lie.

2. Specific False Pretence Situations

Section 320 outlines various types of false pretence offences.

> **320.(1) Every one commits an offence who:**
> **(a) by a false pretence, whether directly or through the medium of a contract obtained by a false pretence, obtains anything in respect of which the offence of theft may be committed or causes it to be delivered to another person;**
> **320.(2) Every one who commits an offence under paragraph (1)(a)**
> **(a) is guilty of an indictable offence and is liable to imprisonment for ten years, where the property obtained is a testamentary instrument or where the value of what is obtained exceeds two hundred dollars; or**
> **(b) is guilty**
>> **(i) of an indictable offence and is liable to imprisonment for two years, or**
>> **(ii) of an offence punishable on summary conviction, where the value of what is obtained does not exceed two hundred dollars.**

Section 320(1)(a) covers the general situation in which property (usually money or "goods") is obtained by false pretences. Anything that is *capable of being stolen* is capable of being obtained by false pretences.

To establish an offence under s.320(1)(a), it is necessary to prove that the accused received more than mere possession of the property. It appears the owner of the property must intend to transfer *ownership,* as distinct from *possession.* This point is illustrated in *R. v. Arsenault.*[1] The accused was charged on two counts of false pretences. The false pretence used in both cases was a "bad" cheque (he lied about the amount of money in his bank account). In the first instance, he purchased electric clippers which were sold and delivered to the accused on the faith of the cheque. In the second instance, a cheque was used as a down payment on a car.

However, the vendor refused to deliver the car to the accused until his cheque had cleared, and his conditional sale agreement had been accepted and discounted by the finance company. The accused then persuaded the vendor to let him test the car, but instead of returning it, he drove it to Mexico.

The accused was convicted of false pretences in the case of the clippers. However, with respect to the car, he was found not guilty. The court held that the accused acquired only temporary possession of the car because the vendor did not *intend to transfer ownership* of it and, as a consequence, he did not commit the offence of "false pretences" within the meaning of s.320(1)(a). The court concluded the proper charge against the accused should have been theft of a motor vehicle. As well, a charge of fraud, (s.338), might have been more appropriate.

Section 320(4) states:

> **320.(4) Where, in proceedings under paragraph (1)(a), it is shown that anything was obtained by the accused by means of a cheque that, when presented for payment within a reasonable time, was dishonoured on the ground that no funds or insufficient funds were on deposit to the credit of the accused in the bank or other institution on which the cheque was drawn, it shall be presumed to have been obtained by a false pretence, unless the court is satisfied by evidence that when the accused issued the cheque he had reasonable grounds to believe that it would be honoured if presented for payment within a reasonable time after it was issued.**
>
> **(5) In this section, "cheque" includes, in addition to its ordinary meaning, a bill of exchange drawn upon any institution that makes it a business practice to honour bills of exchange or any particular kind thereof drawn upon it by depositors.**

In other words, if a person honestly believed that a cheque he gave in payment would be honoured by his bank, he would not be guilty of false pretences for actions that would *otherwise* be criminal under *s.320(1)(a)*.

Subsections 320(1) *(b) (c) and (d)* read as follows:

> **Everyone commits an offence who ...**
> **(b) obtains credit by a false pretence or by fraud;**
> **(c) knowingly makes or causes to be made, directly or indirectly, a false statement in writing with intent that it should be relied upon, with respect to the financial condition or means or ability to pay for himself or any person, firm or corporation that he is interested in or that he acts for, for the purpose of procuring, in any form whatever, whether for his benefit or the benefit of that person, firm or corporation,**
> **(i)   the delivery of personal property,**
> **(ii) the payment of money,**
> **(iii) the making of a loan,**

      (iv) the extension of credit,

      (v) the discount of an account receivable, or

      (vi) the making, accepting, discounting or endorsing of a bill of exchange, cheque, draft, or promissory note; or

  (d) knowing that a false statement in writing has been made with respect to the financial condition or means or ability to pay of himself or another person, firm or corporation that he is interested in or that he acts for, procures upon the faith of that statement, whether for his benefit or for the benefit of that person, firm or corporation, anything mentioned in subparagraphs (c)(i) to (vi).

Section 320(3) provides:

320.(3) Every one who commits an offence under [s.320](1) (b) (c) or (d) is guilty of an indictable offence and is liable to imprisonment for ten years.

Subsection (b) creates the general offence of *obtaining credit* by false pretences. *Subsections (c) and (d)* define specific false pretence situations involving the establishment of a "phoney" *credit rating*.

Subsection (b) would be applicable if a person deliberately gave false information about his assets to a bank officer when negotiating a loan. However, in *R. v. Winning*,[2] the accused obtained a credit card by giving his correct name and address, but lying about his financial worth. It was held that credit was not advanced by relying on the false information but on the basis of an independent credit investigation and, therefore, the offence was not made out. Therefore, in the example about the loan officer being given false information, it would have to be established that he actually relied on the false information in determining whether a loan be granted, before the offence of false pretences could be made out.

The false pretence in subsections (c) and (d) must be made in *writing* with the object to procure one of the benefits listed within the subsection. That is, obtain delivery of personal property or money, or obtain a loan or an extension of credit, etc. For example, A owns a company and he drafts a letter which falsely describes his company's worth. He presents this letter to several creditors and they, relying on the letter, loan him money. In such circumstances, A would be guilty of an offence under s.320(1(c).

Section 322 creates the special offence of *fraudulently obtaining food and lodgings*.

322.(1)   Every one who fraudulently obtains food, lodging or other accommodation at an hotel or inn or at a lodging, boarding or eating house is guilty of an offence punishable on summary conviction.

  (2) In proceedings under this section, evidence that an accused obtained food, lodging or other accommodation at an

hotel or inn or at a lodging, boarding or eating house, and did
not pay for it and
  (a) made a false or fictitious show or pretence of having
      baggage,
  (b) had any false or pretended baggage,
  (c) surreptitiously removed or attenpted to remove his baggage
      or any material part of it,
  (d) absconded or surreptitiously left the premises,
  (e) knowingly made a false statement to obtain credit or time for
      payment, or
  (f) offered a worthless cheque, draft or security in payment for
      his food, lodging or other accommodation,
is, in the absence of any evidence to the contrary, proof of fraud.

B. FRAUD

1. Elements of the Offence

Fraud is defined by section 338 of the Code:

> **338.(1) Every one who, by deceit, falsehood or other fraudulent
> means, whether or not it is a false pretence within the meaning of
> this Act, defrauds the public or any person, whether ascertained
> or not, of any property, money or valuable security**
>   **(a) is guilty of an indictable offence and is liable to imprison-
>   ment for ten years, where the subject-matter of the fraud is a
>   testamentary instrument or where the value thereof exceeds
>   two hundred dollars; or**
>   **(b) is guilty**
>   **(i) of an indictable offence and is liable to imprisonment for
>   two years, or**
>   **(ii) of an offence punishable on summary conviction, where
>   the value of the property of which the public or any
>   person is defrauded does not exceed two hundred
>   dollars.**

The classic definition of fraud is found in an old English case, *Re London and
Globe Finance:* "To defraud is to deprive by deceit: it is by deceit to induce a man
to act to his injury. More tersely, it may be put that to deceive is by falsehood to
induce a course of action."
Applying this definition to the constituent elements of s.338, the following may
be stated: Anyone who (1) *creates a state of mind* in another, (that is *deceives),* such
that the other person (2) takes a *course of action* whereby (3) he *loses property or
money,* is guilty of the offence of fraud.

2. Fraud and False Pretences

There is not a great distinction between the offence of obtaining property by false pretences, (as defined in s.319), and obtaining it by fraud, (s.338) that is by "deceit, falsehood or other fraudulent means." A person can make a false pretence and be charged under s.338, rather than under an offence described in s.320. Fraud is more of a "catch all" offence and, hence, if a person obtains something by deceit that does not amount to a false pretence, he may still be committing the more "general" offence of fraud. A false pretence is a false representation (usually a statement) of a fact known to be untrue and calculated to mislead. In other words, the false statement must be specifically intended to induce the victim to act. Further, the statement must be about an *existing* (or past) fact, as distinguished from a mere promise or statements about the future, or about expectations. Fraud does not require that such a statement be made, or, if a statement is made about a *future* set of circumstances, it will be treated as fraud, and not false pretence. In general, any form of deceit, deception, artifice or trickery which causes a person to part with his money, or property, can be considered as fraud.

3. Examples of Fraud

In *R. v. Kribbs,*[3] the accused was charged with defrauding A of a sum of money. He obtained the money by taking advantage of his relationship with A, who was in a condition of senility and dependent upon him. The accused obtained the money by getting A to transfer his money into a joint bank account. He then withdrew large sums of A's money. The accused was convicted of fraud under s.338. In substance what the accused did was to, by deceit, defraud A of his money.

In *R. v. McLean and Janko,*[4] the accused, M, was charged with committing fraud contrary to what is now s.338. M, a used car dealer, made a practice of getting customers to sign offers (to purchase a car) at a price agreeable to the customer, and said he was willing to give delivery at the set price. Afterwards he would refuse to approve such offers and attempt to get the customer to pay more for the car, or enter into some other deal more advantageous to him. This latter process, known as "bumping" or "jacking," was entrusted to his sales manager. A, a customer, paid the agreed price of $320.00 for a car, was promised delivery and was then sent to J, who tried to get the customer to pay a further $100.00 for the car, or buy another with the money he had already paid. A refused and demanded that he receive the car that had been promised him or his money back. When J failed to deliver the car or return the money A went to the police.

The court held that because M made a false promise (that the customer would receive a particular car for his money), a promise which from the start he never intended to keep, he was guilty of committing fraud.

4. Specific Fraud Offences

Section 338(2) provides:

> **338.(2) Every one who, by deceit, falsehood or other fraudulent means, whether or not it is a false pretence within the meaning of this Act, with intent to defraud, affects the public market price of stocks, shares, merchandise or anything that is offered for sale to the public, is guilty of an indictable offence and is liable to imprisonment for ten years.**

Section 338(2) is a specific type of fraud concerned with the manipulation of price of any article that is on sale to the public. A person or company cannot "fix" prices in such a manner as to cheat the public.

Section 338 (not reproduced) provides that a person who uses the mail to send letters or circulars concerning *schemes designed to deceive or defraud the public* is guilty of an indictable offence and is liable to imprisonment for two years.

Section 340 (not reproduced) makes it an offence for a person to *manipulate the stock market* by creating a misleading or false appearance of active public trading.

Section 358 deals with situations in which companies or shareholders of companies are the object of a form of fraud:

> **358.(1) Every one who makes, circulates or publishes a prospectus, statement or account, whether written or oral, that he knows is false in a material particular, with intent**
> **(a) to induce persons, whether ascertained or not, to become shareholders or partners in a company,**
> **(b) to deceive or defraud the members, shareholders or creditors, whether ascertained or not, of a company,**
> **(c) to induce any person to entrust or advance anything to a company, or**
> **(d) to enter into any security for the benefit of a company, is guilty of an indictable offence and is liable to imprisonment for ten years.**
> **(2) In this section, "company" means a syndicate, body corporate or company, whether existing or proposed to be created.**

Sections 343 and 344 cover any fraudulent behaviour involved in the *sale or mortgaging of property*. That is fraudulent activities on the part of a mortgagor, or vendor of property. Specifically, section 343 provides:

343.(1) Every one ...
(a) with intent to defraud and for the purpose of inducing the purchaser or mortgagee to accept the title offered or produced to him, conceals from him any settlement, deed, will or other instrument material to the title, or any encumbrance on the title, or
(b) falsifies any pedigree upon which the title depends, is guilty of an indictable offence and is liable to imprisonment for two years.

Section 344 states:

344. Every one who, as principal or agent, in a proceeding to register title to real property, or in a transaction relating to real property that is or is proposed to be registered, knowingly and with intent to deceive,
(a) makes a material false statement or representation,
(b) suppresses or conceals from a judge or registrar or any person employed by or assisting the registrar, any material document, fact, matter or information, or
(c) is privy to anything mentioned in paragraph (a) or (b), is guilty of an indictable offence and is liable to imprisonment for five years.

5. Personation

If one person "passes himself off" as another *for a criminal purpose,* he will commit an offence under section 361:

361. Every one who fraudulently personates any person, living or dead,
(a) with intent to gain advantage for himself or another person,
(b) with intent to obtain any property or an interest in any property, or
(c) with intent to cause disadvantage to the person whom he personates or another person
is guilty of an indictable offence and is liable to imprisonment for fourteen years.

In *Rozon v. The Queen,*[5] the accused, upon being asked to identify himself, handed to the police officers a medical insurance card belonging to another person. He did so in order to avoid being arrested on a warrant issued against him. The court held that the words "with the intent to gain advantage," as used in section 361, were to be given a broad meaning. In the circumstances the accused was convicted of "personation" because he deliberately, and in bad faith, showed police the insurance card of another in order to gain the "advantage" of avoiding arrest on a warrant outstanding against him.

In a similar case, *R. v. Dozois,* [6] the accused, D, whose driver's licence was suspended, was convicted of "personation" when he used his passenger's licence, after being stopped by police for a traffic violation.

C. FORGERY

1. Elements of the Offence

Section 324(1) defines the offence of *forgery:*

> **324.(1) Every one commits forgery who makes a false document, knowing it to be false, with intent**
> **(a) that it should in any way be used or acted upon as genuine, to the prejudice of any one whether within Canada or not, or**
> **(b) that some person should be induced, by the belief that it is genuine, to do or to refrain from doing anything, whether within Canada or not.**

Section 324(3) states:

> **324.(3) Forgery is complete as soon as a document is made with the knowledge and intent referred to in subsection (1), notwithstanding that the person who makes it does not intend that any particular person should use or act upon it as genuine or be induced, by the belief that it is genuine, to do or refrain from doing anything.**

Section 325(1) provides:

> **325.(1) Every one who commits forgery is guilty of an indictable offence and is liable to imprisonment for fourteen years.**

Before an accused can be convicted of the offence of forgery, it must be proved that he (1) *knowingly* made a *false document* with (2) *intent* it be used (3) as if it were *genuine* in such a way that someone is "prejudiced."

A. FALSE DOCUMENT Section 282 defines a *false document* as follows:

> **282. "false document" means a document**
> **(a) the whole or some material part of which purports to be made by or on behalf of a person**
> **(i) who did not make it or authorize it to be made, or**
> **(ii) who did not in fact exist;**
> **(b) that is made by or on behalf of the person who purports to make it but is false in some material particular;**

(c) that is made in the name of an existing person, by him or under his authority, with a fraudulent intention, that it should pass as being made by some person, real or fictitious, other than the person who makes it or under whose authority it is made.

The word "false" as it is used in the context of false document has a definition that is different from the meaning it conveys in ordinary conversation. A false document does not mean that it contains untrue statements. A false document is one that tells a lie about *itself,* not about its *contents.* Thus forgery consists *of the falsification of the document itself and not in merely making false statements.* If a letter is supposed to have been signed by A but was in fact signed in A's name by B, without his permission, and a third party is led to believe it is A's letter, the letter is a false document. It tells a lie about itself, the lie being that the letter is signed by A. If the same letter had actually been signed by A, even though the contents of the letter may have been completely untrue, the letter would not be a false document. It does not tell a lie itself. The lie is in the information, not in the letter.

In *R. v. Coté,*[7] the accused was charged with having committed the offence of forgery. The sole question for determination was whether the documents alleged to be forgeries were, in fact, false documents. The documents involved were salary sheets, listing hours worked. Some of the sheets made reference to work done with the assistance of a bulldozer supposedly owned by T. T, in fact, did not own a bulldozer, yet was paid in excess of $2,000.00 for work done by the bulldozer. The salary sheets were signed by the accused, who knew that the bulldozer did not exist.

The court held that although the documents contained false information, they were not false documents within the meaning of forgery. *The documents had not been falsified in order to appear as something they were not.* The court stated: "considering that the wage documents . . . .are not false documents . . . .since they were really prepared and signed by the persons whose signatures appear thereon, and were not altered by the addition or subtraction of any essential elements, although they do contain certain statements which are not true . . . .the evidence does not disclose the committing of any offence included in the offence of forgery."

The court did, however, make the following observation: " . . .if after making out the wage dockets, the accused had changed the amounts appearing therein, with the intent that a larger amount should be paid, the document would become false."

Section 324(2) provides:

324.(2) Making a false document includes:
(a) altering a genuine document in any material part,
(b) making a material addition to a genuine document or adding to it a false date, attestation, seal or other thing that is material, or
(c) making a material alteration in a genuine document by erasure, obliteration, removal or in any other way.

To make a "material addition or alteration," or to change a "material part" of a document, is to change an important part of the document. For example, to change the date on a cheque is to alter a material part of the cheque. In *R. v. O'hearn*,[8] the accused got an 87-year-old man, (L), to subscribe to *Maclean's* magazine for a year. L gave the accused a signed cheque with the marginal figures "315" inserted, but the amount otherwise blank. The accused gave L a receipt for $3.15, the cost of the subscription. The accused afterwards altered the cheque to read $31.50 and filled in the words for that amount in the appropriate space. See Figure 14-1. The court held the alteration of the figures constituted an alteration of a material part of the cheque.

CHEQUE AS ALTERED BY THE ACCUSED

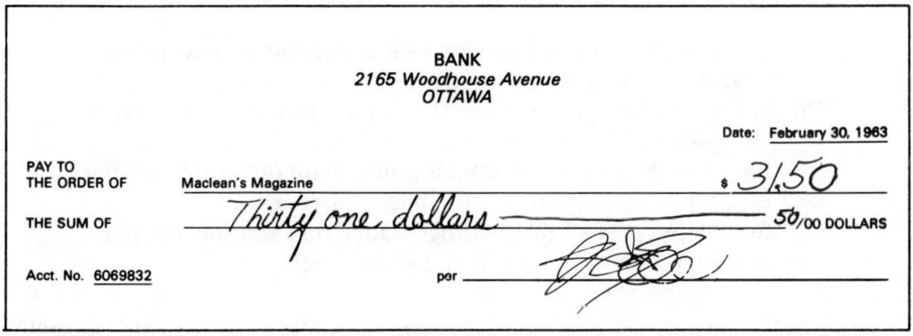

BANK
2165 Woodhouse Avenue
OTTAWA

Date: February 30, 1963

PAY TO
THE ORDER OF   Maclean's Magazine $ *31.50*

THE SUM OF   *Thirty one dollars*   *50*/00 DOLLARS

Acct. No. 6069832   per

FIGURE 14-1

B. CORROBORATION Section 325(2) states:

> **325.(2) No person shall be convicted of an offence under this section upon the evidence of only one witness unless the evidence of that witness is corroborated in a material particular by evidence that implicates the accused.**

"An offence under this section" refers to the offence of forgery.

Section 325(2) means that additional, *independent evidence* is required to strengthen, or support, the testimony of a single witness before a conviction for forgery can be made out.

2.Uttering

Section 326 states:

> **326.(1) Every one who, knowing that a document is forged,**
> **(a) uses, deals with, or acts upon it, or**
> **(b) causes or attempts to cause any person to use, deal with, or act upon it,**
> **as if the document were genuine, is guilty of an indictable offence and is liable to imprisonment for fourteen years.**
> **(2) For the purpose of proceedings under this section, the place where a document was forged is not material.**

Section 326 creates the offence of "uttering" a forged document. Generally, uttering means to pass, or to cause to have passed, as if it were genuine, a forged document. If a person takes to a bank a forged cheque *knowing* it to be forged (whether or not he forged the cheque himself), and attempts to cash it, he is guilty of an offence under s.326. Similarly, if a person, *knowing* a cheque is forged, gives it to another, who has no knowledge of the illegal nature of the cheque, with a request that he cash it, the person who caused the other to pass the cheque is guilty of "uttering."

3. Offences Resembling or Related to Forgery

There are a number of other offences resembling or related to the offence of forgery. Some of these offences are described in the following paragraphs.

A. FORGERY EQUIPMENT Section 327, not reproduced, provides that it is unlawful (without the proper authorization) to make, or possess, *exchequer bill paper, revenue paper,* or paper that is used to make *bank notes,* or any paper that is intended to make bank notes, or any paper that is intended to resemble any of the above. Section 327 also states that it is unlawful to make, or possess, *any machinery,* or *instrument* that is intended to be used to commit forgery. A person contravening Section 327 is liable to imprisonment for fourteen years.

B. FALSE MESSAGES Section 329 states:

> **329. Every one who, with intent to defraud, causes or procures a telegram, cablegram or radio message to be sent or delivered as being sent by the authority of another person, knowing that it is not sent by his authority and with intent that the message should be acted on as being sent by his authority, is guilty of an indictable offence and is liable to imprisonment for five years.**

C. FORGING A TRADE MARK There are a number of offences that deal with trade marks. Generally, a *trade mark is an identification* of a company's product or property. Trade marks are the property of a company. Only that company may use the trade mark, unless it grants permission allowing another company to make use of the trade mark.

Section 364 states:

> **364. For the purposes of this Part, every one forges a trade mark who**
> **(a) without the consent of the proprietor of the trade mark, makes or reproduces in any manner that trade mark or a mark so nearly resembling it as to be calculated to deceive, or**
> **(b) falsifies, in any manner, a genuine trade mark.**

Section 365 then provides:

> **365. Every one commits an offence who, with intent to deceive or defraud the public ...forges a trade mark.**

Section 368 has wider application:

> **368. Every one commits an offence, who with intent to deceive or defraud,**
> **(a) defaces, conceals or removes a trade mark or the name of another person from anything without the consent of that other person, or**
> **(b) being a manufacturer, dealer, trader or bottler fills any bottle or siphon that bears the trade mark or name of another person, without the consent of that other person, with a beverage, milk, by-product of milk or other liquid commodity for the purpose of sale or traffic.**

In *R. v. Irvine,*[9] the accused, a manufacturer, was convicted under s.368 when he filled bottles with his own product and then marked these bottles with another company's name.

D. COUNTERFEIT MONEY

1. Definition

There are a number of offences relating to *counterfeit money*. The *making* of, having *possession* of, and the *uttering* of counterfeit money are all offences. The sections defining these offences are self-explanatory.

Counterfeit money is defined by section 406:

> **406(a) a false coin or false paper money that resembles or is apparently intended to resemble or pass for a current coin or current paper money,**
>> **(b) a forged bank note or forged blank bank note, whether complete or incomplete,**
>> **(c) a genuine coin or genuine `paper money that is prepared or altered to resemble or pass for a current coin or current paper money of a higher denomination,**
>> **(d) a current coin from which the milling is removed by filing or cutting the edges and on which new milling is made to restore its appearance,**
>> **(e) a coin cased with gold, silver or nickel, as the case may be, that is intended to resemble or pass for a current gold, silver or nickel coin, and**
>> **(f) a coin or a piece of metal or mixed metals washed or coloured by any means with a wash or material capable of producing the appearance of gold, silver or nickel and that is intended to resemble or pass for a current gold, silver or nickel coin.**

The word "current" as it is used in the counterfeiting sections usually means that the money counterfeited (copied) must be *negotiable,* or still "in circulation."

In *Robinson v. The Queen,*[10] the accused had in his possession a number of counterfeit U.S. 1941/42 dimes. The peculiarity in their dating, (1941/42) gave them a numismatic value of between $100.00 and $800.00. The accused argued that the dimes were not intended to resemble, or pass as, "current" coins, within the definition of "counterfeit money." They were for the purpose of sale as a numismatic curiosity and not for circulation as legal tender.

A representative of the Treasury Department of the Secret Service in Washington D.C. gave the following evidence with respect to the dimes:

> *Q. I have in this plastic bag one hundred and forty-six 1941/42 U.S. dimes. Are these currency in the United States?*
> *A. Most definitely.*
> *Q. Are they legal tender?*
> *A. They are.*
> *Q. And if they were genuine, would they be legal tender today?*
> *A. They would be, sir.*

The court held that the coins' primary characteristic was that they were counterfeits of "current" coins and that they were intended to resemble such coins. The accused was, therefore, convicted of having counterfeit money in his possession.

2. Offences Involving Counterfeit Money

A. MAKING Section 407 states:

> **407. Every one who makes or begins to make counterfeit money is guilty of an indictable offence and is liable to imprisonment for fourteen years.**

B. POSSESSION Section 408 provides:

> **408. Every one who, without lawful justification or excuse, the proof of which lies upon him,**
> **(a) buys, receives or offers to buy or receive,**
> **(b) has in his custody or possession, or**
> **(c) introduces into Canada,**
> **counterfeit money is guilty of an indictable offence and is liable to imprisonment for fourteen years.**

C. UTTERING Sections 410 and 411 state:

> **410. Every one who, without lawful justification or excuse, the proof of which lies upon him,**
> **(a) utters or offers to utter counterfeit money or uses counterfeit money as if it were genuine, or**
> **(b) exports, sends or takes counterfeit money out of Canada, is guilty of an indictable offence and is liable to imprisonment for fourteen years.**
> **411. Every one who, with intent to defraud, knowingly utters**
> **(a) a coin that is not current, or**
> **(b) a piece of metal or mixed metals that resembles in size, figure or colour a current coin for which it is uttered, is guilty of an indictable offence and is liable to imprisonment for two years.**

D. SLUGS AND TOKENS Section 412 provides:

> **412. Every one who without lawful excuse, the proof of which lies upon him,**
> **(a) manufactures, produces or sells, or**
> **(b) has in his possession**
> **anything that is intended to be fraudulently used in substitution for a coin or token of value that any coin or token-operated device is designed to receive is guilty of an offence punishable on summary conviction.**

262 Part B: Criminal Code Offences

E. CLIPPING Section 413 reads:

> **413 Every one who**
> **(a) impairs, diminishes, or lightens a current gold or silver coin with intent that it should pass for a current gold or silver coin, or**
> **(b) utters a coin, knowing that it has been impaired, diminished or lightened contrary to paragraph (a)**
> **is guilty of an indictable offence and is liable to imprisonment for fourteen years.**

F. COUNTERFEITING EQUIPMENT Section 416 states:

> **416. Every one who, without lawful justification or excuse, the proof of which lies upon him,**
> **(a) makes or repairs,**
> **(b) begins or proceeds to make or repair,**
> **(c) buys or sells, or**
> **(d) has in his custody or possession,**
> **a machine, engine, tool, instrument, material or thing that he knows has been used or that he knows is adapted and intended for use in making counterfeit money or counterfeit tokens of value is guilty of an indictable offence and is liable to imprisonment for fourteen years.**

QUESTIONS

1. Explain the difference between "false pretences" and "fraud."
2. A takes possession of a used car from B and promises to pay for it in one week. A does not have any intention of paying B for the car. What is he guilty of?
3. A buys a motorcycle from B. He gives B a postdated cheque in payment for the "bike." On the date for which the cheque is endorsed B discovers that A's bank account has insufficient funds to cover the amount of the cheque. Has A committed an offence? Explain your answer.
4. What is a "false document"?
5. A is applying to join the Canadian Armed Forces. He must provide the recruiting officer with a copy of his high school marks. A lists all of the subjects he studied at high school but he lies about some of the marks which he received. Has A made a false document? Explain.
6. Define the elements of the offence of forgery.
7. What is "counterfeit money"?

¹ (1970) 11 C.R.N.S. 366 (B.C.C.A.)
² (1973) 12 C.C.C. (2d) 449 (Ont.C.A.)
³ (1968) 1 C.C.C. 345 (Ont.C.A.)
⁴ (1963) 3 C.C.C. 118 (B.C.C.A.)
⁵ (1975) 28 C.R.N.S. 232 (Que.C.A.)
⁶ (1974) R.L. 285 (Que.C.A.)
⁷ (1972) 16 C.R.N.S. 47 (Que.)
⁸ (1964) 3 C.C.C. 296; 44 C.R. 48 (B.C.C.A.)
⁹ (1905) 9 C.C.C. 407 (Ont.C.A.)
¹⁰ (1973) 10 C.C.C. (2d) 606 (S.C.C.)

Chapter Fifteen

Mischief,
Arson and
Cruelty to Animals

A. MISCHIEF

> **387.(1) Every one commits mischief who wilfully**
> **(a) destroys or damages property,**
> **(b) renders property dangerous, useless, inoperative or ineffective,**
> **(c) obstructs, interrupts or interferes with the lawful use, enjoyment or operation of property, or**
> **(d) obstructs, interrupts or interferes with any person in the lawful use, enjoyment or operation of property.**

Mischief that causes actual danger to life is an indictable offence. Mischief in relation to public or private property may be prosecuted as an indictable offence or as a summary conviction offence [s.387(2), (3), (4)].

The term ''property'' refers to both real property and personal property. In brief, real property refers to immovable things (or real estate), i.e. land and things attached to the land (e.g. a house or garage). Personal property refers to movable things such as automobiles, furniture and animals.

It may be helpful to consider examples of the offences in s.387(1) using personal and real property. Mischief in regard to personal property may occur by:

(a) damaging a car by breaking the car's radio antenna;

(b) rendering it dangerous by tampering with the brake system of the car;

(c) obstructing the use of the car by blocking a public highway; and

(d) interfering with a person in the lawful use of the car by striking the driver of the car while he is driving.

Mischief in regard to real property may occur by:

(a) damaging a building by breaking its windows;
(b) rendering the building dangerous by weakening a step in a stairway;
(c) obstructing the use of the building by barricading the entrance so that no one can get in, and
(d) interfering with a person in the lawful use of the building by assaulting a person who works in the building.

The important issue in many mischief cases is whether or not the damaging, rendering dangerous, or obstructing is done wilfully. Wilfully usually means intentionally, or as one judge has put it: "Wilfully means not merely to commit an act voluntarily but to commit it purposely with an evil intention, or in other words it means to do so deliberately, intentionally, and corruptly and without any justifiable excuse."[1]

So, if a student breaks a window in his school building, it must be shown that he broke the window deliberately and with a criminal (i.e. evil) intent. He would not be guilty of mischief if he broke the window accidentally or if he broke it with a justifiable excuse (e.g. to escape from a fire).

Section 386(1) extends the meaning of "wilfully" when it is mentioned in Part IX of the Code to include recklessness:

386.(1) Every one who causes the occurrence of an event by doing an act or by omitting to do an act that is his duty to do, knowing that the act or omission will probably cause the occurrence of the event and being reckless whether the event occurs or not, shall be deemed, for the purposes of this Part, wilfully to have caused the occurrence of the event.

In other words, a person may not intend to damage property but if he did some act and he knew that the damage would probably occur and he took an unjustifiable risk that the damage would not occur, then he will be considered to have wilfully or intentionally caused the damage if it occurs.

The wilfulness of an interference with property was considered by the Supreme Court of Canada in *McKenna v. R.*[2] The accused drove his car onto a railway track, left it there, and walked away. A short time later, a train crashed into the car. When questioned by the police, the accused stated that he parked his car on the track, that he did not think that trains travelled on that track, that he had taken the keys and turned off the lights and that he had walked four miles for help. Later, after being told of the crash, he said the car was stuck rather than parked. At the time of being questioned by the police the accused could walk without assistance but staggered and appeared to be intoxicated. He was charged with wilfully obstructing the lawful use of property and he was convicted of the charge. The court concluded that the interference with the railway track was wilful, but it did not specify whether the accused had acted with criminal intent or had acted recklessly.

In *R. v. Wendel*,[3] the accused and other youths were charged with breaking and entering with the intent to commit mischief. Early in the evening, they had obtained some beer. They drank some of the beer while sitting under a bridge. They then went to an apartment building, and found a vacant apartment with a slightly open door. They went in and drank their beer. Later, the caretaker of the building came to the apartment and could not get in because the door had been locked from the inside. There was no question that they had broken and entered the apartment. The only question was whether they intended to wilfully obstruct or interfere with the lawful use of the apartment. The court held that even under the extended meaning of wilfully in s.386(1), the accused was not guilty. He and the others entered the apartment for the purpose of drinking beer, not for the purpose of obstructing or interfering with the use of the property.

The extended meaning of wilfully (i.e. recklessness) was applied in *R. v. Gotto*.[4] The accused and a group of others ransacked a car. In order to provide light so that he could see under the front seat, the accused set fire to a road map which he found in the car. He left the map near the car when he and the others left. The car caught fire and was destroyed. The accused argued that he was not guilty because he had not wilfully set fire to the car. However, the court disagreed and held that his conduct fell within the meaning of "wilfully" in s.386(1). He knew that damage to the car would probably result if he did not take precautions to remove the risk of the fire destroying the car. He made no attempt to remove the risk and was reckless about whether or not the damage would occur.

A trivial interference with property will not be considered to be mischief. In *R. v. Chapman*,[5] the accused was charged with wilfully interfering with the lawful use of property [s.387(1)(c)]. The accused, who was 18 years old, and two younger companions were walking along a street late at night when they saw a small car parked in the street. As a prank, they pushed the car 10 to 30 feet down the street and left the scene. They did not try to start the car and it was not damaged in any way. The only inconvenience to the owner of the car was that he had to walk an extra 10 to 30 feet the next morning to his car. The court found the accused not guilty. There was no significant interference with the use of the car. And, there was no intention to interfere with the lawful use of the car.

The interference with the use of property may occur by words rather than actual physical interference. In *R. v. Clavelle*,[6] the accused boarded an airplane and told stewardesses that he had a bomb and that he wanted to go to Cuba. The flight was delayed about a half a hour while the plane was searched for the bomb. No bomb was found. The accused was drunk and later claimed that he had only been joking. He was charged with wilfully interfering with the lawful use of property. The court held that because of the intoxication there was a reasonable doubt that the accused had acted wilfully and he was found not guilty.[6a]

B. ARSON AND OTHER FIRES

389.(1) Every one who wilfully sets fire to
(a) a building or structure, whether completed or not,
(b) a stack of vegetable produce or of mineral or vegetable fuel,
(c) a mine,

(d) **a well of combustible substance,**

(e) **a vessel or aircraft, whether completed or not,**

(f) **timber or materials placed in a shipyard for building, repairing or fitting out a ship,**

(g) **military or public stores or munitions of war,**

(h) **a crop, whether standing or cut down, or**

(i) **any wood, forest, or natural growth, or any lumber, timber, log, float, boom, dam or slide,**

is guilty of an indictable offence....

(2) Every one who wilfully and for a fraudulent purpose sets fire to personal property not mentioned in subsection (1) is guilty of an indictable offence ....

1. Arson

The term "arson" is not used in s.389 but strictly speaking it applies to the offences in ss.(1).[7]

Subsection (2) deals with personal property (movable property) and subsection (1) deals with both real property (e.g. a building) and personal property (e.g. materials placed in a shipyard for building).

The extended meaning of "wilfully" discussed above applies to s.389(1) also. So, a person may be guilty of arson not only if he intentionally sets the fire but also if he recklessly sets the fire.

For arson to be committed, there must be a burning of property. In *R. v. Jorgenson*[8] the meaning of "burning" was explained:

> *There must be actual combustion, although it is not necessary for the material to blaze openly, so long as it comes to a red heat. Charring, that is, the carbonization of the material by combustion, is evidence of burning, but blackening of the material not accompanied by any degree of consumption is not nor is mere scorching ....So long as there is burning in that sense, the extent and duration of the fire is immaterial, and the damage may be insignificant.*

In *Jorgenson,* the accused was charged with wilfully setting fire to a building. The only evidence of burning on the building consisted of three blister marks on a small area of the paint on a metal door. The court held that the blistering did not amount to burning because there had been no consumption of material.

Another issue in the *Jorgenson* case was whether the accused had set fire to part of a building or something that was not part of a building. The building involved in the case, owned by the accused, was used for processing movie film. In addition to the blistered door, the prosecution said that some "staging" and a cupboard had been burned. There was no doubt that the door was part of the building but there was a question as to whether the staging and cupboard were fixtures[9] and thus part of the building. If they were not fixtures, then the accused could not be guilty under s.389(1)(a) of wilfully setting fire to a building. The court held that the staging and cupboard were not fixtures. They were not attached to the building. The court went on to say that even if they were attached, other things would have to be considered, such as how firmly they were attached, the circumstances under which they were attached and the purpose of attaching them. These factors would indicate whether or not the thing which was attached was intended to be a part of the building.

The meaning of "building or structure" was discussed by the Supreme Court of Canada in *Springman v. R..*[10] In this case, the accused was charged with arson under s.389(1)(a). The accused had wilfully set fire to a mobile labor camp which included wheeled bunkhouses and a wheeled combination bunkhouse and office. The issue in the case was whether or not the bunkhouse and the combined bunkhouse and office were "buildings or structures" within the meaning of s.389(1)(a). The court held that they were not buildings or structures because they had no fixed or permanent foundations. Thus, the accused was found not guilty.

2. Fraudulent Burning of Personal Property

The offence of fraudulently burning personal property is contained in s.389(2). The essential elements of the offence are (1) there must be a burning of personal property; (2) the burning must be done wilfully; (3) the personal property must not be a type of personal property mentioned in s.389(1); and (4) the burning must be done with the intent to defraud. Thus, if A intentionally destroys his automobile by fire with the intention of defrauding his insurance company so as to collect money under his policy, he would have committed an offence under s.389(2). However, if any one of the four essential elements did not exist, then the offence would not be committed.

3. Other Burning Offences

A person can also commit an offence of setting fire to something that will probably cause something else to catch fire:

> **390. Every one who**
> **(a) wilfully sets fire to anything that is likely to cause anything mentioned in subsection 389(1) to catch fire; or**
> **(b) wilfully and for a fraudulent purpose sets fire to anything that is likely to cause personal property not mentioned in subsection 389(1) to catch fire,**
> **is guilty of an indictable offence ....**

For example: A starts a huge fire in his back yard to burn leaves and trash. The fire is very close to his neighbour's wooden garage. A would be committing an offence under s.390(a) even if the garage did not catch fire. It is enough for the offence to be committed that the garage was likely to catch fire.

Section 391 creates a presumption against the holder of a fire insurance policy:

391. Where a person is charged with an offence under section 389 or 390, evidence that he is the holder of or is named as the beneficiary under a policy of fire insurance relating to the property in respect of which the offence is alleged to have been committed is, in the absence of any evidence to the contrary and where intent to defraud is material, proof of intent to defraud.

Thus, in the example above in which A burned his car, this section would apply. That is, if the prosecution could show that A was the holder of a fire insurance policy on his car, then it could be assumed that A intended to defraud his insurance company. But this could only be assumed if there were no evidence to indicate that A did not have the intent. So, if A could produce some evidence that the fire was an accident, then he would have overcome or rebutted the presumption. It would not be necessary for A to prove that it was an accident. It would be enough to simply produce some evidence that it was. It would then be up to the prosecution to produce evidence of A's fraudulent intent. If the prosecution could not prove the intent beyond a reasonable doubt, then A would be found not guilty.

Other offences involving fire are in s.392:

392.(1) Every one who causes a fire
(a) wilfully, or
(b) by violating a law in force in the place where the fire occurs,
is, if the fire results in loss of life or destruction of or damage to property, guilty of an indictable offence ....
(2) For the purposes of this section, the person who owns, occupies or controls property in which a fire that results in loss of life or destruction of or damage to property originates or occurs shall be deemed wilfully to have caused the fire if he has failed to comply with any law that is intended to prevent fires or that requires the property to be equipped with apparatus for the purpose of extinguishing fires or for the purpose of enabling persons to escape in the event of fire and if it is established that the fire, or the loss of life, or the whole or any substantial portion of the destruction of or damage to the property would not have occurred if he had complied with the law.

It must be kept in mind that "wilfully" as used in s.392(1)(a) means to act with criminal intent or to act recklessly. So, for example, A throws hot coals from his barbecue into a file of flammable trash. He knows that this will probably cause a fire and is reckless about whether a fire occurs. In a short time, a fire breaks out and some of the flames spread to a neighbour's tree, destroying it. A would be guilty under s.392(1)(a).

Under s.392(1)(b), it must be established that (1) the accused violated a law in force where the fire occurred; (2) the violation of the law caused the fire; and (3) the fire resulted in loss of life or damage to property. For example, assume that there is a law which prohibits smoking within ten feet of a gas pump at a service station. While fueling a car's gas tank, A, the attendant, smokes a cigarette. A spark falls from the cigarette and ignites the gas tank. This causes a fire which seriously injures A and the driver of the car. All the essential elements of a charge under s.392(1)(b) would be present and thus A would be guilty of the offence.

Subsection (2) of s.392 was applied in *R. v. Beck*.[11] The accused was the owner of a building which was used for manufacturing toys. He had posted several "no smoking" signs throughout the building. He had also given specific verbal instructions from time to time that smoking was prohibited. However, some employees persisted in smoking and the owner gave them the choice either to stop smoking or to quit their jobs. Rather than stop smoking, they quit. Later, a compromise was reached with the employees by which the owner allowed them to smoke only in rest periods and in the west half of the building, away from the combustible material. A fire broke out in the building when one of the employees violated the owner's orders that no employee should smoke in the east half of the building. This part of the building was being used to manufacture a toy known as "magic slate." One of the ingredients of the toy was celluloid, a very inflammable material. When the employee lit her cigarette, the flame came in contact with some celluloid on the floor of the work area. The celluloid ignited and in a matter of minutes the whole inside of the building was a raging inferno. One employee died from severe burns. The owner of the building was charged with causing the fire. The prosecution argued that the accused had failed to obey a city bylaw which prohibited smoking in any place where there was combustible material. Under s.392(2) the accused would be guilty if (a) he violated the bylaw and (b) the fire would not have occurred if he had obeyed the bylaw. The court decided that the accused had not violated the bylaw. The bylaw put an obligation on everyone not to smoke in such a building. The bylaw did not prohibit an owner from permitting anyone to smoke. Also, the court said that he had neither counselled nor aided and abetted the employees to violate the bylaw. The court was of the opinion that even if the owner had done nothing about the smoking, he would not have violated the bylaw. Finally, the prosecution argued that the owner had violated another section of the bylaw by not getting a permit to keep the celluloid in the building. However, the court said that even if the accused had violated this section of the bylaw, there was no proof that the fire would not have occurred if he had obtained the required permit.

C. CRUELTY TO ANIMALS

402.(1) Every one commits an offence who
(a) wilfully causes or, being the owner, wilfully permits to be caused unnecessary pain, suffering or injury to an animal or bird,
(b) by wilful neglect causes damage or injury to animals or birds while they are being driven or conveyed,

(c) **being the owner or the person having the custody or control of a domestic animal or bird or an animal or bird wild by nature that is in captivity, abandons it in distress or wilfully neglects or fails to provide suitable and adequate food, water, shelter and care for it,**

(d) **in any manner encourages, aids or assists at the fighting or baiting of animals or birds,**

(e) **wilfully, without reasonable excuse, administers a poisonous or injurious drug or substance to a domestic animal or bird or an animal or bird wild by nature that is kept in captivity or being the owner of such an animal or bird, wilfully permits a poisonous or injurious drug or substance to be administered to it,**

(f) **promotes, arranges, conducts, assists in, receives money for, or takes part in a meeting, competition, exhibition, pastime, practice, display, or event at or in the course of which captive birds are liberated by hand, trap, contrivance or any other means for the purpose of being shot when they are liberated, or**

(g) **being the owner, occupier or person in charge of any premises, permits the premises or any part thereof to be used for a purpose mentioned in paragraph (f).**

(2) Every one who commits an offence under subsection (1) is guilty of an offence punishable on summary conviction.

The meaning of "unnecessary suffering" in s.402(1)(a) was discussed in *R. v. Linder*.[12] The charge of causing unnecessary suffering to a horse was laid by an officer of the Society for the Prevention of Cruelty to Animals. The horse was a bucking horse and was being used in a bucking contest in a rodeo. The prosecution argued that unnecessary suffering was being caused by the use of a "bucking strap." The procedure was to place the horse in a chute with this strap loosely around the back of the horse's belly and in front of its rear legs. When the chute was opened to let the horse out, the strap was drawn tight which had the effect of making the horse buck more strenuously. The bucking, which lasted for about ten seconds, loosened the strap. The court held that no offence had been committed. The intent of the section was to make it an offence to cause unnecessarily substantial suffering to any animal. The court found that the strap did nothing more than excite or irritate the horse to more strenuous bucking. This did not cause any injury, not even an abrasion of the animal's skin.

Under s.402(3) a person who fails to exercise reasonable care or supervision of an animal, thereby causing it pain, will be considered to have "wilfully" caused the pain. However, this is only a presumption and may be rebutted if the accused can produce some evidence that he did not wilfully cause the pain, even though he may have failed to exercise reasonable care.

Another presumption is in s.402(4) which states that a person who was present at the fighting or baiting of animals or birds will be considered to have encouraged or assisted at such fighting or baiting in violation of s.402(1)(d). This can be rebutted by the accused showing some evidence that, even though he was present, he was not encouraging or assisting.

The purpose of s.402(1)(f) was considered in *Prefontaine v. R.* [13] The court held that the subsection was intended to prevent the use of live captive birds in trap shooting of any kind.

Finally, it is an offence to wilfully (a) kill, maim, wound, poison or injure animals, or (b) place poison in such a position that it may easily be consumed by animals. If any of these acts are done in regard to cattle, then it is an indictable offence under s.400. The term "cattle" is defined in s.2 and includes a horse, mule, ass, pig, sheep or goat. If any of the above acts are done in regard to animals that are not cattle and are kept for a lawful purpose, then a summary conviction offence is committed under s.401.

D. LEGAL JUSTIFICATION AND COLOUR OF RIGHT

When a person is charged with any of the offences discussed in this chapter — mischief, arson, and cruelty to animals — he will not be guilty if he can rely on s.386(2):

> **386.(2) No person shall be convicted of an offence under sections 387 to 402 where he proves that he acted with legal justification or excuse and with colour of right.**

If a person acts with "legal justification or excuse," it means that his actions are permitted by law. This legal permission for acts which would otherwise be unlawful can be based on either the common law or statutory law. For example, there are provincial statutes which allow the killing of a dog that is found injuring or killing cattle.

"Colour of right" means an honest belief in a state of facts which, if it actually existed, would be a legal justification or excuse.[14] However, simply having an honest belief is not enough. There must be reasonable grounds for the belief.[15]

Following are three cases in which colour of right was a defence to a charge of wilfully damaging property:

In *R. v. Pimmett,* [16] the accused was charged with wilfully damaging a telephone pole which was located on his land. Many years earlier, a telephone line to a summer hotel was erected across the property of the accused. The telephone company had never acquired a right to use the land for this purpose. Without deciding whether or not the accused actually had the right to remove the pole, the court held that the accused was not guilty because he reasonably believed that he had the right to remove the pole which he considered to be a nuisance.

In *R. v. Adamson,* [17] the accused was charged with wilfully damaging another's land by crossing the land with a load of hay. The accused believed that she had a right to cross the land because the municipality had passed a resolution authorizing the accused to do so. The municipality had the authority to open temporary roads across private property but a resolution of the municipal council did not have the effect of opening the road. In short, the resolution was merely a preliminary step before the municipality's decision became law. The court held that the accused had colour of right for crossing the land because the municipality had the right to open temporary roads and the accused had an honest belief, based on reasonable grounds, that the resolution had that effect.

In *R. v. Johnson,*[18] the accused was charged with wilfully damaging the fence of Mott. In this case, there was some confusion as to whether or not the accused had a right of way over Mott's land. The court held that the accused had reasonable grounds for honestly believing that he did have a right of way. Therefore, he had colour of right for taking down part of a fence which was blocking his use of the right of way. In other words, the accused may not, in fact, have had a legal right or justification for damaging part of the fence. But, he had an honest belief, based on reasonable grounds, that he had such a right. Therefore, he was not guilty of the offence of wilfully damaging Mott's fence.

If a person acts with colour of right, then he is not guilty of the offences in this chapter because he does not have the *mens rea* which would make his actions criminal. However, he may still be liable in civil action for damages. For example, in the *Johnson* case, Johnson could have later been sued by Mott for the damage caused to the fence. However, if Johnson could show not only that he acted with colour of right, but also that he did actually have a legal right or justification for damaging the fence, then he would not be liable for civil damages. In short, colour of right would be a defence to the criminal charge, but not the civil action. On the other hand, legal justification or excuse would be a defence to both the criminal and civil actions.

Finally, s.386(2) says that the accused must prove "that he acted with legal justification or excuse and with colour of right." This seems to mean that both legal justification or excuse *and* colour of right must be proved in order for the accused to have a defence. However, the courts have interpreted "and" to mean "or." Thus, the accused may prove either legal justification or colour of right as a defence to a charge of mischief, arson or cruelty to animals.

In general, a person who owns something may legally damage or destroy it. However, s.386(3) should be mentioned:

> **386.(3) where it is an offence to destroy or to damage anything,**
> **(a) the fact that a person has a partial interest in what is destroyed or damaged does not prevent him from being guilty of the offence if he caused the destruction or damage, and**
> **(b) the fact that a person has a total interest in what is destroyed or damaged does not prevent him from being guilty of the offence if he caused the destruction or damage with intent to defraud.**

Under paragraph (a), it is no defence to a charge of mischief, for example, for an accused to say that he was partial owner of the thing which was damaged. If A, B and C jointly own a building, A's partial ownership of the building does not give him a right to tear down the building and replace it with a swimming pool. He would have to get the permission of B and C. Under paragraph (b), even if A had total ownership, he would not necessarily have a defence to a charge of arson if he burned the building with the intent to defraud his insurance company.

QUESTIONS FOR REVIEW AND DISCUSSION

1. What types of conduct are covered by the offence of mischief?
2. What is the meaning of "property" in Part IX of the Criminal Code?
3. What is the meaning of "wilfully" in Part IX of the Criminal Code?
4. Why was the accused in *R. v. Chapman* found not guilty?
5. Which of the following would be sufficient evidence of burning in an arson case: (a) blackening of the material, (b) scorching of the material, (c) charring of the material, (d) flames on the material, (e) blistering of the material.
6. Which of the following would be considered buildings or structures within the meaning of s.389(1)(a)? (a) a partially completed house (b) a portable out-house (c) a tool shed (d) a house trailer.
7. A is irritated with his neighbour because the neighbour drives a noisy motor-cycle which keeps A awake at night. So, A solves the noise problem by setting fire to the motorcycle. Under what section should A be charged?
8. What are the main differences between s.389(1) and (2)?
9. What is the reasoning behind the presumption against the holder of a fire insurance policy [s.389(1)]? Is it fair to have such a presumption? Why?
10. What must be shown in order to rely on s.392(1)(b)?
11. A operates a slaughterhouse. He slaughters hogs by shackling a hind leg, hoisting the hogs to a height of 15 feet and then slitting their throats. He is charged with causing unnecessary pain and suffering to an animal, contrary to s.402(1)(a). Should he be convicted? What, if anything, else do you need to know? See *R. v. Pacific Meat Co. Ltd.* (1958) 119 C.C.C. 237, 27 C.R. 128 (B.C.)
12. Explain the difference between legal justification and colour of right.
13. A's cattle frequently break through weak spots in a fence and graze on B's property. B is willing to share in the cost of building a new fence, but A refuses. In frustration, B puts poison on the area of his property where the cattle graze and one cow dies as a result. B honestly believed that he had the right to use the poison because A had refused to have the fence repaired. Is A guilty of an offence? Why?

[1] *R. v. Duggan,* 12 C.C.C. 147 (Man.C.A.).

[2] (1961) S.C.R. 660 (S.C.C.).

[3] (1967) 2 C.C.C. 23.

[4] (1974) 3 WWR 454.

[5] (1969) 3 C.C.C. 358.

[6] (1963) 10 C.C.C. (2d) 127 (B.C.).

6a It is questionable whether the accused should have been found not guilty because of his intoxication. Mischief appears to be a general intent offence and intoxication may be a defence only to a charge of committing a specific intent offence.

[7] *Mortimer v. Fisher* (1913), 11 D.L.R. 77 (Sask.C.A.).

[8] (1955), 111 C.C.C. 30, 20 C.R. 382 (B.C.C.A.).

[9] A fixture is a thing which is attached to a building (or land) and is intended to be a permanent part of the building (or land).

[10] (1964) SCR 267, 42 CR 407.

[11] 99 C.C.C. 325, 11 CR 351.

[12] 97 C.C.C. 174, 10 C.R. 44 (B.C.C.A.)

[13] (1973), 26 CRNS 367, (Que.C.A.).

[14] See the defences of mistake of fact and mistake of law in Chapter Four.

[15] *R. v. Ninos and Walker,* 48 MPR 383 (N.S.C.A.).

[16] (1931) 56 C.C.C. 363 (Ont.C.A.).

[17] (1916) 56 C.C.C. 440 (Sask.C.A.).

[18] (1904), 8 C.C.C. 123 (Ont.C.A.).

Appendix

Narcotic and
Drug Offences

The Narcotic Control Act (N.C.A.) and the *Food and Drugs Act* (F.D.A.), together outline several offences aimed at controlling the illegal use of drugs. The two main offences under each are: "possession" and "trafficking".

The N.C.A. deals only with those drugs described as being narcotics by the Act. Opium, Heroine, Methadone and Cocaine are all described as narcotic drugs. At the time of writing this book, cannabis (marihuana and hashish) is also described as a narcotic. It is likely that in the future cannabis will not be described as a narcotic but will, rather, be considered as a "restricted" or a "controlled" drug under the *Food and Drugs Act*.

A. FOOD AND DRUGS ACT

1. Restricted Drugs

The Food and Drugs Act defines both restricted and controlled drugs. Restricted drugs include LSD, MDA, harmaline, mescaline and peyote. It is illegal to have in your *possession,* or to *traffic* in, any *restricted* drug without a special licence.

Section 41 of the F.D.A. states:

41.(1) Except as authorized by this Part or the regulations, no person shall have a restricted drug in his possession.
(2) Every person who violates subsection (1) is guilty of an offence and is liable

(a) upon summary conviction for a first offence, to a fine of one thousand dollars or to imprisonment for six months, or to both, and for a subsequent offence, to a fine of two thousand dollars or to imprisonment for one year, or to both; or

(b) upon conviction on indictment, to a fine of five thousand dollars or to imprisonment for three years, or to both.

"Possession" as it is used in the F.D.A., and N.C.A., has the same meaning as it does in section 3(4) of the Criminal Code, (see page 238). Generally, possession of a drug consists of two elements: (1) knowledge of the drug and (2) a measure of control over it.

If the drug is in the physical possession of the accused he is presumed to have control over it, unless he can demonstrate he had no knowledge of its presence. If the drug is not in the physical presence of the accused, in order to constitute possession, the accused must have more than mere knowledge. He must also have some measure of control, or right of control, over it.

Section 42 of the F.D.A. states:

42.(1) No person shall traffic in a restricted drug or any substance represented or held out by him to be a restricted drug.

(2) No person shall have in his possession any restricted drug for the purpose of trafficking.

(3) Every person who violates subsection (1) or (2) is guilty of an offence and is liable

(a) upon summary conviction, to imprisonment for eighteen months; or

(b) upon conviction on indictment, to imprisonment for ten years.

Trafficking for the purposes of both the F.D.A. and N.C.A., is defined by section 2 of the Narcotic Control Act as follows:

"traffic" means (a) to manufacture, sell, give, administer, transport, send, deliver or distribute, or (b) to offer to do anything mentioned in paragraph (a) otherwise than under the authority of this Act or the regulations.

2. Controlled Drugs

Controlled drugs include amphetamines, barbiturates, benzphetamines, and methamphetamines. Only *trafficking,* and *possession for the purpose of trafficking,* in *controlled drugs,* is illegal. In other words, the mere possession of a controlled drug is not an offence. However, it should be remembered that possession of large quantities of amphetamines, for example, without good reason, will raise a strong suspicion that the amphetamines are in possession for the purpose of trafficking.

Section 34 of the F.D.A. provides:

34.(1) No person shall traffic in a controlled drug or any substance represented or held out by him to be a controlled drug.

(2) No person shall have in his possession any controlled drug for the purpose of trafficking.

(3) Every person who violates subsection (1) or (2) is guilty of an offence and is liable

(a) upon summary conviction to imprisonment for eighteen months; or

(b) upon conviction on indictment, to imprisonment for ten years.

B. THE NARCOTIC CONTROL ACT

The N.C.A. specifies five different offences with respect to narcotic drugs:
1. possession;
2. trafficking;
3. possession for the purpose of trafficking;
4. importing and exporting; and,
5. cultivating of opium poppy or marihuana.

1. Possession

Section 3 of the N.C.A. provides:

3.(1) Except as authorized by this Act or the regulations, no person shall have a narcotic in his possession.

(2) Every person who violates subsection (1) is guilty of an indictable offence and is liable

(a) upon summary conviction for a first offence, to a fine of one thousand dollars or to imprisonment for six months or to both fine and imprisonment, and for a subsequent offence, to a fine of two thousand dollars or to imprisonment for one year or to both fine and imprisonment; or

(b) upon conviction on indictment, to imprisonment for seven years.

The following cases provide examples of various situations in which the accused were charged with possession of a narcotic.

In *R. v. Harvey,*[1] the accused was a passenger in a motor vehicle when it was stopped by the police. A search of the car uncovered marihuana and methedrine in a box hidden under a mat near the gear shift. The accused denied knowledge of the drug's presence. He stated that he was riding in the car because the driver needed someone with a licence. The court held that even if the accused was aware of the drugs' existence, he did not have them in his possession. There was no evidence that he and the driver were engaged in joint ownership of the drug. That is to say, the accused did not have a measure of control over the marihuana and methedrine.

In *R. v. Brady; R. v. Maloney; R. v. McLeod,*[2] the accused were charged with possession of hashish. The accused were present while two others produced hashish and made cigarettes containing the substance. The accused did not smoke, or in any other way handle the hashish. The court held that the accused knew the other two persons present were handling a narcotic. However, they did not have any measure of control over it, and their *mere presence* while others were smoking hashish, was *not* enough to constitute possession.

In *R. v. Caldwell,*[3] the accused, with a number of other persons, was found in a house during a drug raid. The accused had lived in the house for two weeks. Large quantities of drugs were found, some in a bathroom, some hidden under a mattress. No drugs were found in the accused's physical presence. The court concluded that the accused was in possession of the drugs. Although he did not have physical possession it could be *inferred* from the above facts that he did have *knowledge, and control, or a right of control,* over the drugs.

2. Trafficking (or having in possession for the purpose of trafficking)

Section 4 of the N.C.A. states:

4.(1) No person shall traffic in a narcotic or any substance represented or held out by him to be a narcotic.

(2) No person shall have in his possession any narcotic for the purpose of trafficking.

(3) Every person who violates subsection (1) or (2) is guilty of an indictable offence and is liable to imprisonment for life.

For the definition of "trafficking" see page 277. Conveying, or carrying, or moving a narcotic from one place to another for one's *own use* does not constitute trafficking.

The following cases considered the question of whether or not the accused trafficked in narcotics.

For the offence of trafficking to be completed, the accused does not have to actually handle the drugs. He need only exercise control over them. In *R. v. MacFadden*[4] the accused phoned a delivery service and asked that a parcel be delivered to a garage operator. The parcel contained cannabis. The accused was aware of this fact but the garage operator was not. The accused was arrested before he could retrieve the parcel after it had been delivered to the garage. The accused argued that his actions did not amount to trafficking. The court disagreed and concluded that the accused "did traffic" the cannabis because he exercised control over it.

In *R. v. Chernecki*[5] the accused was asked by an undercover police officer if he could get hold of some heroin. The accused stated that he could. The two traveled by car to a cafe. The officer gave the accused $20.00 and the latter went into the cafe. The officer waited in the car. On his return the accused told the officer that they would have to go to a hotel room to pick up the heroin. On the way to the room the officer arrested the accused and charged him with trafficking. The accused was convicted. The accused undertook to procure the narcotic, and deliver it to the officer. In such circumstances a conviction for trafficking was made out.

In *R. v. Young*[6] the accused was living in Vancouver and his friend, G, lived in Sechelt. The accused and his wife planned to take up residence with G in his house in Sechelt. G, with money provided by himself and the accused, in equal portions, arranged to buy one kilo of marihuana in Vancouver for $225.00 and arranged with the accused to transport the drug to Sechelt. The accused was arrested and charged with trafficking in the process of delivering the marihuana. G, called as a defence witness, said that it was for, "our own personal use." G also admitted that the drug was "half mine."

The accused contended that he had purchased the marihuana on behalf of himself, and G, for their personal use, and that therefore it could not be said he was trafficking when he transported the drug to his friend's house. The court, however, stated that the fact the accused was transporting the marihuana not only for himself, but also for another, *and the fact it might be used by others,* sufficed to support a conviction of trafficking. The facts demonstrated there was something more extensive than mere conveying, or carrying or moving of the marihuana incidental to one's own use.

3. Importing and Exporting

Section 5 of the N.C.A. provides:

>   **5.(1) Except as authorized by this Act or the regulations, no person shall import into Canada or export from Canada any narcotic.**
>   **(2) Every person who violates subsection (1) is guilty of an indictable offence and is liable to imprisonment for life but not less than seven years.**

4. Cultivation of Opium or Marihuana

Section 6 states:

>   **6.(1) No person shall cultivate opium poppy or marihuana except under authority of and in accordance with a licence issued to him under the regulations.**
>   **(2) Every person who violates subsection (1) is guilty of an indictable offence and is liable to imprisonment for seven years.**

[1] (1969) 7 C.R.N.S. 183 (N.B.S.C. App.Div.)
[2] (1972) 19 C.R.N.S. 328 (Sask. District Ct.)
[3] (1972) 7 C.C.C. (2d) 285; 19 C.R.N.S. 293 (Alta. S.C. App.Div.)
[4] (1972) 16 C.R.N.S. 251 (N.B.S.C. App.Div.)
[5] (1972) 16 C.R.N.S. 230 (B.C.C.A.)
[6] (1971) 14 C.R.N.S. 372 (B.C.C.A.)

INDEX